Conversations with American Writers

Conversations
with
American
Writers

CHARLES RUAS

 Alfred A. Knopf   New York   1985

THIS IS A BORZOI BOOK
PUBLISHED BY ALFRED A. KNOPF, INC.

Library of Congress Cataloging in Publication Data

Ruas, Charles.
   Conversations with American writers.

1. Authors, American—20th century—Interviews.
2. American literature—20th century—History and criticism.
3. Authorship.   I. Title.
PS225.R8   1985   810'.9'005   84-47848
ISBN 0-394-52787-9

Manufactured in the United States of America
FIRST EDITION

To my mother and the memory of my father

I WANT TO EXPRESS MY gratitude for the cooperation and contribution of the writers in this collection: William Burroughs and his agent, James Grauerholz, Truman Capote, E. L. Doctorow, Joseph Heller, Norman Mailer, Toni Morrison, Susan Sontag, Scott Spencer, Robert Stone, Paul Theroux, Gore Vidal, Eudora Welty, Marguerite Young, and the trustees of the estate of Tennessee Williams.

I want to thank Marnie Mueller, who, as program director, supported my work at radio station WBAI, and Judith Sherman, Bill Kortum, Rick Harris, and Suzanne Oboler, for their assistance.

This book came into being as the result of a long continuing artistic and critical dialogue with Alice Quinn, my editor, the generous assistance of Joellyn Ausenka, and the unfailing encouragement of Rob Wynne.

Contents

Introduction   xi

Part One
  Eudora Welty   3
  Norman Mailer   18
  Truman Capote   37
  Gore Vidal   57
  Tennessee Williams   75
  Marguerite Young   91

Part Two
  William Burroughs   131
  Joseph Heller   143
  Susan Sontag   180
  E. L. Doctorow   197

Part Three
  Toni Morrison   215
  Paul Theroux   244
  Robert Stone   265
  Scott Spencer   295

Introduction

THE ART OF THE LITERARY interview is transforming a particular interrogation into a universal dialogue. The interview as a genre is the tangible record of a moment's discourse. In the editing of the transcript the interviewer cuts and splices to emphasize the quality and dynamism of the exchange, which has depended as much on what is implied and resonant as on what has been articulated. The finished interview strives to deliver the complete experience of the encounter.

The interviewer's interpretation of the work and his essential curiosity about the author shape the direction of the discourse. It's a curiosity that comes from a literary background, a fund of information, and a specific reading of the writer's works which the interviewer must now convey to the author. This curiosity, at the level of human sensitivity and intellectual interest, provides the reader with an identifiable focus on the author.

The dynamism of the exchange lies not in the sequential logic of questions and answers, but in its undercurrent of understanding and response. The writer will set the limits of what can be articulated. In order not to intrude upon the writer's sense of privacy, whether in daily life or the domain of the creative process, the interview tacitly respects these set limits. Within this situation of nuanced adaptation by both parties, the role of the interviewer ranges from serving as looking glass or window, impartial witness, appreciative audience, or critical authority, to being the unobtrusive quiet voice in the background that provides the continuity. Yet in the formulation of the questions he must maintain an openness that is both incisive and responsive to the author, lest, as in the dialogue between Socrates and the irritated Meno, he be considered an "electric fish."

The territory being explored is not the rational, since the writer's personality is structured by imagination, the same configuration of faculties involved in the creation of a novel. The subject of the interview is the realm of artistic imagination.

The fiction writer unfolds a self-portrait for the interviewer which is composed of many layers of images—the public persona, the individual in front of his work, the archetypal writer. These overlapping shades may be contradictory, but are a fundamentally unified aspect of the writer's psyche, and, ideally, in the full extent of the interview each aspect will have found expression.

A body of work is always present as both the starting point and the basic territory. For the writer, the work has said it all, and often the interviewer who steps outside of the novel is rebuffed: "Go read the book." Thus, the interviewer uses the body of finished work as a bridge of communication which he crosses question by question. In exploring the work by questioning the various aspects of the writing, and by addressing these questions to the author, the interviewer has reversed the role of the author and the work. The author is placed in a position outside the work, and at the same time is made to speak for the work, and, in being questioned about his thoughts and experiences at the time of the writing, in essence he is being asked to return to his original state of creative flux.

In the guise of recalling the process, the writer is asked to observe himself in it. A distinction must be made between the appreciation of the work revealed in a literary interview and the real grasp of the work on its own terms delivered through the insights of literary criticism.

The understanding that an interviewer strives for places the finished work in relation to the author's development, which occurs within the larger social and artistic framework. The advantage in the immediacy of the interview is that by referring to other current works it defines the artistic climate in microcosm, as opposed to the long perspective of literary history, which focuses on the significant accomplishments of an age in a sense through those works that transcend their period. Thus, the interviewer's contribution is to immerse the work in the psychological, social, and political trends of the culture.

The ideas that went into the writing of the work must be kept in perspective as statements of intention. The interview remains a backstage view of the final work. This gives a clear sense of the development of the writer's thoughts from work to work, and the artistic aspiration the work embodies. The validity of the genre remains as biographical document.

The historical place of the literary interview as a source of information is analogous to the position of the epistolary genres in the past. If the intimate letter was akin to the diary, because the seal of confidentiality permitted an openness of communication equal to the writer's exploring his own feelings and thoughts, the interview is akin to the letters addressed to one person in the knowledge that they would be circulated. The interview retains the integrity of discourse but is addressed to the journalist as a representative of the public, knowing that all statements may be printed. That is the risk of the literary interview—that it remains not merely a public platform, which it fundamentally is, but a public arena controlled by the writer to shape a view of himself. This can turn the interview into a monologue without the rigors of the written essay. Certain celebrated writers have been overinterviewed and have developed defenses against hearing the same questions covering the same ground. As a result, writers who are most in demand have of necessity developed a public-speaking persona to blunt the monotony, protect their privacy, and safeguard their sanity—and, sometimes, to protect their work from a reductive and trivializing level of discussion.

An example of the creative use of journalistic interrogation is Boswell's *Life of Samuel Johnson*. Worked into the text are both interviews and created situations in which Boswell confronts Johnson with opponents such as John Wilkes. These are integrated to document different aspects of Johnson's intellect and character.

An aspect of the author's control of the interview situation is the development of a repertory of set anecdotes and ideas called into play for the public, which eventually consolidates into a monologue that is a barrier to genuine discourse. Another style is represented by those who use the interviewer's questions as a middle ground, redefining the terms and thus opening up each question to admit its largest implications. In a way, they are protecting their privacy and drawing a line by moving the discourse from the particular to the universal, which can result in a richer texture of thought. On the other hand, some authors have such a strong sense of public responsibility and their particular role in society that it is almost impossible for the interviewer to ask them a question that they have not already thought about. And yet their scope allows for a total freedom within their public personae, and the interviewer feels that there is no question they will not answer. Mailer has written, "In an interview, one answers the questions out of one's experience—out of the church—if the word may be allowed—of one's acquired knowledge." Thus, Susan Sontag out of her philosophical training creates an intellectual discourse by stating her position, anticipating objections, and integrating them within her answer. Toni Morrison's response to the questions starts from the personal, but will always include her sense of cultural responsibility. These writers have a public role and speak from that position of authority. Their social conscience permeates all aspects of their discourse, and the result of the individual exchange is to benefit the public at large.

By contrast, to speak to writers such as Marguerite Young or William Burroughs is to enter into the realm of their imagination. Other writers who remain essentially private speak from a disarmed openness that calls upon the interviewer's protective impulses as an individual. Still others concentrate on a discussion of their craft, and make a strong distinction between the writer and his work.

Ideally, the reader will be engaged in the dialogue and will derive a sense of the imagination at work and a renewed understanding of the synthesis that is the created work. He may also be encouraged to consider the entire body of work by the facts of the individual's road to that achievement. Certainly for other writers the compelling interest of the literary interview is not only in the information gleaned but in the continuing dialogue stimulated within the imagination.

Here the ideas of the masters of the art can be heard echoing in the voices of contemporary writers, Rabelais and Cervantes, Balzac and Dickens, Flaubert and Henry James, Dostoevsky and Tolstoi, Joyce and Proust, Faulkner and Fitzgerald are invoked as tablets of the law or seminal experiences, as catalysts or as touchstones whose importance is rediscovered in the process.

The writers selected for this collection span three decades of American fiction, and the interviews are ordered with respect to when their work first appeared in print. The three general groups are those writers who first published immediately after the Second World War; the writers of the sixties; and the writers who began publishing in the seventies. In this scheme, Joseph Heller is in the second group, because *Catch-22* was published in the sixties, although the subject is the Second World War. For the same reason, Toni Morrison appears as a writer of the seventies despite the fact that her general affinities are with fiction writers of an earlier generation.

The focus is on the state of contemporary American fiction as defined by its practitioners. The book begins with those novelists who are in a position to sum up their achievements and culminates with new writers who have just won recognition. The selection of writers in this collection must seem arbitrary to some extent. For every writer who appears there are countless others of equal importance to the literary world, and whose work I admire enormously, who are not represented. The selection was necessarily determined by who was available, who was willing, and whose recent work prompted the press to encourage my interest in obtaining an interview. Within the limitations of space, I hoped to achieve a representative selection of writers whose artistic concerns and individual stance towards "mainstream" American literary culture would express the full gamut. But as with the capture of Proteus in the *Odyssey*, each manifestation of fiction is in effect a transformation, and the attempt to seize the essential form only leads to the spectacle of a multiplicity of forms.

The ordering by time of publication addresses the issue of

changing cultural attitudes towards the novel. We live in an age of fiction, as we have since the nineteenth century. There is a prolific variety of talent working in the genre, although many new writers, as well as the majority of those who write experimental novels, are published by small presses or academic presses, which often results in limited distribution. In this aspect, the predicament of the novel seems parallel to that of poetry. We live in a silver age of poetry, with countless talents working in an infinite variety of forms, all in the shadow of the giants of the first half of this century. This has caused the public to perceive poetry as a diffuse field with few strong central figures. Whereas, even if the novel no longer occupies the central artistic stage for the public, it remains nevertheless the basic form, which in its fecundity generates the popular forms of entertainment.

The post–Second World War writers were first published when the literary community as well as the reading public at large had inherited the ideal, and the expectation, of "The Great American Novel." This ideal existed at all levels prior to the Second World War, and writers ranging from Margaret Mitchell and Thomas Wolfe, to Fitzgerald, Faulkner, and Hemingway espoused it. Whether the idea developed in response to the great masters at the beginning of the twentieth century who accomplished the ultimate artistic synthesis and summation within their own individual oeuvres and for their respective cultures, such as Joyce, Proust, and Thomas Mann, or whether the idea developed as a response to the supreme powers of innovation reflected in the poetry of T. S. Eliot, Ezra Pound, William Carlos Williams, etc., it is clear that this idea existed in the larger arena of culture, encompassing a cosmopolitan definition of literature.

This is the aesthetic context of such diverse works as *The Naked and the Dead, Catch-22*, the epic novel *Miss MacIntosh, My Darling*, and *The Naked Lunch*. The writer was the center of attention in a society that was culturally conservative. This created the paradox grounded in a reverence for high art coinciding with a social conservatism that repudiated the artistic experience. With McCarthyism, the political and cultural extremes in American history were eclipsed.

In the literary climate of the sixties the thrust was towards experimentation with form, as with Burroughs's novels, the fictional constructions of E. L. Doctorow, and the early novels of Susan Sontag. This is also the period of Truman Capote's redefinition of *naturalism* in terms of his own concept of "faction," a description of the techniques used in writing *In Cold Blood,* the history of a criminal case written in the tone of a fictional account. He has further described this technique as journalism raised to an art form. Throughout this period, writers again became politically engaged. The pugilistic young Mailer who, upholding the Hemingway ideal, used boxing as the metaphor for writers, now turns to the essays of *Advertisements for Myself* and *The White Negro.* In the work of William Burroughs, we first see the sudden emergence of the drug culture as the image of capitalism, preying upon the psychic resources of a people and victimizing most of those it has carelessly abandoned or been unable to enlist. Here, too, is the post-apocalyptic vision that would preoccupy such diverse imaginations as Thomas Pynchon and Doris Lessing. All of the writers who emerged during the sixties adopt strong artistic, cultural, and political stances, thus retrieving the writer's prerogative of an earlier generation.

Henry James predicted that the novel as a genre would increasingly concentrate on exploring and portraying a slice of life, a particular realm of experience from a personal point of view. It is with the writers who emerge during the seventies that this seems most true. A transcontinental sweep and regionalism closes off the cosmopolitan view of the novel. This does not diminish the importance of Beckett, Borges, or the Latin American novelists, but the dominant focus of contemporary fiction in the United States remains American. The American experience is investigated in private terms, and the novelist, speaking from a particular background, begins creating a mythology, such as that of *Song of Solomon* and *Ragtime,* retrieving the history of particular cultural groups, or reinterpreting individual myths and mysteries in the manner of *Grendel* or *Ancient Evenings.*

The cultural transformation is exemplified by the change in critical terminology used by writers, editors, and critics. The criterion of a writer's *style* has been redefined as a measure of the writer's *voice.* "Style" referred to the mastery of the written word on the page and the distinct artistic command of technique, whereas the term "writer's voice" encompasses a larger definition of individual traits. Originally it referred exclusively to the author in relation to the work, with the meaning of "inner voice." Its common and broader usage now reveals important aspects of our present cultural situation.

If "style" is about consciousness, will, consummate artistry, and execution, "voice" is about the opposite quality inherent in writing, the "authenticity" of language and execution. This authenticity is then extended to include attitudes towards the world, manifest in all other forms of writing, and even the spoken word. In this current usage of the term "writer's voice," the assumption that the person is the work and the work is the person becomes explicit. These interviews attempt to record the writer's voice—in writing; and the role of *voice*—how writers perceive the issues of *style* and *voice*—makes up a significant portion of the interest of these conversations.

In preparing for an interview, I consult standard reference books for biographical data and then I read the body of the author's work, looking for certain constant elements or thematic developments. For example, William Burroughs's initial creative momentum carried him straight through three novels, once he had come into his subject matter and style. By contrast, Toni Morrison's novels suggest a continuous progressive development, with each novel starting exactly at the point where the previous novel raised issues and questions. However, it's the unexpected statement, the unpredictable aperture, that shapes the course of the interview. The discussion is about how the imagination manifests itself as the work comes into being. In general, writers correct or edit themselves as they speak; they improve the phrasing or nuance of words until they achieve the sentence that most closely approximates their style. Even the interviewer listening to Truman Capote's laconic voice has no clue that the phrases when placed end to end on the page create strong paragraphs almost as precise, clear, and pungent in style as his written words. Or that Toni Morrison's lucid speculations and anecdotes have a powerful emotional resonance kindred to the special quality of her novels.

I hope that the reader will gain a perspective of these varying literary aspirations, evoking in turn vastly different literary archetypes. For the interviewer, each writer's articulation of that psychic figure, the archetype within his own imagination, reveals the essential fiction behind the fiction.

PART ONE

Eudora Welty

EUDORA WELTY WAS RECOGNIZED early as a master of the short story in the Southern tradition. *The Collected Stories of Eudora Welty*, published in 1980, reveals the whole range of her artistry over four decades of writing.

Our meeting was set for four o'clock in the lobby of the Algonquin Hotel. I recognized her stepping off the elevator, a pale woman of medium height with white wavy hair. She walks carefully, due to a touch of arthritis. Her greeting is gracious—friendly, but reserved. The strong Southern lilt in her voice places her vividly in Jackson, Mississippi, where she has always lived.

We selected an out-of-the-way corner of the dim paneled lounge to settle down undisturbed. Eudora Welty was uneasy about being taped but readily entered into the conversation. Her melodious drawl, reminiscent of the dialogues in her stories, created a sense of spontaneity. There was also in her attention a great perspicacity. She weighs her words, pausing to select a nuance or else to edit herself. When she is absorbed in a moment of thought, her expression is that of someone completely absent, but when she speaks, her eyes become luminously intelligent. In laughter her face is illuminated by the afterimage of the young woman and the child she must have been, so open is her merriment. It reminded me of the way she described herself in *One Time, One Place*: "My complete innocence was the last thing I would have suspected of myself." Her recollections of childhood, her family, and her artistic maturation are the subjects of *One Writer's Beginnings* (1984).

She was born in Jackson, Mississippi, in 1909, and after college and a year at the Columbia University School of Business in New York, she returned there to live in the house that her father had built back in 1925. During the Depression she obtained a job with the WPA, which sent her traveling all over the state of Mississippi. She began photographing what she saw on these trips. Through the photographic medium of observation she understood that "A fuller awareness of what I needed to find out had to be sought for through another way, through writing stories. . . . I knew that my wish, indeed my continuing passion, would be to part a curtain, that invisible shadow that falls between people, the veil of indifference to each other's presence, each other's wonder, each other's human plight."

The Collected Stories of Eudora Welty includes four volumes—*A Curtain of Green* (1941), *The Wide Net* (1943), *The Golden Apples* (1949), and *The Bride of the Innisfallen* (1955)—as well as two later, uncollected stories. Alternating with these volumes, Eudora Welty has published five novels and novellas: *The Robber Bridegroom* (1942), *Delta Wedding* (1946), *The Ponder Heart* (1954), *Losing Battles* (1970), and *The Optimist's Daughter*, which was awarded the Pulitzer Prize in 1972. Her photographs of the WPA era are gathered in *One Time, One Place* (1971), and her essays and reviews in *The Eye of the Story* (1978). *The Shoe Bird* is a children's story she published in 1964.

The conversation had bounds tacitly set by Eudora Welty's not wishing to speak about her private life or that of her friends, and by her modesty about her work. In contrast, she revealed a great generosity of spirit towards the works of other writers. Her unassuming demeanor conveyed at once a profound detachment and a harmonious sense of her work and her life as a writer.

CR: You've just brought out your collected short stories. The last pieces are from the mid-sixties, and you've been writing novels since. What are you working on now? Can we expect another novel?

EW: I'm working on something, I don't know exactly what. Since the last of these stories, I've written two novels, a book of criticism, and a collection of essays. Short stories are my favorite form, though, and most of the novels have become novels accidentally. I'll lead myself into them thinking they'll be short stories, and then I have to go back and work on them as novels.

CR: If the material determines the form, don't you project a final form when you begin writing?

EW: Well, I'm just not smart enough. I think the short story is my natural form. That is, the long short story, about the length of "The Demonstrators." When I realize that it has the scope of something I should explore further and really treat differently, then, of course, I'll recast the whole thing totally. It was a waste, it was a delusion on my part to think it was a story. That has happened nearly every time I've gotten a novel. But I love the short story and I intend to go on writing them. This is not the end. But I was very glad to have the book done.

CR: It must be satisfying to see them all collected in one volume.

EW: It just made me feel very good that my publisher wanted to do it.

CR: So many critics see you as a regional writer, because your stories are set in the South. That doesn't differentiate between your particular vision as a writer and your subject matter.

EW: I think it's probably because there's a long history behind me of Southern writers, and people want to fit me into that frame. Of course, I grew up in that. I don't "classify" myself, naturally. What I'm trying to do is write about life as I see it, and I have to define it. I set a stage within the framework I see around me, which I think I would do wherever I lived, whether it was Norway or Tokyo, because I feel there is a close connection between fiction and the real world. No matter how far you might range in fancy or imagination, I feel that your life line is

connected to the real life around you. I couldn't take off without a firm base, so I do use the real world as well as I can. It helps me, defines things for me, and makes me understand my feelings about life in general. Unless any story connects with life, it doesn't have an impact on anybody, does it?

CR: Does this intimate connection also entail a responsibility towards the culture?

EW: I don't think so. In the South a lot of times people say, "Oh, we're so glad you're writing, because you're doing this for the South." And I say, "No, I'm doing it for the story."

CR: That sort of generalization is so self-conscious that I think the speaker doesn't connect with the artist or the culture. Do you find that the idea of the Southern writer is becoming more abstracted as the phenomenon becomes less true?

EW: I believe that it becomes less and less true for the simple reason that the great founders are dying off, I'm sorry to say. I'm thinking of Katherine Anne Porter, who just died last week, the poet Allen Tate, Faulkner, and some of the great figures who are no longer here. Of course, in Mississippi they always say, "What about you and Faulkner?" It was just a coincidence that we lived there. I am happy that I came from the same place, but I can't see any other connection.

CR: Regional distinctions have, sadly, all but disappeared nowadays.

EW: I think the whole country is much less a matter of regions now than it used to be. The distinctions are much less easy to define. I happen to think there always will be a Southern character or feeling, which may not even be definable when a town looks like Illinois or anywhere else. It's an attitude towards life, a way of looking at things that may not last long, but I think it will last longer than other places, except possibly New England. But the sense of family which gives you the sense of narrative and drama, that's where we draw our stories.

CR: You draw on the custom of family histories and storytelling.

EW: I think so. Then, also, the fact that you are able to follow a person's life from beginning to end, almost. You know the people who went before him, and you know the result of all his actions, and what happened in the end. You don't just know people in little segments, or minutes, or only under certain circumstances. You know them under all circumstances. It can't help but develop your sense of narrative, the continuity in history of the life there. I think that will persevere somehow in the Southern attitude, but maybe not in the form that you were asking about, the old, absolute Southern regional variety. It's much more connected with the world, and I'm glad of it.

CR: As the old order disappears, I think people turn to their artists to keep the culture alive. Do you think that's what people look to find in you and your work?

EW: It intimidates me so, that anyone wants me to speak for a culture. I'll leave that to those other girls [Carson McCullers and Flannery O'Connor], and they can't speak now. Some group was doing a seminar on the three of us, and they sent me a tee shirt on which were drawings of Welty, O'Connor, and McCullers [*laughs*], so I guess that's what they want. I don't know why we are combined, except that we are all females and come from south of the Mason-Dixon Line. I think that all of us as writers knew what we wanted to do. Part of it was the time when we were all alive and working at the same time. But I'm not very good at seeing connections anyway, just at reading people's work. Then I feel in direct touch with the writer.

CR: Since you're often compared to them, let me ask, were you aware of the works of Carson McCullers and Flannery O'Connor at the time? Did you ever meet?

EW: I met Carson McCullers when we were both given fellowships, I guess you'd call it, to Bread Loaf [Writers' Conference]. Carson had already published her first book [*The Heart Is a Lonely Hunter*], and I was just beginning on my stories. We were up there for a week at the same time. We never were intimate, and it never came about that we were later. Flannery O'Connor I only got to meet, I am sorry to say, towards the end of her life, when we both worked at giving college readings, and we corresponded some. I was crazy about her, and I wish I could have known her better. It took me a while to realize the things I didn't know about her work, the spiritual force of them. I wasn't acquainted with the Roman Catholic Church and concepts like grace, I had to find out. Of course I loved her stories on any level. I didn't realize how much more was in the stories until I got it from her, hearing her lecture and talk. Terrifying power, and so true to the idiom, the way she's got those Georgia country people down.

CR: Paul Theroux thinks that a regional writer has to leave his place of origin to acquire the perspective to know his material. I know you studied in New York. What made you decide to return to Jackson, Mississippi?

EW: I knew I wanted to be a writer, but I went to Columbia Business School because my father was very practical and down to earth. He said, "It would be fine to be a writer, but you still have to earn a living." At that time most all that girls could do was either teach school or go into business. I knew I didn't want to teach school, so I spent over a year in New York going to school. I didn't get any kind of business degree. All I did was take courses in business so I could apply for jobs. But that was when the Depression came along, and my father became ill and the next year died, and life was changed. I had thought that I could get a job supporting myself in advertising in New York, and go to the theatre and everything else, and write at the same time—a dream. I'm glad I didn't get caught up in any of that. I did get jobs, but they were back home, they were part-time, and they happened to be jobs that showed me a lot about Mississippi, about which I didn't know much at the time, except for Jackson. I traveled all over the state.

CR: Was that part of your work with the WPA?

EW: I was a junior publicity agent. I wrote about it to explain those photographs in *One Time, One Place*. I went on from there and just sent stories to magazines and did everything by mail. That was very lucky for me. I don't know what I might have turned into if I stayed up here. But I still love New York.

CR: When you say you don't know what you might have turned into, does that mean you've thought about "the road not taken"?

EW: No, I'm sure I would have written stories, but I don't know where I would have laid the stories. Later I wrote one story set in New York, which I don't think was successful since I didn't even know enough about my own home grounds, much less a vast city. You can't tell what you might do. But I know I would have written stories.

CR: Did the Depression affect the way you saw things and wrote about them?

EW: I hadn't really started then except for myself. In fact, the Depression in Mississippi could hardly be told from the normal way of life. It was already so poor. But I was seeing it for the first time. If you've seen those photographs, you'll know what I mean. We've always been so poor in that part since the Civil War. It was burned from one end to the other and there was nothing left to start on, and recovery was very slow. As Walker Percy says, "There was no Marshall Plan for the South after the war."

CR: Your interest is in psychology also, so that a story such as "Why I Live at the P.O." is a comedy of hysteria. The humor comes out of a pathological behavior.

EW: No, I tell you I don't think of them at all as being pathological stories. I know Katherine Anne Porter refers to the girl as a case of dementia praecox in the introduction [of *A Curtain of Green*]. She believed I thought so, but it's far from what I was doing in that story. I was trying to show how, in these tiny little places such as where they come from, the only entertainment people have is dramatizing the family situation, which they do fully knowing what they are doing. They're having a good time. They're not caught up, it's not pathological. There is certainly the undertone, you're right, which is one of wishing things would change. Even though Sister goes and lives in the post office, she'll probably be home by the weekend, and it could happen all over again. They just go through it. I've heard people talk, and they just dramatize everything—"I'll never speak to you again!" It's a Southern kind of exaggeration. There is something underlying it, needless to say. That's what gives it its reason for being.

CR: But the current beneath the humor is despair, isn't it?

EW: I know in those early stories I have a number of characters where something visibly is wrong, they're deaf and dumb. Although I didn't think about it, it was a beginning writer's effort to show how alone some of these people felt. I made it a visible reason which is, of course, inside everybody. I must have chosen that as a direct, perhaps oversimplified way. I was not aware at the time that that was what I was doing—for instance, the story about the feeble-minded girl, Lily Daw. Nearly every little town had somebody like that in that part of the world, and the whole town made it their business to take care of her. They wouldn't usually send her away to the Institute for the Feeble-Minded unless they really reached an emergency, which they felt this was. Everybody takes care of everybody to the point where it's not taking care at all. You could see the futility of what they were doing. It was something I observed, just as I observed how people talk in exaggeration. All these things are rooted in a reality which I can use for the story, but I didn't invent it.

CR: "The Wide Net" is a comedy of misunderstanding between newlyweds. The young wife threatens to kill herself, and the husband calls the community together to drag the river for her body. Your description of the forest in autumn is elegiac, knowing that all things must come to an end, and yet inevitably return.

EW: That's exactly how I felt when I was writing. They were going on an excursion. Old Doc says, "The excursion is the same when you go looking for your sorrow as when you go looking for your joy." Young love is a mysterious thing, and anything might have happened. Things could have been very terrible. William Wallace, who was so inarticulate, could fish and dive down to the bottom of this water. That's part of it, because they wanted the presence of mystery and the possibility to be there. That's about the season of the year, the fall and the changing times.

CR: Young lovers acting out the drama in the fall reminded me of Chekhov, and I wondered if he influenced your concept of the short story.

EW: He certainly was my ideal. I didn't consciously try to base things, although that is an acknowledged method of teaching yourself. I guess I never thought I could base anything on a master like that.

CR: Did your reading determine your direction?

EW: I'm sure it must have done it indirectly, but not directly. I feel that when I'm really working on something, I'm not aware of anything but the story. I'm not thinking of myself, or of another writer. I'm just trying to get the story the way I want it. Those things can certainly help and bear down on me, but it's done at other times. Then they are worked out in the story without my conscious knowledge.

CR: When you began writing, did you identify with the Southern tradition?

EW: I'm self-taught, so I really didn't. I just wrote stories. I was befriended by Robert Penn Warren and Cleanth Brooks, who published me in *The Southern Review*; I met Katherine Anne Porter fairly early; and they were already long-established writers, but we had no group. We're all such individuals, I hardly see how we could. I'm thinking of Walker Percy and Peter Taylor and many more. We all met in the course of things without seeking one another out, just meeting as life opened and enjoying each other.

CR: Katherine Anne Porter was a lifelong friend, and I wondered if she was involved with the direction of your writing.

EW: I don't know that I would have known how to take any kind of direction. What she did for me that was so great was to believe in my work. This was like a bolt of lightning from the sky, that people whose work I loved thought well of mine. It made me feel that I was really in the world, that I had understanding and some readers. That's the greatest thing you can do for somebody.

CR: You have this independence in your work. Does it carry over also to publishers, because they are at such a geographical distance?

EW: I don't think about that end of it when I write. All I want to do is write that story, and I had such a long wait before stories appeared. I began writing six years before a story appeared in *The Atlantic Monthly*, which was my first national magazine, but from the beginning they were welcomed by university and college magazines. I was published, which gave me a sense of reaching somebody. I don't know what would have happened to me if I'd waited to be published to write the next story. One blessing about living at home—although I imagine I would do it anywhere—is that I write just the way I want to, and when I want to, until I get it nearly as I can to what I want. Then its fate is up to the other end. I've always been blessed with wonderful editors and agents. I didn't even realize how extremely lucky I was.

CR: How would you interpret the development of a writer such as Truman Capote? He began by writing stories and novels set in the South. Then his later works change completely and become a synonym for all that is most urbane and sophisticated.

EW: I think he is a man of great talent, but I like his talent in his earlier work. I truly can't subscribe to, and I don't think there is such a thing as, "faction." People are free to do whatever they wish, but then I think it stops being fiction. It becomes whatever it is, and I like it so much better when it is purely in the world of imagination. The introduction of real people, especially when it's blended with other motives than the imagination, to me detracts from what can be done. I would not want to do it myself. I would feel like I was amputating something of myself, taking away the main equipment I work with. It's such a waste. Why have you worked all these years to try to develop this tool that you just keep wanting to use better, if you can, and then just deny it? I don't understand it—that's my real answer.

CR: You have such a strong sense of what you want to accomplish in your writing. Having just seen the film version of Flannery O'Connor's *Wise Blood*, I wanted to ask if you were interested in other media?

EW: I think there is a definite connection between short stories and films. The methods of making them are similar, the use of flashbacks, for instance, the seeing of a town, being able to show what people are thinking or dreaming, things you cannot show on stage but which you indicate in a story. You have that much freedom and even more in a film, it's much more fluid. You can use shading and speed the way a short-story writer does. But it's in the abstract I'm speaking.

CR: What was your reaction to seeing your work adapted for the stage?

EW: I was interested because the forms were so different. One form needs to take off from the other and have a life of its own. Once I was prepared for that, I enjoyed it. I can see lots of other ways *The Ponder Heart* could have been treated. In fact, a film is the way I would best imagine it.

CR: You said that the Depression was scarcely different from normal circumstances in Mississippi when you began writing. Was it the Second World War and Hiroshima that was the major shock to you as an artist?

EW: Oh, yes. I was at the age where my brothers were in the war, and all the men and boys I knew. Everybody was personally caught up in it—before the atomic bomb was dropped—just the war itself. I went to the wedding of some friends. We didn't know it, but on the day of the wedding was Pearl Harbor; we just turned from the celebration to the whole world engulfed in war overnight.

It's hard for young people today to conceive of how the country felt about the war. It was not like the Vietnam War in any respect. Everybody honestly believed we were trying to save the world from Nazism. We believed in our country; well, I still believe in my country. It was a very pure kind of wish to accomplish this victory, and we were in it heart and soul. Members of our family were over there fighting. My brother was in Okinawa, and my friends were in the landings in Normandy and Italy.

That was a terrible time to live through. I couldn't write about it, not at the time—it was too personal. I *could* write or translate things into domestic or other dimensions in my writing, with the same things in mind.

CR: In contrast to the Second World War, the civil-rights movement and the war in Vietnam brought dissent right to your doorstep.

EW: Of course, that war's another world. At home we have a good small amateur theatre, and one of the things we've done is programs on different songwriters, such as Cole Porter and so on. We did one on George M. Cohan, who wrote "Over There." I would go and watch the rehearsals. It was so hard for the young people to realize that all these songs were really ardent and meant. It was a strange thing to realize that belief had evaporated in the young.

CR: In the time span of your volume of collected short stories you've seen the South become part of the mainstream. There has even been a president from the South.

EW: Mississippi is very conservative, and I'm surprised that they gave their vote to Carter in the first place. Reagan carried the state because he came down there and he talked about "We'll be having states' rights" and a whole lot of things like that. You know, that was very wicked of him. A lot of old conservative die-hard elements think that indeed he is going to turn back the clock, whereas Mississippi as a whole, I think, has really done very well in its adaptation. We have a far better [civil-rights] record than up north. Once we did it, we did it. [Race] relationships, as far as I know, and I know something about living in Jackson, are on the whole sound and fluent. We have things come up that are bad, but nothing on the scale that happens in the big cities. We now have a progressive up-coming governor, and his whole idea is to connect Mississippi with the rest of the world. We're part of the Union or we can't live.

CR: Your stories "Where Is the Voice Coming From?" and "The Demonstrators" are about desegregation and the civil-rights struggle. You've written about suddenly understanding the assassin of Medgar Evers.

EW: Well, I knew the situation because I lived there, but it had never occurred to me that I could write something about it from within an assassin's mind. At that point any writer putting himself or herself into another person was sticking his neck out, but I had been so put out by stories I had read written in a synthetic way about Southerners and their attitudes. They were so "simplistic," as people say now, with no distinctions made between one kind of person and another. They lacked understanding. I knew many people who came down and helped work for civil rights, and I was a friend of theirs, and I knew they were good people. But journalists and other people would telephone me in those times, because I was a writer—they didn't know me. "Why aren't you going out there and writing about those devils you live with down there?" Nobody made any distinctions of character. I thought, I know how bad this man is, and I'm just going to try to imagine what it would be like to be in his skin, because I ought to know. They don't know. It was a story writer's challenge.

CR: You've captured his voice, and I was wondering how you would read it as compared with your well-known readings of Sister and your other characters. You've experienced all these transformations around you.

EW: It's been interesting to watch all of this. I have had an opportunity to know some of the people bringing these things about, because I've lived there all my life. For instance, no one thought our new governor could ever be elected, except he was defeated before by a scoundrel, so when he ran again, for the third time, I think everybody thought, Well, look what we got when we didn't vote for him. When he had his inaugural, he invited leaders in different fields from all over the country, who were either born in the state, or had lived there, to come present a symposium on what Mississippi should do to connect herself with the rest of the world. I was part of the team, so was Margaret Walker, a black writer who lives in Jackson, and Leontyne Price came down and sang for the inauguration. It was all so joyous. Everybody just thought, The top rail is on top instead of on the bottom, where it had been for so long.

Norman Mailer

IN 1959 NORMAN MAILER MADE a summation of himself as a writer in *Advertisements for Myself:* "The sour truth is that I am imprisoned with a perception which will settle for nothing less than making a revolution in the consciousness of our time."

Mailer's stance was taken in opposition to an American cultural context that was a combination of high literary standards, great political conservatism, and rigorous self-censorship. In this spirit he became a co-founder of the *Village Voice.* He represents the vital link between the earlier, prewar novelists and the contemporary development of the writer as a public figure. Mailer received unanimous acclaim for his first novel, *The Naked and the Dead* (1948), which turned to critical condemnation of his second novel, *Barbary Shore* (1951), on political grounds. *The Deer Park* (1955), after being set into galleys, was rejected by his publisher over an issue of censorship, and turned down by eight other publishers in a row. It is now considered one of his most important novels. His two books of essays, *The White Negro* (1959) and *Advertisements for Myself,* contain seminal ideas that would be the banner of the cultural transformation by the end of the decade.

Subsequently, Norman Mailer has made his public involvement the subject of his journalism with *Armies of the Night* (1968), *Of a Fire on the Moon* (1970), his film *Maidstone* (1971), and his running as a candidate for mayor of New York City. And even his lighter social commentaries are the basis of *Of Women and Their Elegance* (1980).

He commands media attention, while having an ambivalent and antagonistic attitude towards mass media. Even in *Pieces and Pontifications* (1982), he discusses his bewilderment at how television misrepresents him, complaining that the cool, reductive scale of the TV screen does not convey his impassioned point of view, whereas the laconic drollness and understated wit of a Truman Capote are delivered vividly to the audience. To some extent a part of Mailer is uncomfortably surprised at seeing his image on the screen, framed, and reduced to the medium's bland context. On the other hand, he is disdainful of the trivializing effect of this mass attention.

Norman Mailer, who publicly talks about his development as a writer, embodies the popular transition from writer's "style" to writer's "voice."

In literary matters he is conservative, as was Hemingway, upholding the highest ideal of a writer's artistic, moral, and political responsibility. In his latest works, *The Executioner's Song* (1979) and *Ancient Evenings* (1983), we see him return to subjects of vast scope. By contrast, *Tough Guys Don't Dance* (1984) is a brisk turn at a murder mystery, set in Provincetown and Cape Cod, where he spends his summers.

Before the latter two novels, his collection *Pieces and Pontifications* was published and Mailer himself was caught up in the trial of Jack Abbott (author of *In the Belly of the Beast*, prison letters addressed to Mailer) for the murder of young actor-playwright Richard Adan. The issues in this case pointed out all of Mailer's social and political ideals as confronted by a criminal act and judged in a changing political climate. He spent ten years working on *Ancient Evenings*, in which he turns towards the mythic, and the spiritual mysteries of death and regeneration.

In his editor's office at Harper & Row, I met Norman Mailer, with his shock of silver-white hair and brilliant blue eyes, looking tanned and vigorous, someone physically aware of his force of character. We set out a time limit for our discussion, and with great good humor and relish he asked me to fire away.

CR: I was surprised to discover that the title *Executioner's Song* comes from a poem you had written long before the book. This theme has been with you for some time, then, and in some way *Executioner's Song* was a title looking for a work to embody it.

NM: I love the title, there's no question of it. At one point I thought of putting the poem called "The Executioner's Song" at the beginning of the novel and using it for an epigraph, but it didn't really fit the novel and I thought just made it more confusing than it's worth. Looking back, I could have used it. It could be the voice of Gary Gilmore speaking about himself. But I wanted to keep the book very simple, because I felt we were dealing with such complexities [in *The Executioner's Song*] that the ideal way to go with it was to stay as simple as one could as long as one could. The title stayed in my mind, and I saw it pretty quickly as the title for the book. Even when I didn't use the poem it didn't matter to me; I thought, That's legitimate, I've done that before. *The Naked and the Dead* was originally the title of a play about a mental hospital I wrote while I was in college. The play never succeeded, and the title stayed there. It's happened to me two or three times in my life that a good title's hung around. Recently I answered a questionnaire that asked if I have any titles that I have not used yet that I wanted to use. I do have one, *The Saint and the Psychopath*, and I'm just waiting for the right book.

CR: I ask about the long-term feelings and themes behind *Executioner's Song* because you've often talked about—and I'm quoting from *Cannibals and Christians*—the "occult forces of a work of art" and how the author has to pay a price for each work.

NM: A given work of art can set loose forces.

CR: When you became caught up once again in the Jack Abbott murder trial, I wondered whether you felt a recognition that indeed this was the price for *Executioner's Song*.

NM: I wouldn't say no to that straight out. I don't know if I've ever really thought of it that way. You know, Abbott helped me a great deal on *Executioner's Song*. In a way, it's hard to describe. But actually he was a correspondent for a couple of years and there was an awful lot in that correspondence that never got into his book. In certain ways his letters weren't, obviously, as well edited as the book—we're talking about thousands of pages—but over the whole, they had to be richer. I ended up with a good sense of the psychology of hard-core convicts. That was a great help. Because I didn't have to spend a year or two trying to figure it out for myself, I was able to understand Gilmore more quickly. So I thought I had a debt to Abbott. In my mind, part of paying off that debt was to help him get out of jail.

CR: At some point was there an identification between Abbott and his talent, as shown by the letters, and your subject, Gary Gilmore?

NM: There was to this extent—I don't know how to put it—as I was writing the book I felt, This is really going to engage me in more unforeseen consequences than most books I do. I did have that feeling. When Abbott wrote to me and said he thought he had a chance of getting out of jail, since I knew him pretty well by then I did feel, This is part of the price for *Executioner's Song*, and it was probably a fair price. Now, of course, in all this I thought that I might have a lot of trouble with Abbott at one point or another, because I didn't know him *that* well, and I had had trouble before with convicts, so I know when a man gets out of jail he's not always the easiest guy in the world to live with or have around. It had never occurred to me that it might be trouble for someone else, so that part of the responsibility I feel, looking back at it now, is that I was so egocentric about it. I saw it as a test of myself rather than as a test for strangers. Part of the shock of it afterwards was to have looked at it so narrowly. It's like when people come up to me and they say, "Well, don't feel bad about it, it's not your fault," and my feeling is, I don't feel bad about helping a man out of jail—some people come out of jail and they do all right and some don't, and that's part of it all. I feel bad about having looked at it with such tunnel vision. I feel bad about the lack of sensitivity I had to the dimensions of the problem.

CR: Your motivation was based on the talent you saw in him. Did you have a sense of impending crisis that Abbott, who had always fought the system, would get out and receive all this public attention?

NM: I was aghast. Jason Epstein and I had once had a difference about something and we hadn't even spoken to each other for years. When the book was taken by Random House, I knew nothing about it. My secretary, Judith McNally, took most of those letters and put them together very well, I thought, and that was what was printed in *The New York Review of Books*. The next thing I heard was that Random House wanted to do a book, and I thought, Fine. When Jack said, "What do you think of Random House?," I said, "Well, they're a very reputable house, etc., go ahead." It never occurred to me that the book was going to come out within a month after he was getting out of jail. I don't think it occurred to Random House, either. Actually, the thought probably was that the book would come out and that might help him to get out of jail a year later. He got out of jail much faster than any of us thought. If I had been able to see it all, I would have said, "No, the one thing that must not happen is that the book comes out within a month to six weeks after he gets out of jail," because if I know anything, I know about first novels—and the most stable first-novelist in the world is half crazy when his first book comes out. It's the worst climate.

   The accusation that this was an exercise in radical chic is absolutely off the point. No one was sitting around saying, "Oh, isn't this marvelous, he's going to have all this publicity, we're playing with this wonderful toy, etc.," it wasn't like that at all. Jack's editor, Erroll McDonald, and I, when we'd ever talk about it, when we looked at each other, it was as if we were saying silently, "Oh boy, let's fasten our safety belts," because we saw what Jack was going through. I don't feel any regret for saying nothing about it, because you don't say to a publisher with whom you're not on close terms, "Hold up this book for six months," after they had set the wheels in motion and after Jack got out. It was a series of very unfortunate—what would the word be?—call it coincidences, if you will.

CR: Do you feel that the prison authorities in some way deceived you?

NM: No, I don't feel that. I didn't ask them anything and they didn't tell me anything. How do you mean "deceived me," in what way?

CR: In his letters, Jack Abbott constantly describes the severe punishment meted out to him, and in retrospect one questions how extreme a case he was and whether the prison authorities withheld that information from the parole board or his sponsors. I know there isn't a clear measure of criminality.

NM: No, I think there's something about the prison system that's just not recognized by many people, which is that he was very close to getting out, and they have a general policy that if a long-termer is ready to get out in a year or two, they'll let him out before the end of his sentence because they feel it's safer if you keep him on parole for a year or two than if you just let him out cold. So they often let a man out before the expiration of his term. Now, the last time I spoke to Abbott, I don't know if it's true or not, but he said that he figured that one reason they discharged him is because he was within a year of getting out what with automatic time off for good behavior that he had acquired. This is apparently standard operating procedure in many prison systems. In other words, you can have twenty-five infractions and be in solitary all of the time but you pick up this automatic good time, three months off each year of the sentence, or whatever it is. So, given that, they just let him out a year earlier.

Now, what people simply don't recognize is that the problem for which society sends people to prison in the first place mainly gets exacerbated over the years, because you have a man who's lived most of his life in jail. Nonetheless, there comes a time when his sentence is over. Now, let's suppose that they don't parole him early, that the guy serves out twenty full years, whoever he is, not Abbott, anyone. They have to let him out at the end of the twenty years by law. Now, when they let him out they know he's still dangerous, but they let him out—they have to. All right, so what do you do—the alternative is keep the guy in jail forever and let some set of officials make a decision that this man is too dangerous to let loose. That sets up an incredible capacity for the abuse of human rights. To me one of the incredible incongruities of the modern temper is that people are frothing at the mouth—"What! You want this man to get out in fifteen years instead of twenty-five? And are you willing to engage in the risk this is going to create for society?" The hard-core convicts also wear out just like all of us. By the time they're fifty they're usually not nearly as dangerous as they are when they're twenty-five or thirty-five or what have you. They're terrified about what Jack Abbott is going to be in ten, fifteen, twenty years and furious at me for wanting him not to get life. And at the same time, literally, we engage in these incredible saber-rattling operations with nuclear bombs. We're engaging in risk on twenty orders of magnitude greater than anything involving Jack Abbott. I simply can't understand the passion of the matter.

CR: I suspect the passion is stirred not so much by the larger issue of global war as by the more immediate issue of violence on the street, the threat to one's family. The reaction is, Keep the criminals in jail for the maximum duration of their sentences.

NM: The grim conclusion you can come to is that people would rather be wiped out by a nuclear war, which doesn't involve courage or cowardice, which is absolutely passive, than have the hideous experience of being killed on the street by a mugger. That's very interesting, though. In other words, people do not want that ultimate confrontation before they die. They want a death without confrontation. I think that may be part of the passion that is aroused by this. That this one man or any criminal like Abbott poses for people—the notion that you might have to die in a confrontation—that's odious.

CR: I think that because you were sponsoring him, you were identified with the nonfunctioning of the whole system, which can be blamed on liberal reforms—that mental hospitals don't give care, prisons don't rehabilitate, etc.—a lot of that resentment was pointed at you. And this gets us to *Pieces and Pontifi-*

cations again. Norman, when you said that you wanted to save the talent, I think that was the least understood statement.

NM: Well, of course, the reason that it was so little understood is that probably it involves certain mystical notions that I have. There are very few writers that come out of prison. I think the scheme of things destroys a man's ability to write. The noise, which is tremendous in a prison. The paranoia—you literally do have to be afraid of just about everybody around you, there's very few people you can trust, if anyone. The tension—you threatened someone three weeks ago, when you were feeling strong, and now you're feeling weak. That guy is working out with weights every day in the yard and giving you bad looks or not looking you in the eye or whatever. All that tension always proliferates all over the place. The daily injustice, which is inevitable. Most convicts may not have a very good sense of the rights due others, but they sure have a sense of what's due them, and they're not getting it most of the time. So they walk around with a burning sense of injustice. Injustice breeds obsession. Obsession blots out the power to write, because, after all, obsession is like a magnetic field. Every time you start to say something or write something, you're pulled back to your preoccupation. All this militates against writing, makes it almost impossible. When you think about it, there have been so few good writers that have come out of jail in all these years. Given that incredible experience you'd think that writers would ferment like a yeast, but they don't.

And so, to find this fellow who had had no education—he had educated himself—who literally could not pronounce words that he knew how to read, just as Lenin learned German to the point where he could write German fluently but if he tried to speak German nobody could understand him. Here was a fellow who was doing practically the same thing with English, and actually, if you talk to Jack, he does not sound nearly as bright as his work. He sounds like somebody who's been in jail for twenty-five years, out in Western jails mainly. He has that accent that comes out of a prison system, which is laid-back, laconic. I wouldn't say it's a typical Western accent, it's kind of Southern, Midwestern. It's just that he speaks very simply, and not terribly connectedly. He doesn't speak in paragraphs, he doesn't speak in sentences, he speaks in phrases.

What happened is, he took this mighty leap inside prison with his mind. His mind was way ahead of his emotions, his physical powers, his knowledge of the world—all of it. I feel that in a way something is gained from the cosmos when you have that sort of transcendental activity. Just because a man's violent doesn't mean that he's beyond the pale altogether. He may be beyond the pale for most people most of the time, but to assume that a man who is a murderer is not to be considered in the same human scale as ourselves is, I think, one of the roots of all evil. Certainly, it's the foundation for the sort of complacency that creates social sludge. I think that when someone has talent, he really represents something special in the cosmos; that is, it's a victory against entropy, if you will.

CR: You feel that social outcasts have a special fund of knowledge that's inaccessible to us and lacking in the culture. You have always wanted to introduce that sort of raw talent and acculturate it through writing.

NM: Well, take another example. Look at what Genet did for French culture. Obviously you can't compare Abbott and Genet in the same sentence. Genet is a great writer; he's a genius, and Abbott was a gifted young writer who might have developed or might not at that point. But nobody's ever mentioned the sort of marvelous things Genet did, not only for the French intellectual mind but for the French idea of themselves. The peculiar pride they took in Genet: here is one of our worst who ends up being one of our best, and the reason is because he's French. Only in France could this have happened—and they're quite right, probably. It wasn't that I was looking for an American Genet—quite the contrary, because Abbott is very different from Genet—but it's something worth working for. My feeling is, if anything is ever going to be salvaged from this absolutely wasteful business that was a disaster all around, it's if Abbott ends up able to do some truly serious writing. I think that's going to be very difficult now. At least we would have that out of it. It's much better to get something out of a disaster than nothing. Again, this is a mystical equation that I have.

CR: Norman, I think the extraordinary violence of the attacks on you is because people in some way blame you. They bring up your stabbing of your wife, Adele, implying that you were the hand behind the hand that held the knife.

NM: Hmmm. That I inspired him?

CR: No, by association with Abbott's brand of violence, they formulate a psychic drama because he killed another aspiring writer, an actor-playwright. I also wanted to ask you, will going through these awful times bring you any resolution or new understanding?

NM: If there are going to be any benefits, I haven't discovered them yet. You know, there are certain experiences where you don't want to think of it in terms of any benefits. Finally, there is that young man's life. He was a very talented actor, I hear, and he's dead. The first thing you remarked on—I think people who think like that tend to have hothouse minds, because, if we're going to get into it, what was the result of stabbing my wife, after all? My children had to carry it. They won't be able to lose their temper without wondering, "Do I have a truly dangerous temper?" So when you have nine kids, as I do, you tend to live with that a lot, with the fact that you've given them that particular burden all through their lives. You're not looking for fulfillment. In other words, you're not feeling like "I botched the job [as a father], let someone come along who can fulfill the job." Quite the contrary, when that happened, years ago—after all, it's now twenty-two years ago—I felt it wasn't the end of my life. I had to rebuild from there, but it more or less worked—so it gave me a certain optimism about what others could do. Now, that optimism may have been misplaced. I may have felt that the chances were better for Jack Abbott than they truly were, but I should have had enough sense not to take my own reactions and carry them over. But anyone who comes up with a theory like that is taking pleasure in easy constructions, and he's feeding his desire to dismiss me. And, naturally, I'd like to frustrate that desire.

CR: I think that theory echoes the newspaper articles accusing you of romanticizing violence.

NM: I'm not romanticizing violence. The language of "The White Negro" doubtless is a little more romantic—in quotes—than the language I would use today in discussing it. But the fundamental equation is still there. What I said in "The White Negro" is that individual violence is the antidote to collective violence, just as collective violence is the antidote to individual violence. What I was formulating about collective violence is that the bad architecture that proliferates everywhere, the superhighways, the freezer foods, the monotony of existence, and all that is making criminals of sensitive ghetto kids. One of the ways in which potential violence is alleviated is if you become interested in your environment and everything in the scheme of things. These corporate products divorce us from our environment, and I call that collective violence. You don't have to put people in a concentration camp to dehumanize them; you can dehumanize them right down on the street—and we do. And not just in America, in all the countries in the world. The twentieth century is going through the most peculiar period of mass dehumanization, and it's too easy to say the fault is all American capitalism. In fact, it's something even deeper than that. It's almost as if there's a titanic battle going on about the nature of the continuation of man.

CR: In *Pieces and Pontifications*, Norman, that is precisely your battle with television and mass media. This surprised me, because I think of you as being able to command media attention.

NM: I can always get the ball pitched to me, but then I end up getting a lot of fouls. If I were a golfer, always hooks and slices—I'd never end up on the fairway.

CR: You are frustrated with mass media because they cannot understand you, nor can they carry your message to the public.

NM: Well, I have a mathematical equation for it. The more people you reach in any mass-media form, the less you will be able
to say per unit. If you're talking to three people, you will affect
history as much as if you talk to three million or thirty million
people. By the time you're talking to thirty million people, you
will say things like "We've got to balance the budget."

CR: Which leads us to Reaganomics, a favorite topic of yours.

NM: Well, I love Reaganomics. I'm beginning to come to the set
conclusion that Reaganomics is simply a rip-off. It's "Let 'em eat
cake." The wisest fat cats in America have said at a certain
point, "This thing can't go on for more than another four or five
years. We're through, we're caught in insoluble contradictions,
let's make all the money we can and get it over to Switzerland
before the deluge." If you have an honorable economy, it can be
anything, radical or conservative. To wit, they're either honest
or dishonest to their own principles. Stockman was a wonderful
example of that. He thought we were going to have true conservatism. It didn't matter whether you were rich or poor. If your
claim against the government was weak, you'd get it taken
away. Well, what he discovered was that this was only going to
be exercised with the poor; that when rich interests had weak
claims against the government, they were going to be honored.
That was a great shock to him; he finally ended up saying there
are no conservatives in Congress.

CR: Even before Watergate you had discussed the CIA within
the CIA. Your sense of corruption inherent in the system is extreme.

NM: I look upon it as totally corrupt. I once thought about using
as an image of America a three-hundred-pound giant holding a
heavy beam up, and everything wrong—high blood pressure,
hair falling out—well, let's not get into it. As a creature, the
American economy by now is a beast. It's a sick human beast of
small pleasure to any of us. We're living within that creature.

CR: I never thought that one day people would debate whether
to give schoolchildren lunches.

NM: I don't mind that, I'm not a moralist that way, I'm more of a philosopher. I think you can separate the two. A philosopher is someone who says, "At a certain point morality must cease; this is philosophy." What I ask for in politicians is that they have a consistent philosophy, because that's the only way you can ever learn. Any political philosophy has a certain amount of natural injustice built into it. Socialism does, conservatism does. Conservatism does because it says at a certain point, "Those people who finally can't survive, maybe they don't have a right to survive." It's a very hard view, but it's a consistent point of view. You can learn from it whether that's one of the fundamental constituents of human nature or not. Socialism can err in other directions. They can say that individual effort, finally, always proves obscene because it goes against the common good, and you can be consistent about that and be very hard on artists and a great many people. It's perfectly consistent for conservatives to, say, stop school lunches. If parents aren't willing to sacrifice enough to give their kids a lunch, then let the kid learn what reality is. Conservatism is only saying that if we divorce ourselves too far from reality, we'll have no reality at all. And I'm not altogether opposed to that. It's just that I think they are unconscionable hypocrites. A conservative has more moral demand to be prudent and have a fine sense of proportion, and counterbalance greed with all the correctives, such as a certain respect for justice and the rights of others. Conservatism isn't necessarily saying the emphasis should be on the rights of others, but it recognizes that there have to be many equations or the thing falls apart. So it's the inconsistencies in Reaganomics that offend me profoundly.

CR: You've always taken on social issues. Has it taken you from the novel to journalism and all the other activities that have involved you directly with the public?

NM: I don't really know. I always want to understand why I do certain things, and I use a funny metaphor: people sixty, seventy, or eighty whose sexual instinct is still functioning don't go around and ask themselves why. I'll often do things on instinct and, I suppose, on a very simple basis, if it feels right generally to do it, I'll do it. In other words, if I've got to write a book that's going to take care of some debts, I want it to be a book that I want to write. I've never written a book because there's going to be a lot of money in it, because I know that's the surest way to take five years off your life.

CR: With *The Executioner's Song* and now *Ancient Evenings*, are you returning to the ideal of The Great American Novel that runs through all of your statements about fiction from the very beginning?

NM: You mean, am I trying to write a great novel?

CR: I assume you're always trying to write a great novel.

NM: Not always, no. There'll be certain books you just know when you start that the last thing you want to say to yourself is, "This is going to be a great novel." When I did *Of Women and Their Elegance*, I was trying to write something that would be charming and sufficient unto itself. I don't know if I succeeded, but that was all I was trying to do there. With *Ancient Evenings*, I'm trying to do something that's as good as I can. I want to just see what I'm capable of, so this is the largest demand I've ever made on myself.

CR: After the America of *The Executioner's Song*, you have gone so far from your usual subject with a historical novel. Will you return to a contemporary subject?

NM: I think so. I tend to react against what I've done with my last work. *The Executioner's Song* was a reaction against *Ancient Evenings*, which I was in the middle of writing. I really wanted to write about America again, and so *The Executioner's Song* came along at a perfect time. It was fun to just get in touch with America, literally, by going out and doing all those interviews in Utah and Oregon. But when it was done, it was agreeable to go back to the Egyptian novel, because now I didn't have to be dealing with daily life in America but could imagine what life was like in Egypt.

CR: When I heard that your subject was ancient Egypt, I had a number of speculations about why you made that choice.

NM: It was the burial customs that drew me first.

CR: The burial customs in *The Egyptian Book of the Dead?*

NM: Well, yes, because I finally understood them. I suppose that's a vainglorious remark. I read *The Egyptian Book of the Dead* and it was one of the most difficult books I've ever read in my life, and in fact I don't think there's anyone alive outside of E. A. Wallis Budge who's ever read all of it. But on the one hand, this thing was impenetrable, it was opaque, and on the other hand, it is fascinating. The second thing, of course, was the Egyptian belief in an afterlife, which is so profound that they literally believed in the idea of dying a second time. Do you know about that? Well, they believe that when you die, one of your seven souls or spirits almost certainly goes on. That's your ka, your double, or your genius. There're any number of words for it. The ka looks like you, acts like you, has various properties, is virtually yourself. This ka can either live forever and be immortal, or it can perish. And if you die a second time, the second death is the true one. Now, of course, it's almost impossible to think about the Egyptians without the dualities. Egypt was called The Two Lands, and in every way they were living as the most dialectically inclined people. When I started I thought I was going to write a chapter about Egypt in a picaresque novel and go through many countries. Then I just never got out of Egypt. I had no idea it was going to take ten years when I started.

CR: Are you drawn to Akhenaten and the problem of pre-Mosaic monotheism?

NM: No, I stay far away from that, because I find that impossible to comprehend. Egypt is full of enigmas. It's really like trying to solve equations with eight unknowns and you only have three equations with which to tackle these eight unknowns. With all the prodigious, marvelous work done on Egyptology, most of Egyptian history is still just a series of debates—whether A or Z is true in a given moment in a given period. Even to this day the dates of the various pharaohs and the dynasties are being re-calibrated. So for that reason I picked a period about which not a great deal is known. It's a safe period, rather, because a great deal is known about periods before and after. At one point in this book there's an immense flashback that takes up half the book, to an earlier period about which a great deal is known, the era of Rameses the Second. Now, Akhenaten was before Rameses the Second and he was one of those people who were almost absolutely forgotten. He was one of those heretics absolutely expunged from the record for all practical purposes. What he did was incredible, but I felt I would not know how to write about him. I wouldn't know what to think of him. He's the one that draws everyone, but I was much more interested not in the monotheism of Egypt, but the polytheism, which for my purposes was much more interesting. What you say about Egypt is not that it was a monotheistic country but, on the contrary, it was a polytheistic country and a most interesting one.

CR: Were you going to do a Herodotus picaresque novel in the manner of Gore Vidal? I was convinced you were going to history to do a revelation of the mysteries—to have that freedom of *Thus Spake Zarathustra.*

NM: No, no, no. It's possible that if a sophisticated reader picked up the book with no identification, he or she could read it and not necessarily think that I had written it. I may be one of six or eight authors they would name as the possible author of it but they'd probably say, "No, no, this is an unknown author."

CR: The only novels I know about Egypt are one by Théophile Gautier and *Palimpsest* by H.D. Did you read fiction set in Egypt?

NM: I started to read the *Joseph* novels and then decided I'd better not. I just thought, I don't want to be thinking of Thomas Mann all the time when I'm writing my book, either writing away from him or writing next to him. I just didn't want to have that on my mind.

CR: Was the appeal of history the fact that it gives you freedom to project your imagination? History can be a projection of an ideal on the past, or, on the contrary, it can be read as the present, repeated in a cycle.

NM: I wanted to create a psychology that's absolutely foreign to us and yet by the end of the novel would be comprehensible, so that one is thinking the way they thought. Of course, this is my assumption of how they thought. You have to make these large assumptions, because there are such holes in our understanding of Egyptian culture. So if you don't make the assumptions you've got nothing. You just have contradictions. You're dealing, after all, with a primitive people who at the same time were capable of incredible feats and had an unbelievable sense of order and a highly developed aesthetic. I wanted at least with my assumptions to create a world that existed before the Old Testament or Christ. There's nothing of the Judeo-Christian temperament in any of these people. You can take Freud and throw him right out the window. Freud's absolutely—I don't want to say inadequate, because one doesn't want to speak too cavalierly about old Freud—but he's not applicable that way.

CR: In your last three works—*Why Are We in Viet Nam?*, *An American Dream*, and *The Executioner's Song*—there is an in-depth sounding of psychopathology, and I thought that that would be the direction you would continue in *Ancient Evenings.*

NM: I want to get away from those words. Indeed, I think when people read this book they'll see that a word like "psychopath" isn't really useful. One of the things they did quite normally in ancient Egypt was to cut off malefactors' hands. A psychopath is what we would call someone today going around doing that. But in Egypt it was *de rigueur*—if you got caught stealing, off came your hand. It's as different from our world as life on Mars. I thought, It would be a splendid aesthetic shock for the reader, getting to know that world, if I can bring if off.

CR: This is also a spiritual investigation, in the sense that you've discussed good and evil and God. Since primitive people have the most absolute sense of spirituality in their laws, are you investigating that aspect of psychology?

NM: It's hard to talk about, because I wasn't trying to write a book in which I would take my ideas further. I wanted the reader to inhabit a new land, and wander about in it, and see where I got and what I would discover.

CR: It's an imaginative leap—in *Ancient Evenings* are you coming to a synthesis? Because you've spoken of Capote's *Answered Prayers* as his attempting a synthesis, I wondered if that was part of your goal?

NM: *Ancient Evenings* is the first of three that are going to be related umbilically although not sequentially. The first one is there, the next one is about a spaceship sometime in the future, and the third will be contemporary. They'll probably all be big, each of them. I finished *Ancient Evenings* a couple of weeks ago, and it's 1,744 double-spaced pages. I haven't counted the words, but it must be close to 400,000 words. I think I'm going to want to cut it, because it seems a little too long. I think it will end up being somewhere between 300,000 and 350,000 words, and the other two books may be as long. If I'm going to put everything I know into one immense novel in three parts, of which this is the first, maybe, then, we can say, "This is all I know."

CR: Is your artistic synthesis one of multiple vision? This triptych encompasses the past, present, and future.

NM: The artist that I feel the greatest kinship with is Picasso. I almost wrote a book on Picasso once, years ago. I understand one thing about him very well, which is he wasn't interested in his own identity. He was interested in various attacks on the nature of reality, and he preferred to make each attack from a separate base so that he'd move his techniques and his psyche and his wit and assorted spiritual equipment over to the other side of the mountain. What I find most interesting in writing at this point is always making a new attack on the nature of reality. Reality has some subtle desire to protect itself, and if we keep going in the same direction, reality is able to handle us, just in the same way organisms become resistant to various pesticides and herbicides and start thriving among them. Reality will do that if you keep taking the same approach to it. You've got to sneak up on it from the other side. So I have no idea what the next book I'll do will really be like. I have an idea, but all I know is, it'll be different from the last one.

Truman Capote

TRUMAN CAPOTE'S APARTMENT AT the UN Plaza overlooks the United Nations building and park. The East River, brilliant as mercury in the light, winds under the bridges down to lower Manhattan, along the towers and rectangular blocks cut through by avenues and intersected by the threads of side streets half visible among low buildings. His apartment is elegantly furnished with antiques—a Victorian settee and side chairs, a yellow lacquer breakfront decorated with gift chinoiserie figures, and papier-mâché tables inlaid with mother-of-pearl. His collection of paperweights is arranged on all the surfaces. On the coffee table among the curios rises a giant rattlesnake coiled to strike—a specimen of the taxidermist's art. In the next room, on top of a bank of filing cabinets, Truman Capote eagerly shows me stacks of snake-bite kits in which he stores paper clips and sundry office supplies. This is not where he works, he explains. The studio where he writes is on a lower floor. It's the only way he can have the isolation he needs for concentrated work.

Truman Capote was born in 1924 as Truman Streckfus Persons, Capote being the name of his stepfather. He grew up with relatives in the deep South and attended school in Greenwich, Connecticut. During his apprenticeship in writing short stories, he worked as an office boy at *The New Yorker*.

His early stories were set in the South and the other locales of his childhood; his subject was the imaginative world of dreamers and outcast personalities, as in his first novel, *Other Voices, Other Rooms*, published in 1948, and the short stories collected in *A Tree of Night* in 1949. His second novel, *The Grass Harp* (1951), was adapted for stage and television. He turned his story *House of Flowers* into a musical in 1954. In 1956 he published *The Muses Are Heard*, his journalistic report about touring Russia with the company of *Porgy and Bess*. *Breakfast at Tiffany's*, a novella about a New York café society playgirl, Holly Golightly, appeared in 1958. It was eight years later that he published *In Cold Blood* (1966), the story of a real crime written as a novel, using a blend of fictional and journalistic techniques he called "faction."

Music for Chameleons (1980), a collection of stories, journalistic pieces, and a "faction" report on the mass murderer of "Handcarved Coffins," is Truman Capote's first book since *Esquire* published three chapters of his projected opus, *Answered Prayers*. Those friends who appeared in the excerpts were vociferous in their protest, creating the scandal of the day. Capote's critics took the opportunity to question the validity of writing about real people and events in the name of Art. In the preface to this new collection, Capote reaffirms his intention to use journalistic forms to create a work of art—to refine his style in a synthesis of techniques drawn from cinematic, reportorial, and fictional writing.

The last piece in the book is a dialogue between the author and his alter ego, drawing upon Flaubert's "La Légende de Saint Julien l'Hospitalier." Capote sees his own development reflected in the story of the adored only son who turns into a hunter of insatiable bloodlust and inadvertently kills his parents. At the end of the story Julien, now a penitent, encounters a leper who asks him to kiss his lips. When Julien complies, the leper is transformed into God. Thus Julien becomes Saint Julien. "But I'm not a saint yet," Truman Capote defines himself in this dialogue. "I'm an alcoholic. I'm a drug addict. I'm a homosexual. I'm a genius."

Truman Capote wanted to be interviewed over lunch at La Petite Marmite, directly across the street from his apartment. The staff was quite familiar with the situation and had a table ready for us. Truman Capote walked in looking very summery, dressed in a white Ungaro sweater with black bands down the sleeves and white slacks, and his blue cap worn at a rakish angle. His skin is translucent, showing a delicate tracery of veins. His hair is fine and gold-colored. He speaks in that familiar nasal drawl, varying his rhythm with his expression. He immediately asks me if I've read the reviews.

———

CR: I see that you dedicated *Music for Chameleons* to Tennessee Williams.

TC: I dedicated my book to Tennessee Williams because of the incredible infidelity of the American people and audiences and what not. No other country in the world treats artists the way this one does. Behavior like that would be inconceivable in Italy, France, and even Spain, or anywhere. They would never turn on a person. After all, you owe them some gratitude for the past, even if you don't like what they've done in the present. I liked Tennessee's new work. I liked *Clothes for a Summer Hotel.*

CR: Has it always been this way, the cannibalizing of the artist the moment a person reaches a certain stature? You can sense when the tide begins to turn.

TC: They do it to everybody in this country. They do it to film stars, they do it to writers, they do it to painters, they do it to composers. They'll build somebody up and then totally destroy him. I think the toughest thing in the world is to survive decades of creative work, working creatively and consistently, trying to do what you want to do and survive. Look at me. They build me up, tear me down, build me up, tear me down, up, down, up, down.

CR: You always manage to stay ahead. Do you also make time to keep up with works of other writers?

TC: Oh, yes, I certainly do. That's one of the things that I find so strange, because I read more than any other person I know. I read more magazines, more newspapers, more books. I don't watch television, that's why I have time to do it. Yet I'm continually reading things in the newspaper about so-and-so superstar was there with the superstar so-and-so, and I never heard of either of these people. I can't recognize the names of any of these so-called big-time celebrities. I must be losing my mind, I've completely lost touch with everything, because I can't imagine anybody, in a certain way, more *au courant* than I am, and I just don't know who these people are. The same thing happen to you?

CR: Probably they are the television soap-opera celebrities. You're more interested in films. Have you worked a lot in Hollywood?

TC: I did the adaptation of James's *Turn of the Screw, The Innocents,* and I had to be on the set all the time because of the way the director worked. I really thought being around movie sets, and going to the thing day after day, intolerably boring.

CR: Did you hate doing that performance in *Murder by Death?*

TC: I thought it was going to be kind of an amusing thing to do. But, again, it went on for three months and it was very boring. I thought that I would be able to get a lot of work done. I didn't, I couldn't, because there were always interruptions about this, that, and the other. It's something I would never do again.

CR: Is it true you had a fight with Bogart when you first went to Hollywood?

TC: Oh, is it ever true! I'd written the script for the movie called *Beat the Devil,* with Humphrey Bogart, Peter Lorre, Robert Morley, and Gina Lollobrigida. It had an all-star cast and it was made in Italy. Bogart was always, between scenes, doing this hand thing with other people, you know, *whuuuuu,* and I watched him push them down, and he said, "You know how to do this?" I said, "Yes."

CR: Arm wrestling, was it?

TC: Hand wrestling, as we say down south, down home. He said, "Well, come on, give me." Um, um, um, and I pushed his hand right down. He just sat there and didn't say anything for a long time, and he said, "Do that again." And I said, "Sure." And um, um, um, it went right down. He jumped up from the table. I don't know what he was doing, I think he thought it was funny, he was sort of hugging, tickling me. I said, "Cut that out"; I said, "I mean it, cut that out!" And I just put my leg behind his, turned around it, pushed him back, and broke his elbow, which, unfortunately, wasn't so funny, because it put the film out of commission for about five days.

CR: Are you working on the film script for "Handcarved Coffins" now?

TC: I'm not going to do it. The way it's written, it's already a film script, but it needs a certain new conception from a certain angle which I'm going to work out with the person who does write the film script.

CR: Did the studio buy the script before finding the director?

TC: They bought "Handcarved Coffins" a long time ago. I had a lot of offers long before it was published, and everybody thought it was such a high price, five hundred thousand dollars for a short novel. I had much, much higher offers than that, but I gave it to Lester Persky.

CR: Did you feel that you needed to write a preface to explain your present position in *Music for Chameleons?*

TC: Oh, no! I wrote a preface to explain my position as a literary artist in general. It was really written for myself. Why should it be difficult to survive as a creative artist in any country, not just this, but especially this one?

CR: Why do you think that is the case in this country? What are the forces that make it almost impossible?

TC: Envy!

CR: You think it's envy rather than power and money.

TC: Envy, envy, envy! The people simply cannot endure success over too long a period of time. It has to be destroyed. If a person survives, then he goes on and comes back stronger than ever. I know, because I've been through this three times.

CR: When was the first time?

TC: Well, *Other Voices, Other Rooms*, wham! You can't imagine. And after *Breakfast at Tiffany's*, which ended a whole cycle of books, they said, "Oh, Truman Capote is finished." I didn't publish anything for six years. They said, "He isn't doing anything." What I was doing was living on the plains of Kansas, working on something that I think very few writers could survive, in the most remote place, this horrendously depressing atmosphere, for six years. Then I published *In Cold Blood*, and they said, "Well, maybe we were wrong." Time goes by, and *Answered Prayers* doesn't appear because I decided to rework it. I do this book and they had already decided to bury me again. Do you know that famous line of Scott Fitzgerald, "American writers never have a second act"? Well, I'm going into my fourth act. But after I finish *Answered Prayers*, which has been such a fantastic, agonizing, long struggle, I think I'm going to go on writing short nonfiction novellas, and then go back to just straight fiction, but in short form.

CR: In the preface you set out your literary criteria by the references to Flaubert, and you state that you want to accomplish a work that would assimilate all of the elements of your life, to create an opus like Proust.

TC: No, no, no. Proust, no. If I had any model at all, it was Flaubert. The only thing that I have in common with Proust is that if Proust was American and living in New York City in 1980, he would write about the same things that I do. Other than that, we have nothing in common.

CR: There's also the underlying idea of transforming personal experience into art.

TC: Well, the most interesting review of this book I read was written by John Fowles, and it was published in, of all places, *The Saturday Review*. I wish you would read it, because he agreed with everything in there. His last paragraph is very touching, because he says that Flaubert, de Maupassant, and Marcel Proust, who all are obviously Mr. Capote's masters, have been sitting in Parnassus a long time alone, and it will be pleasant now that Mr. Capote will soon be joining their company. that couldn't be a nicer review, could it? [*Laughs.*]

CR: You had brought up all of the problems that Flaubert and the Naturalist writers such as de Maupassant and Zola were working with, with *In Cold Blood*, and here you are again defending your idea of journalism as an art form, your art form.

TC: Yes, you see, they are my favorite writers, along with about five or six others, such as Turgenev, and I love Willa Cather.

CR: You first threw out the problem of these masters with *In Cold Blood*. Why did you again feel the need to discuss it in this work?

TC: Well, you see, it had to go beyond that. I'm not saying *In Cold Blood* is *Madame Bovary*, in the tradition of realistic writing in the same sense. But I didn't do it as fiction at all, I did it as pure factual writing. That's what all of this argument is about, that is why these people keep beating me over the head with baseball bats. Part of it is, I think, that something frightens them about the whole idea of what it is that I am doing. I am saying that fiction as art is not any more important than factual, journalistic writing, as a highly developed art. That is what I'm saying. It's such a simple thing, you know. On the "Dick Cavett Show," if you watched it, I had this argument with this man and finally I just ended up by saying, "There's no sense talking to you, you simply don't understand English. You don't understand one single word I'm saying." Nobody seems to understand this very simple little statement: that factual writing with all the techniques of fiction—which the journalist would never think of using—is as high an art as, and capable of being a higher art than, modern fiction. I haven't read any modern fiction in so long that I thought was good, and it's not that I don't read. The last fiction that I can remember being really impressed with, and that was just the short stories, was Flannery O'Connor. That was the last American writer I can remember being impressed with!

CR: Do you think that alcohol is helpful to writing?

TC: Oh, I think it's not helpful at all. Nobody can drink and write at the same time, and drinking's not good for anybody anyway, period.

CR: You know the line by Williams where he says, "Alcohol narrows the world to a fine point."

TC: Well, I've been through that whole orgy, but my drinking thing was compulsive drinking. It was very short-lived but very intense, and was caused by about four or five different things happening at the same time. I could have handled two of them, or maybe three of them, but I couldn't handle all five of them. So I just began to drink compulsively, even when I didn't want to drink at all, to just try to shut this thing out. Of course, all I was doing was making it worse and worse.

CR: Is that the same for the drugs?

TC: I never was taking drugs, even though they said in the papers that I was.

CR: You feel that meeting both public pressure and private crisis is what made the drinking get out of hand?

TC: No, no, no, no. It was jumping between my work and two or three other problems. No, the only drugs that were causing the trouble were Librium, Valium, stuff like that. The only drug I would take with any consistency—and then I will for three weeks and then I won't for three months and then I will for three weeks, depending on my energy level—is cocaine. I don't know, do you like cocaine?

CR: Some artists use speed to work.

TC: Oh, I can't stand that, that's death on wheels for me. I can't take it at all, it makes me hysterical. You see, cocaine—I mean, at least very good cocaine—is so incredibly subtle that there is no feeling, there's no speed to it. There's no rush, there's no nothing. Most cocaine, you see, has been cut. Usually they cut it with speed, and that's what gives the people who take cocaine this rush from it, the exact opposite of what is supposed to happen. It's just this very slow, rising thing. When I started giving it to people, they said, "But what is it? There's nothing to this." The reason is that this cocaine is 94-percent pure. Most people have never tasted in their life cocaine that was more than 70-percent pure. It's the rarest thing in the world, and the most expensive, I might add. [*Laughs.*]

CR: Do you use it to sustain energy when working or to concentrate?

TC: I have used it working. I don't understand why anybody takes cocaine as a social-recreational drug. Because there's nothing to cocaine that could possibly contribute to anything recreational. Everything about cocaine is that if you use anything else with it, it ruins it. For instance, you can't take a drink, you can't do any other thing, you can only just take the cocaine—then it will work. Any other thing you mix with it works the other way around. I never was interested in it at all. Then I read this long thing of Freud's, a whole volume devoted to cocaine, and how it helped him to work, to concentrate when he was tired. Then I started using it. At first it didn't work at all; I mean, I didn't get any effect from it. I went to a doctor before I started using it, because I was afraid to get started on something. Of course, as you know, cocaine is not physically addictive. Actually, it had exactly the effects Freud describes. When I started to do all this rewriting on *Answering Prayers*, working much longer hours, along about the fourth hour I would use it for about two hours. It lasts forty minutes. It's a serious drug. You really should try it. It's curious, because you can just let go of it like that. When I was tired I didn't use cocaine for about a month, and a few days ago, when I came back and was tired, I started to use it to brace my energy level.

CR: Did it affect your work when you were using it?

TC: No, because what I was doing was, I was rewriting something that was already written. I was using it as a kind of energy concentration.

CR: It didn't affect your perception and style in any way?

TC: It doesn't do that. All it does is, it brings a terrific sense of concentration. I've never tried writing something from scratch, I mean from a standing jump, using cocaine. I just never have tried.

CR: I wanted to ask you about the way you describe yourself in this book. You say, "I'm an alcoholic," and then you say, "I'm a homosexual," and I was wondering whether being gay has affected . . .

TC: I hate that word. It's one of my real *bêtes noires*. But I don't like the word "homosexual" because it sounds so clinical. Christopher Isherwood says, "I wish people would just say I was queer."

CR: You've always projected an image to the public. On the dust jacket of your early novels there's a photo of you lying on a sofa, looking poetic and decadent.

TC: That photograph was done by a brilliant photographer called Harold Halmer who was very young and unfortunately died of cancer two years later. Did you like Irving Penn's photograph on this book?

CR: Yes, very much.

TC: Irving Penn photographed me for the last thirty years over and over, at different times. I like his work, but I didn't like his pictures of me, and I said I liked this one because it's the first picture of me that has something in it that isn't like any other photograph ever taken. He said, "Maybe you like it because it doesn't look like you." And I said, "Well, maybe it doesn't look like me, but it looks more like me than all those *bons vivants*."

CR: After that early photograph, what do you think of the bisexual vogue?

TC: I think people that say they're bisexual are sort of saying something like, "Oh well, you see, there's really nothing wrong with this because I'm bisexual." I just don't believe in bisexuality. I've known hundreds of people who lead bisexual lives, but I don't think that's the emotional balance. It's one way or the other. I know people who are far more heterosexual than they are homosexual, but lead homosexual lives, mostly, in a way, to get ahead.

CR: I think that you're one thing or another, at any one time.

TC: I know what you're saying, but I don't believe that. I think that people do have affairs with a man or a woman, or a what not, and they're perfectly sincere in whatever the moment is. But that's not what I call bisexuality. That's an emotional preference rather than a sexual preference. It's amazing, one great friend of mine of a great many years who is a very straight banker, living in an extremely Catholic, conservative world, has five children—he's one of the most active homosexuals that I have known. About three weeks ago I was having lunch with him, and he turned to me—I mean, I know absolutely everything that you could conceivably know about this man because I had an affair with him myself for a few years—and he said, "You know, I'm not homosexual at all, really." And I said, "Oh, yes? When did you come to this conclusion?" And he said it's because he's having an affair with some young girl at the moment and he's all carried away. But that's what I mean by this confusion of the emotional involvement and something other.

CR: Do you feel that people are still as repressed as they've always been about their sexual identity?

TC: I don't think most people have any idea what their sexual identity is. I've always said that if you decide you want somebody, I don't care who it is, if you really want, and you concentrate exclusively, you will get that person. I have proved that little theory over and over. People are whatever they are under different circumstances, under whatever particular pressures they are. It doesn't mean anything.

CR: Your story "Dazzle" is about a crisis of sexual identity.

TC: A critic wrote me a note about that story, and his point was, did I think that I was doing something startling, telling this story

about when I was a child, about having this woman in New Orleans. Well, that wasn't the point of the story. It was a true story;
it was exactly what happened.

CR: Do you mean the wanting to be a girl? Children wanting to
change their sexual identity? Some children seem to go through
that.

TC: Well, I did. I went from the age of about four to about ten,
and then it stopped, exactly like you turn off a faucet. I know a
lot of people have that thing, but I think I had a rather specific
reason, more than most. I had such an extraordinarily difficult
childhood, because my mother was only a child herself, and I
was continually shifted from one relative to another. My father
was an educated roué, a New Orleans gentleman, whose only interest was in gambling. He's now in his eighth marriage, and he's
in his late eighties. If you know my story named "Christmas
Memories," it was right after that that I went to boarding
school. I literally lived in boarding school until the day I walked
in and started working at *The New Yorker*.

CR: So you still feel that you have control over your public
image?

TC: That's so funny. I was reading a review in *New York Magazine*, and the person who wrote it said there really was no point
in writing a review about Truman Capote because it was like
trying to appraise the Hudson River, Chanel, or chocolate.
There is a point where a person—except for people he knows
very well—just stops being and becomes something that's fixed
in people's minds, no matter what he does. I was complaining to
Tom Wolfe about some nonsense, and he said something to me
which really amused me a lot because suddenly I realized the
truth of it. It was an insight that had never occurred to me, at
least not in a positive way. He said, "Oh, Truman, what does it
matter what anybody says? Don't you realize that you're one of
the few people in the world who are absolutely fireproof?"
There's just nothing that you can say about me that's going to do
me either any harm or any good, really, one or the other.

CR: Have you been involved in the political life of the country?

TC: I have absolutely no interest in politics at all, because I don't think it makes any difference. I think the only time I remember being interested at all was during the Senator McCarthy period—I thought he was really a scary person. But everybody else, they're just like something that they hang up in these gyms. People get these punching gloves on and whack them around for four years, and then they hand up another one. I just couldn't care less. I've known every single one of them, but not well. Jack Kennedy was interesting in a way.

CR: Is his assassination going to be a pivotal event in *Answered Prayers?*

TC: It's mentioned just once, in reference to Jackie at the dinner party. No, it's not in the book. I know it's not, in any sense which you would notice, but I can't be absolutely certain that there isn't special reference to it. There is to various other members of the Kennedy family.

CR: Yes, I remember the piece published in *Esquire*. .

TC: Especially old Mr. Kennedy raping a sixteen-year-old girl, which is actually true, he did. Every publisher, every lawyer, and everybody in America said, "How in the world can anybody get away with it?" I say, quite simply, they know that every word that I say is true, and they're not about to bring a lawsuit against me about it because I could prove it, fact and fact.

CR: You were a childhood friend of Oona O'Neill, Carol Marcus, and Gloria Vanderbilt. They appear as themselves in *Answered Prayers*.

TC: Yes, when I started working at *The New Yorker* I was only seventeen, exactly the same age as they were. Well, I was seventeen, they were sixteen, to be exact. The reason that they came into my life was because Carol Marcus—her name was Marcus then—was having this great affair with Saroyan. But Oona and Carol were my great friends. I always liked Gloria very much. I felt sorry for her. I just had lunch with Oona; she's so changed since Charlie died. She led the life of a chief wife of a Bedouin chieftain. She was so isolated, she had practically no friends. I have a house in Switzerland, not very far from her; and fortunately we've known each other forever. He had this terrific jealousy of her about everything. I was literally the only friend that she could actually see for years and years. Now she's bought an apartment in New York, so she'll be living here part of the year. She's a wonderful person, she's really one of the saints.

CR: But she had a terrible life until she married Charlie Chaplin?

TC: Yes. She had two brothers. One committed suicide, and she has another brother called Sidney, but they were never close. You see, Oona married Charlie when she was only seventeen years old, and her father would never speak to her again. She just devoted her life to this man. It was the most extraordinary relationship I've ever seen.

CR: And she has a huge family.

TC: But they lived a life of such total isolation and exile. She really has changed extraordinarily in the years since Charlie died. This is an exact image, you see. She's like someone who has been living in a nunnery for thirty or forty years, and suddenly emerges into a world that she didn't know existed. I had lunch with her—so absolutely amazing, because I hadn't seen her since Charlie died. She's full of this fantastic kind of sense of extravagance. I mean, Charlie wasn't a stingy person or anything. Yes, maybe he was, and I just never noticed it, you know. We had lunch, and the next day she's sending me two pounds of Beluga caviar. When I first knew Oona, she was always the poor little girl, because her father wouldn't do anything for her, and her mother was married to a garage attendant in New Jersey. She was like an orphan, but, I mean, beautiful. She got lots of publicity, because she was debutante of the year. She didn't have a dime, and all these girls were very rich, and she married Charles and all these years went by. She inherited something like a hundred million dollars—that's what the papers say, I don't know. What amuses me is, now she's so much richer than the people who were giving her their hand-me-down sweaters and being so kind and gracious to have her for the weekend because she had no place to go. Fabulous story there about Oona. Bet you she could tell it.

CR: Does the time scheme of *Answered Prayers* come up to the present?

TC: *Answered Prayers* moves in time between 1940 and 1965. The actual ending is in 1965. I have to make a limitation in it because of the sheer amount of detail.

CR: Are you incorporating all the materials from your journal into this work?

TC: Oh, most of it, I would say two-thirds of the book. Some of the pieces in this collection, like the Marilyn Monroe, came intact from my journal. I changed about seven or eight things. My journals are really extremely complete.

CR: Is the piece on Robert Beausoleil, the cause of the Manson murders, also from your journals?

TC: It's a fantastic piece of writing because of the way it's put together, the line of it. That's the only good piece written about
the Manson Family trial. You were talking about my journal.
You know, when I finish *Answered Prayers* I'm going to have my
journals locked away for one hundred fifty years because there
are things in them that are hilarious but that have nothing to do
with the material for the book. I've always kept these journals
since I was a child, but started doing them really seriously about
1943. I also have a fantastic memory about just anything, and
you'd better watch out, because I can repeat everything on your
recorder. [*Laughs.*]

CR: Did you take a memory course?

TC: No, no, no. I have a fantastic memory to begin with. I didn't
take a course, I invented a thing to use in interviews so that I
never had to take a note. I can repeat almost verbatim any conversation up to as long as eight hours. I've proved it over and
over, to some people's regret. It's the best way. There are many
reasons that it's better, especially in the kind of work I do. This
tape recorder doesn't matter, because you're interviewing somebody who's very used to being interviewed, so it doesn't have
any quality of inhibition. I could never have written *In Cold
Blood* if I had ever produced a pencil, much less a tape recorder.
But I had already trained myself to do it anyway. The first time I
did it totally was in a book called *The Muses Are Heard,* and then
this thing I did for *The New Yorker* on Marlon Brando in which I
just let Marlon go on and on, talking and talking and talking
himself into his grave, for eight solid hours. No notes, nothing. I
went back and I typed the entire thing verbatim. Then I spent
two months cutting it, shaping it into what it was, into what he
could never forgive. I thought my piece about him was essentially sympathetic. I think it made him into a real person, in the
end there, that moment with his mother. His mother is drunk
and he's holding on to her, and suddenly you realize the whole
real fragility of the person. He simply couldn't forgive that. But
that was a real portrait of that person at that time. At that time
the piece was very startling. People just weren't doing that kind
of thing. That's when I was beginning my journalism as art. I

realized there was no way that I could explain to him why I did what I did, because he wouldn't understand it. His contention was that this was meant as a private conversation with me. He agreed to do it with me, and you can't say, "But I didn't know he was going to write that." Well, if you didn't know he was going to write that, what did you say it for? A couple of months ago I reread that piece, and I thought, My goodness, how really mild it is. I do think it's a very sympathetic portrait of a man who became really unsympathetic.

CR: Is the focus of *Answered Prayers* documenting and defining the identity of different people at different times in the social panorama?

TC: You could say that that was the underlying theme of it, because, in fact, it's really devastating. The title page of my book—I hate people using quotes of things, but Camus was a great friend of mine, he was my editor at Gallimard. Anyway, I had lots of letters from him, and in one of his letters he was referring to something he had written and he said, "I've only written a quarter of the truth and already people are screaming." [*Laughs.*] But they're going to be doing a lot more than screaming when I finish, because now I'm so glad I published those chapters of that book. At first I didn't really think anything about it. I really didn't think it was going to cause such an incredible furor.

CR: Who do you rely on as a barometer of your work?

TC: I never show anybody a single thing that I write. But, you know, I never did as a child, when I began writing. I never showed anybody anything ever, and I still don't. I write it and I finish it and this is the way it's going to be. And then, also, I never *submit* something for publication. I like to keep things a year or two, so I can think about it and look at it again. When I decide I'm going to publish it, then I decide where will I publish it—shall I publish it in *The New Yorker*? If so, I call up Mr. Shawn and I say, "I've got something for you, but I want to have lunch to talk about it." I'm not about to let anybody see anything of mine until they have already taken it.

CR: In your preface to *Music for Chameleons* you say you feel you still have all of this talent that is untapped.

TC: I think it's because in writing it I was, curiously enough, trying to use a certain amount of tact about those things. Now, tact is the least of it. [*Laughs.*] I'm really free. I'm in the meadow. I'm wild as a horse. I'm going to let it all come. When I decided to publish this book, I started taking certain risks. It's actually extremely sophisticated, literarily speaking, but so few people are sophisticated. One of the most extraordinary pieces of writing I've ever done in my life, "Music for Chameleons," is in this book. But some people didn't understand it was all about lust and passion and murder. They thought it was about having tea with an old lady in Martinique.

CR: I read reviewers who are puzzled because the mass murderer in the story "Handcarved Coffins" isn't caught.

TC: "Quinn" couldn't be caught because they never had a case against him. I talked to him on the phone only two weeks ago.

CR: You're still talking to Quinn after publishing his story?

TC: Oh, sure. He was never accused. If you read the story carefully, you will see that they never had a legal case against anybody in the book. In fact, they had only one case that they thought they could prove, which was the Roberts murder: giant rattlesnakes injected with amphetamines. So I think he's one of the most fascinating cases in criminal history.

CR: Is there going to be a movie version?

TC: I finally got the director that I wanted to do my film of "Handcarved Coffins." His name is Hal Ashby; I think he's just right. He did a film I didn't especially like called *Shampoo*, he did *Coming Home*. But he has certain qualities I think would be very interesting—a man of that kind of mind doing a mysterious Western town with that limited, enclosed, claustrophobic atmosphere. I mean, Roman Polanski would have done it like a shot, but you can't get him into the country.

CR: In the story—your reviewers insisted it was just a detective story, since the identity of the murderer is established by a subjective association on the part of the narrator.

TC: But I know Mr. Quinn. I've done this thing for years and years, this research on multiple murders. And I have 222 files of American multiple murders in great detail. If I live to my old age, I'm going to do a book called *Meditation on Murder.* I've got these files from here to there, but the book's going to be short. It's just going to take parts and parts of these people and how they connect in my mind—what causes and creates a multiple murderer. Listen, you should read my mail. You know the man who murdered thirty-five boys—well, he writes me practically every day. Mr. John Gacy. You should read his letters; they are all very prim and proper, as if written by a high-school principal, so full of virtue.

CR: The character Quinn creates a dreadful sense of the absence of justice.

TC: Most people didn't believe Mr. Quinn did it. It was just a very small group of people who believed that. If you knew the whole true story! The way I ended that story is my all-time favorite piece of writing. My restraint was just like reining in a horse.

You know, I have this other theory about American writers as highly specialized, trained racing animals. I began being trained when I was seventeen by both *The New Yorker* and by an editor at Random House. This is even before the war, so, let's say at the start there were maybe three hundred fifty young writers in that second generation. Let's say that one generation ended with Fitzgerald and Faulkner, and then this one begins—Norman Mailer, Salinger, and me, Gore, William Styron—there were so many really talented kids. Out of that three hundred fifty most of them, for one reason or another, have dropped by the way. They just didn't make it.

And so here you are coming around now. I figured this race track is here, the starting place. Everybody comes out of the gate and you go around the ring like that, and then you come

back around here and there's nobody left except about five or six
people. There it is. It's got about five or six years to run, and that
last long terrible stretch. Who's going to win this race?

　　Well, I have this feeling that I'm going to win this race.
[*Laughs.*] Because I have a big ace up my sleeve, which I don't
think any of these gentlemen have.

Gore Vidal

GORE VIDAL, AS MAN OF LETTERS, has taken the position of legitimate arbiter of contemporary American politics and culture. With rationalism and wit, he has been the scourge of know-nothing popular culture, as well as a vigilant critic of prejudices, misconceptions, and facile writing among his peers. His essays and literary criticism have been collected in four volumes which target the political and cultural issues of the country for the last three decades.

Born in 1925 at the Military Academy at West Point, New York, where his father was posted and teaching, Gore Vidal grew up in Washington, D.C., under the influence of his maternal grandfather, Senator Thomas Gore. From him Gore Vidal derives his intimate knowledge of American politics and history as well as his grounding in the classics and modern literature.

He enlisted in the army in 1943, upon graduating from Phillips Exeter Academy, and his war experiences were the subject of his first two novels, *Williwaw* (1946) and *In a Yellow Wood* (1947), which established his reputation as a postwar novelist. His third novel, *The City and the Pillar* (1948), was a *succès de scandale* for its depiction of homosexual life. This was followed by *The Season of Comfort* (1949), *A Search for the King* (1950), *Dark Green, Bright Red* (1951), *The Judgment of Paris* (1952), and *Messiah* (1954). The failure of his next six novels caused Gore Vidal to write the Edgar Box murder mysteries, and to try writing for television, films, and the stage—*Visit to a Small Planet* (1957), and *The Best Man* (1960). In the same year he ran in New York State for election to the House of Representatives. Again in 1982, he ran for the Senate as a Democrat from California.

With the publication of *Julian* in 1964, Gore Vidal triumphantly returned to the novel form, and has continued his historical and satirical depictions of contemporary mores, in *Washington, D.C.* (1967), *Myra Breckinridge* (1968), *Two Sisters* (1970), *Burr* (1973), *Myron* (1974), *1876* (1976), *Kalki* (1978), *Creation* (1981), *Duluth* (1983), and *Lincoln* (1984).

Members of the press were leaving Gore Vidal's Plaza suite when I arrived for my appointment. His reluctance to speak about himself or his work notwithstanding, he is a favorite with the media and had been giving interviews all day. His suite has a view of Central Park, which from this height is sharply outlined as a green rectangle fenced in from every direction by irregular rows of concrete apartment blocks. The green surface is slashed across by dark roadways. From here, trees are puffs of foliage growing densely along the perimeter and thinning as they spread towards the center, the dusty yellows, browns and greens giving the impression of rampant growth in a neglected planter. I examined the view as Gore Vidal picked up the phone to tell the operator to take messages, so that we could speak undisturbed.

Gore Vidal is tall and, surprisingly, slightly heavier than he appears in photographs or on television, because the camera brings out his strong bone structure—wide brows, straight thin nose, and firm jawline. His eyes are pale, almost a yellow-brown, and quizzical in expression—he sometimes squints. His dark-brown hair, streaked gray, is parted and combed straight back. He appears athletic, and dresses with elegance. When he is not mimicking characters, his conversation is equally elegant, rapid, almost clipped, and has the bite and brilliance of his written style.

CR: In your novel *Julian*, the Emperor of Byzantium becomes an apostate because he attempts to revive the pagan gods and the cult of philosophy in opposition to the state religion, Christianity. Again, in your novel *Creation*, an enlightened and skeptical narrator encounters the world's major religions. Whether you are writing about antiquity or American history, the subject is the nature of governments, politics, and the wielding of power. The position you take, as expressed by various narrators, is like Julian's, the opposition from within.

GV: Unfortunately, I never achieved the high office that Julian did as Emperor of Rome, but I certainly was an apostate. A political family is an unusual background for a writer, a novelist. In the American context, a writer whom I think I resemble in some ways is Henry Adams. But there was no model for me when I began. I wanted to be a politician. I was constantly reading to my blind grandfather Senator Gore. We read everything—a great deal of history, particularly classical history. He was born in 1870. That means between his memories and my memories, we encompass half the history of the United States. The Reconstruction in the South—in Mississippi, where he came from—was as vivid to him as my race for Congress when Jack Kennedy was running for president is to me. So I know half the history of the country, as it were, first hand. In due course I got very interested in the half I didn't know—before his birth and mine.

CR: Is that the reason why artistically you turned to history as your subject?

GV: Inevitably, one brings to bear upon these reflections about the American past a knowledge of the political life of the present era. I know what politicians are like because I was around them; I know what presidents do and don't do; what the Congress is like. That's why I was always startled in school by textbooks that were neither interesting nor truthful. I was as bored taking history in school as everybody else was. Eventually, I decided that I would go back to the Revolutionary period to find out what the country's founders had in mind. And, as I suspected, American history was extremely interesting. Out of all this reading came the American trilogy—*Burr, 1876, Washington, D.C.* Now, God

help us, a tetralogy—with *Lincoln*. What little the average thoughtful American—that is, the 5 percent of the country who read books—what little they know about American history, I taught them. [*Laughs.*] I never intended to do this. I certainly wasn't trained to do it—I was self-taught. Rather an awesome responsibility. Fortunately [*smiles*], someone else will come along in another generation or sooner and take my place. I was happy to have made a contribution. Simultaneously, I was curious about the invention of Christianity [*Julian*]. Most of it was done about the fourth century A.D., when the mystery cults and so forth were absorbed into Christianity. That, in a sense, was also the inspiration for *Creation*, which then goes back five or six hundred years before Julian, when suddenly the entire human race began to write and to ask such questions as: How was earth created? Every system, philosophic, ethical, religious, and scientific, was really all present in the fifth century B.C. in embryo form. I want to know everything—that is temperamental—and, combined with the accident of being born into an active political family, I had the sort of background that made it possible—inevitable—for me to write about men of power from first-hand knowledge, as Henry Adams could, and as the great Thucydides could.

CR: Did the development of your political sense as a child, listening and reading to your grandfather, cause you to start writing at an early age?

GV: I was taught to read by my grandmother at the age of five. By six I was reading tales from Livy, the first grown-up book I read. By seven or eight I was attempting to write novels and a great deal of poetry. Between the ages of fourteen and nineteen I had started five novels. The fifth was completed; that was my first book, *Williwaw*.

CR: Did reading create the impetus to become a writer?

GV: I never wanted to be a writer. I mean, that's the last thing *I* wanted. I expected to be a politician. My grandfather at one point thought he might have been president, and once you get that in the family, the family never gets over it. That was the unfinished business of his life. I was very close to him, and his son was a disappointment, and my mother, his daughter, equally a disappointment. I was the oldest grandchild, and I lived with him. I would be his political heir. That's what I wanted, too. Unfortunately—or fortunately, as the case may be—I was a writer. I simply could not *not* write. A writer is someone who writes, that's all. You can't stop it; you can't make yourself do anything else but that. I took ten years off, hoping I could kick the habit. I turned to politics and to writing for the stage, movies, and television. I don't regard those things as proper writing; writing they are, in a way . . . but God!

CR: But that's just transferring your skills to another medium, so I don't understand why you did it.

GV: I did it partly for financial reasons. I inherited no money and I had to make money. Also, it amused me: Maybe I can finish with this thing; maybe I can go into politics. But by 1960 I found myself writing again, *Julian.*

CR: In 1960—that's when you ran unsuccessfully for the House of Representatives in New York State.

GV: But I did very well in that race, was the leader in five counties of the Mid-Hudson. I ran twenty thousand votes ahead of John F. Kennedy, who was the head of the ticket. I lost by about twenty-two thousand votes, which means that if Jack had done a little better, I would have won. In '62 I was offered the nomination for the Senate to run against Javits, and I turned that down. In '64, when I was in Rome finishing up *Julian*, I was offered the seat for the race upstate again, and I would have won. We had turned the district around. I said, "No, I don't want to be in the House of Representatives. I am now a writer again."

CR: The kind of mind that engages in writing and politics has a historical perspective. Even *Kalki*, with its scenes about the end of the human race, reveals a historical imagination, so that your fiction is always informed by a sense of history.

GV: I divide my novels between reflections and inventions. Reflections on Christianity and history, as in *Julian* and *Creation*; reflections on American politics in the tetralogy. In these books I'm doing the work of a historian or biographer, reflecting upon the past and making narratives out of it, in much the same way as the historians who interest me the most do . . . Thucydides, say, who was a proto-novelist. I enjoy the reflections. But I much prefer the inventions, because I make them up out of my head. If I'm remembered at all as a writer it will be for *Myra Breck-*

inridge, Myron, and *Kalki.* The reflections may be superseded by other reflectors, but my inventions are not going to be de-invented.

CR: Didn't the publication of *The City and the Pillar* affect your chances in running for office, since the subject of homosexuality was considered so scandalous at the time?

GV: No. If it did, it would have come up in 1960, when I ran. I got the most votes of any Democratic candidate for Congress in that district in fifty years. It didn't seem to cause any distress to the crowd. Mind you, the press's axes were constantly grinding. I have a great deal of problem with the print media. But as long as I have television, I can counteract what they do.

CR: It constantly occurs to me that as a man of letters, you are a political writer in your essays, always in the public eye, yet the media present you as a personality rather than as a political commentator or as a novelist.

GV: The media trivialize everything and everyone. What are they going to do with ideas they can't cope with? Nothing. So they just do personality. They create a fictional character called Gore Vidal, which bears no relationship to me. Also, I never try to present my work as a writer. That's for the critic to do, that's for the publisher to do, that's for the books themselves to do. I go on television to try to change people's minds.

CR: In your essays I can define your stance as that of arbiter; how do you see yourself when you address the public directly?

GV: What I do when I make an appearance is—well, be political. I am seen in political terms and newspapers tend not to like what I say. Why should they? I regard them as very much a part of the problem. I am attacking the ruling class of the country, and the economic interests that dominate the United States, and the fact that we have no politics, etc. But on those occasions when I am able to go on television and talk directly to the peo-ple, a fair proportion apparently like what they hear. What they like is that I am attacking something that they sense is all wrong, and I am trying to define a prospect which is obscured, to say the least. But then it is meant to be obscured because the great interests in the country do not want to illuminate the darkness.

CR: Your early work was highly praised. How do you explain this conflict with the print media?

GV: *The City and the Pillar*—it started then and it was relentless. Orville Prescott, a reviewer of enormous power in the daily *New York Times*, wrote a marvelous review of *Williwaw*. But then he read *The City and the Pillar*, and he said to my publisher, "I will not only never review another novel by this disgusting writer, but I will never read one." So my next five books were not reviewed by the *Times*—or by *Time* or *Newsweek*. I was excluded, when the previous year *Life* had pictured me as *the* young war novelist.

CR: Are you saying the issue was homophobia?

GV: Oh, nothing but fag bashing, going on all the time. They never let up.

CR: How do you think that Truman Capote's early novels escaped that?

GV: Fairly obvious. He played the part. He was entirely what you would expect a person of that sort to be.

CR: The whole persona he created then?

GV: Exactly. They don't mind hairdressers. They are not threatened by someone who is effeminate and freakish and amusing; he's good copy. I was a six-foot soldier with a much-admired war novel who had suddenly written a book of the sort that nobody else had ever done [in this country], showing the normality of a certain sort of relationship. This was unbearable to the media. From then on it was trouble. The other writer who had the same problem was Norman Mailer. They really turned on him for radical politics [*Barbary Shore*], for radical statements about life, and sex, and so on. But he set to work, doggedly, to get them to accept him and they did.

CR: You believe the media try to control artistic careers?

GV: Take Tennessee Williams—he commanded Broadway for ten years, which is a long time in that business. Brooks Atkinson at the *Times* was quite autonomous. Although the people who ran the *Times* did not like Tennessee or degeneracy, Atkinson was just too big, they couldn't handle him. But the literary reviews of Tennessee were poisonous. *Time* magazine's Louis Kronenberger never gave him a good review; he attacked everything from *Glass Menagerie* on. But then it was house policy, because I asked Henry Luce.

My stepfather was his roommate at Yale and put up about a fourth of the money to start *Time*. So, Uncle Harry, as we were taught to call him, and I were on a shuttle from Washington to New York. I said, "You know, I think it is disgusting, what you do in your magazine in the theatre reviews"—they were unsigned in those days. "We have only one great playwright in the United States, who is Tennessee Williams, and he has never had a good review in *Time* magazine. This makes *Time* magazine look silly, because he is read around the world and everybody is doing his plays, and they pick this up." And Luce said, "Well, I don't like him." And I said, "Yes, but other people do." And he said, "Well, it's *my* magazine." That is right from—as they say—the horse's mouth.

Finally, Tennessee was put on the cover of *Time* for *Night of the Iguana*. Kronenberger was gone by then and Luce was dead or withdrawn. So I did a piece for *Esquire*, unsigned. On one side, I quoted every *Time* review of Tennessee's work, each one a blast. Beside it, I put all the words of praise from the cover story. The article was illustrated with a painting of Tennessee emerging out of the swamp, busy typing away. The heading was from Ecclesiastes, "In *time* all things shall come to pass." Tennessee was annoyed. He said [*imitating voice*], "Why did you remind them about my bad reviews, why did you do it? You did it deliberately!"

CR: You've often said that your work is not autobiographical, but your first two novels are about the war. I was wondering how *The City and the Pillar* affected your family.

GV: My father quite liked it. But then we always got on well. For one thing, I have supported myself since I was seventeen. I enlisted in the army. When I was twenty my first book was published. I have supported myself ever since, which is probably the rarest story in American literature—all by writing. Fathers tend to like that. I have never been a teacher. I did not marry money, as some of my wise confreres have done.

CR: Was it right after the war that you met Anaïs Nin?

GV: I was still in the army when I met Anaïs. A friend was giving a lecture at the YMHA and I sat next to her. This must have been in '45, when I was stationed at Mitchel Field, just back from overseas. And thus began our relationship, capital R, and that went on and on, and then on and off. Then she came down to Guatemala and stayed with me, and I went to Acapulco and stayed with her, and nearly died of hepatitis, which she nursed me through. We had a great row over *The City and the Pillar*. She thought I depicted her badly; she gave it much thought and read a position paper on it.

CR: If anything, I thought the character of Maria Verlaine was idealized.

GV: Anaïs said the character was sordid. What bothered her, I think, was the fact that the woman was twenty-two years older than the young man. But Anaïs wasn't really the character, and God knows I wasn't the character. I know when Tennessee read it—he almost never read a book of any kind by anybody—but he sat down and read that one straight through—and he hated the ending. He said [*mimicking voice*], "You didn't know what a good book you had. Why did you tack on such a melodramatic ending? Of course, I liked particularly your family." I said, "What?" "You know, that Virginia family, exactly like my own background." I said I had made it all up, I got it all out of James T. Farrell. I would have liked to be the tennis player that Jim Willard was, but not the hustler. He was quite startled. Most people think that you can't write a book like that at such a young age, that you can't invent. But it's all an invention. Closest to life was the character of Anaïs, someone *like* her, but not her.

CR: But that didn't cause the final break between you.

GV: That was the first break. She was forever denouncing people. She'd write out a position paper, why she could no longer see you, you had betrayed her. She wrote one to Maya Deren. She fell out with Jane Bowles when Jane published *Two Serious Ladies*, of a brilliance beyond anything Anaïs could achieve. It had the *succès d'estime* Anaïs lusted after. Paul Bowles described in his memoirs walking down a street in the Village. A funny little woman darts out of a doorway, grabs Jane, and pulls her to the corner. He sees them talking very intensely, gesticulating, and Jane looking bewildered and finally breaking away. "What on earth is that?" Jane says, "That was Anaïs Nin." "What on earth was she carrying on about? You don't know her, do you?" She says, "No. She was just telling me what a bad writer I was." Anaïs took it personally that Jane could have had such a success.

CR: Anaïs Nin was very frustrated at having such a hard time bringing out her work and meeting with so little understanding.

GV: There's a lot to be said on Anaïs's side. What she did wasn't really very good unless you managed to fall in love with her. She just didn't fit into any category. She wasn't a novelist; she wasn't a short-story writer; she wasn't an American. These were all things which mattered in *those* days in *this* world, particularly in the New York publishing world. To get her published by E. P. Dutton, I forced them to take her, and no reference is made to this in the diaries. She did dedicate *Ladders to Fire* to me, but the dedication was removed from later editions.

CR: You satirize these traits in your novel *Two Sisters*. But was Maya Deren your introduction to filmmaking at that time?

GV: My mother had spent the war years in Bungalow No. 1 at the Beverly Hills Hotel, and that put me right in the center of the stage. She was surrounded by film people, and they liked the

idea of a great Eastern lady living among them. She was an alcoholic, the life style of many people then. Later she worked for
Alcoholics Anonymous. I'd been frozen—got arthritis in the
Aleutians—and I was in Birmingham General Hospital in Van
Nuys. So I used to hitchhike every now and then over to Hollywood and hang around the studios. I was there about three
months, until I was restored to active duty. Later, after the war,
with Maya, I saw experimental filming. Anaïs and I acted in one
of Maya's films. We stood around and made symbolic gestures. I
never saw the movie. I'd like to see what we all looked like then.

CR: That was your first encounter with the surrealist movement?

GV: Anaïs was on the fringe of the surrealist movement, and I remember she took me to a party at Peggy Guggenheim's where I
met André Breton, Charles Henri Ford, Parker Tyler, and Jim
Agee. Ford and Tyler used to put out *View Magazine,* and I was
charmed and intrigued. After all, I was a war novelist in the tradition of Stephen Crane, and it was miles different from what I
thought literature to be. Later, I was to absorb some of the
paradoxes of surrealism—which you can find in Myra/Myron.

CR: Do you see your first eight novels, before you left off with the
genre, as having a direct line of development?

GV: Only *Williwaw* works aesthetically, because I knew what I
couldn't do. There wasn't much that I *could* do, but I knew how
to deploy it. It's a small book, but it works. *In a Yellow Wood* is
small and terrible. *The City and the Pillar* is a kind of innocent
book, rather flawed. With *The Season of Comfort* I attempted a
major breakthrough. By then I was a modernist, reading Joyce
and so on; and the result was a mess. I have never allowed it to
be reprinted. Then came *A Search for the King,* my first historical novel, twelfth-century, which has a certain charm, like an
E. B. White kind of legend. *Dark Green, Bright Red* is about the
revolution in Guatemala, and very good on action. It generally
bores me to read battle scenes, but they are interesting to write
because they are so difficult. Then I was trying out different
voices in the short stories, *A Thirsty Evil.* At the age of twenty-

five, I settled down in the Hudson Valley and wrote *The Judgment of Paris*, my first good book. I found my voice, and the style is what it has been ever since. Next came *Messiah*, which became an underground favorite for many years. Then came my oblivion, because without *The New York Times*, *Time*, and *Newsweek* my books were vanishing. So I quit for ten years.

CR: Seriously, was it mixed reviews or lack of attention that forced you into this decision?

GV: It was financial. I couldn't live. I had a best seller in *The City and the Pillar*, but the others were, literally, unnoticed. I had a marvelous reputation in England and certain European countries, but I couldn't live on my royalties, so I had to do something else. I went into television.

CR: Is that also the reason you started writing those wonderful Edgar Box detective novels?

GV: Well, because I was broke, I really had only two choices: one was to write under a pseudonym, and the other was to quit and go off and do something else for a while till the troubles blew over. So I did both. I went off to television, and I published three mystery stories, all written in one year. I wrote each one in eight days. Each has seven chapters of ten thousand words. I would do ten thousand words a day, and on the eighth day I would revise. They were published under the pseudonym Edgar Box and received glowing reviews. I did it because my editor had said, "We have Spillane. Now we need an up-to-date S. S. Van Dyne." They are still in print around the world, and certainly more translated than most of my novels.

CR: How do you think writing for television, the theatre, and films affected your style when you returned to the novel?

GV: You learn a great deal. What you learn is something you ought to know anyway but you don't. The novel in English has always tended to be discursive, and if you add that to the tendentiousness that is so natural to Americans, the result is often windy and garrulous. A detail is there just because the writer put it there, and there's no selection. What you learn in the theatre is that every line must mean something, must have a purpose. This is extraordinary news to most novelists, because most of them just go on and on until they finally stop. Occasionally you get a perfectionist like Flaubert who desperately tries to remove double genitives and so on, but that is very rare. You can see in James an immediate difference from his early books and *What Maisie Knew*, *The Awkward Age*, and *Turn of the Screw*, which came right after his long period of trying to break into the theatre. My career was the reverse of his. I went into the theatre and made the money that James dreamt of making. Then I went back to the novel having learned better how to make scenes work—and how *not* to write.

CR: During this early phase of your career, having grown up in Washington with your grandfather who was from Mississippi, you never identified with the Southern writers.

GV: I didn't really like them. Maybe I got too much of it at home. Anyway, I was drawn to European writers. Earlier, when I was a kid, it was Somerset Maugham—and James T. Farrell: *Studs Lonigan* was my first sexy book. Then, as I started to read seriously, D. H. Lawrence immediately captured me. Now, of course, I wonder what it was I saw in *Women in Love*. With great admiration I read and reread Thomas Mann. *Dr. Faustus* may be the best novel of our period. Then Balzac. Then, Stendhal, who is a young man's writer. I couldn't read Proust then; you have to be over thirty to enjoy Proust. These were the writers I looked to, in what you call my "early phase."

CR: Which of the great Americans did you read?

GV: I couldn't take Hawthorne; I still can't. I don't like anything he wrote except *The Blithedale Romance*, which is almost a novel. The others are romances. I do detest *Moby Dick*, and I never finished *Pierre; or the Ambiguities*. But then, I don't like Melville's writing. It is windy and pretentious, it is bogus Shakespeare.

CR: Some of the very best American writers were working in the South then.

GV: At that time Faulkner had done his best work, but he wasn't very popular. I admired *All the King's Men*, Huey Long and politics, but I can't think of any of the other Southerners. Faulkner came from not far from my family's place in Mississippi. Mary Gore Wyatt, my great-aunt, had been his Latin teacher. We only met three or four times, but when we got together, we would talk kin. We would review what had happened to Cousin Addie and what happened after the fire. Southerners make such good novelists; they have so many stories because they have so much family. I adapted "Barn Burning" for television and I saw him after that. He said [*mimicking voice*], "I myself did not see it, I do not have the television"—as he called it—"but members of the family in town told me it was very good." I said I was going out to Hollywood. I had a contract with MGM. He had one with Warner Brothers. He was a cold little man, very impersonal. He said [*mimicking voice*], "If I may give you some advice, never make the mistake of taking films seriously. Fitzgerald did, and I think that was a mistake. You do it, you get your money, and then you go and do your own work." What he would say about the *auteur* theory would be wildly funny, because he knew what actors and directors were.

CR: But aren't you passionate about films?

GV: Yes, I was brought up on films. I am the generation of sound, which came in when I was four years old. I barely remember the silents, and I certainly remembered the heyday of MGM, the greatest studios, and all the great stars of the thirties and forties. By the fifties, I was writing movies. The curious thing is that as a child I saw *A Midsummer Night's Dream*, and by the time I was fourteen I had read all of Shakespeare with pleasure because I had seen this "great" movie. Now, I don't think that happens when a child today watches television.

CR: I see what you mean. Films stirred people to read more, whereas television refers only to itself. Except for the tie-ins, it positively discourages people from reading. Was the culture less materialistic, less blatantly commercial, when you began publishing your novels?

GV: No. It was somewhat different, but it was the same. The same commercialism, the same dullness prevailed, duller in some ways. The one exception is that the novel was at the center of the culture, and now the novel is off on the periphery. I never thought that would happen.

CR: In the writing of your novels, is the awareness that they might be turned into films a consideration?

GV: I always regarded it as two different sets of muscles. You use one set to make a movie and another set to make a novel. The better the novel is, the more untranslatable the tone of the author's voice is. That's why *Myra* doesn't work. *Portnoy's Complaint, The Great Gatsby, Madame Bovary* don't work, because there was a tone to them that doesn't translate.

CR: My next question, then, would be, Is your imagination verbal or visual?

GV: When you imagine, you *image-in.* I hear things much more than I see them, but I can start seeing after a time when I am writing. I hear voices, I am a mimic. I have just so many actors in my repertoire, and I know what they can do, and I make the scenes for them. As a novel, *Kalki* was like a movie. I even adapted it.

It may well be that the cinema has affected the novel, but, on the other hand, there were cinematic novels long before there were films. I was reading *Jude the Obscure* the other day, and, God, Hardy writes absolute movie scenes. There is a scene in *Jude* where the boy is being slung around by his father and as he goes around he sees the towers of Christ Church and Oxford in the distance. That's cinematic.

CR: In the second phase, with your return to fiction, people start describing your work as novels of ideas, beginning with *Messiah* and *Julian*. The point of view is one of wit and skepticism. And the central characters are adversaries from within. Is that the perspective that brought you back to fiction?

GV: After my ten years of "commercialism" I returned to fiction with *Julian*, which, of course, by the ultimate irony, proved to be more successful than any of my commercialism. It was followed by *Washington, D.C., Myra Breckinridge, Two Sisters, Burr*, and *1876*. I try out different voices which is why I do all those first-person narratives. I like impersonation. I like going into another character. I really believe *mimesis* is one of the highest aspects of art. So the "I" is mimetic. When you are in the first person, you have to have some connection with the character, though I come back to the mystery of Myra/Myron, which I think must be unique. I have nothing in common with Myra Breckinridge except total admiration. She is magnificent, she is mad as a hatter, and yet that is one of my voices. It just came to me one day. People are now talking about the "urbane, familiar tone" of my narrator; now, that really irritates me. In *Julian* I have four voices: Julian as emperor, trying to sound like Marcus Aurelius; the private Julian, who is frantic; Priscus, who is dry, cold, and sardonic; Libanius, who is feathery and oratorical. These four voices go all the way through the book and provide the variations.

CR: What of the Proustian idea that the novelist has one book to write, so that all of a writer's future development will be found in a germinal state in his very first work? Are your novels part of a larger structure?

GV: A unified-field theory? Well, if it is there, it is still inside of me. I have no master plan that I am conscious of. It may be that I am doing something instinctively, a bit the way a coral reef gets made. The little corals do not know, as they cling to the debris of their predecessors, exactly what kind of a creation they are going to make—a barrier reef. It may be that in the accretion of all these books and themes and characters I am constructing some whole, but I don't know what it is.

CR: You said that *Creation* came out of your work on *Julian*. Is there a continuum through the historical novels?

GV: I'm sure the lines converge. There is only so much a writer does. I use somewhere the idea that every writer has a given theatre in his head, a repertory company. Shakespeare has fifty characters, I have ten, Tennessee has five, Hemingway has one,

Beckett is busy trying to be none. You are stuck with your repertory company and you can only put on plays for them.

CR: At some point have you considered bringing all these aspects
of yourself together in one work?

GV: No, because it would be necessary for me then to sit down
and consider what it is that I have been doing for thirty-five
years, and I'm not about to do it. I'm not very personal, as I keep
saying, and I am not even personal about the books. "It is not
wise to investigate these things," as Tennessee would say.
"There should always be an air of mystery in the work." To
which my answer was, when I was having a little trouble in
adapting one of his plays [*Suddenly Last Summer*], "Yes, but
there should not be an area of confusion. Mystery is one thing,
confusion is another."

CR: Would you consider doing a document such as Tennessee
has done, an autobiography?

GV: After I read *Les Mots* by Sartre, I realized I would have to
find a form as unique as he found. He created a small masterpiece. Between *Les Mots* and *The Education of Henry Adams* I
am abashed. Unless I could find an arresting form, I wouldn't do
it. But to remember personalities is probably worth doing, and
now that I have lived so long and known so many people, I think
I'll do more and more essays of the sort I did on Tennessee and
Isherwood, in which I'm able to bring myself in as a sort of
counter-memoirist, to show them from another angle—mine not
theirs.

Tennessee Williams

THE LIVING ROOM OF Tennessee Williams's New York apartment at the Elysée Hotel had that impersonal elegance of white walls and white French furniture. The few mementos, such as framed photographs and books scattered around the rooms, only heightened the impression of transience. By contrast, Tennessee Williams, relaxed in casual dress on the sofa, was welcoming and smiling with contentment about his recently published memoirs.

His secretary, Joe Uecker, who maintained their schedule, had refreshments prepared on the coffee table. Tennessee introduced me to his sister, Rose, a petite woman, powdered and rouged and wearing a red tulle dress and bolero jacket. She smiled sweetly and sat with a drink, watching us as we talked—she would doze, wake up, take another drink, and then doze off again. Tennessee spoke to her as to a child, which seemed his customary way. He explained that Rose always visited him from upstate New York when he was staying in town.

Tennessee Williams entered the conversation with good-humored curiosity and spoke in a drawling nasal Southern twang. His mood was mercurial, at once laughing and anxious, stoical and sentimental, kindly and caustic. As he became more relaxed with each drink, he was more confiding, laughing at himself and the folly of the world. Only fatigue put an end to the conversation.

Thomas Lanier Williams was born in Columbus, Mississippi, in 1911. He changed his name when he left home for New Orleans.

It had been a college nickname because his father was from Tennessee, and he wanted to break with his early attempts at writing. Tennessee Williams wrote two novels, *The Roman Spring of Mrs. Stone* (1950) and *Moise and the World of Reason* (1975), and a novella, *The Knightly Quest* (1966); his short stories are published in *One Arm* (1948), *Hard Candy* (1954), and *Eight Mortal Ladies Possessed* (1974), and his poetry collected in *In the Winter of Cities* (1956) and *Androgyne, Mon Amour* (1977). He published a volume of memoirs in 1975, which was the occasion for this conversation.

He dominated the American theatre for twenty years, beginning with *Battle of Angels* (1940), a title taken from Anatole France; it was the first play to bring him public attention, and it evolved into *Orpheus Descending* (1957), and the basis of the film *The Fugitive Kind*. He won national acclaim with *The Glass Menagerie* (1945) and *A Streetcar Named Desire* (1947), *Summer and Smoke* (1948), *The Rose Tattoo* (1950), *Camino Real* (1953), *Cat on a Hot Tin Roof* (1955), *Garden District* (1958), *Suddenly Last Summer* (1958), *Sweet Bird of Youth* (1959), *Period of Adjustment* (1960), *The Night of the Iguana* (1962). All these plays were made into films, and he wrote an original film script for *Baby Doll* (1956). In the mid-sixties, he started writing the darker plays of his late phase, beginning with *Slapstick Tragedy* (1965), which includes *The Mutilated* and *Gnädiges Fräulein; The Seven Descents of Myrtle* (1968); *In the Bar of a Tokyo Hotel* (1969); *The Two Character Play* (1969), later rewritten and staged as *Out Cry* (1973); *The Red Devil Battery Sign* (1976); *Vieux Carré* (1977); *A Lovely Sunday for Crève Coeur* (1979); and a play about Scott and Zelda Fitzgerald entitled *Clothes for a Summer Hotel* (1980).

His style and concept of theatre underwent a change after his conversion to Catholicism in 1968. In the plays of his last period the action is secondary to the monologues of the characters, who explain themselves to the audience. Beautifully as these plays may read, the stage productions failed; the last fifteen years of his life presented a harsh contradiction: his earlier works were in production around the world, as part of the international theatrical repertory, while each new work failed on stage, almost unanimously lambasted with dismissive cruelty by theatrical critics. This situation has been variously explained. One theory has it that he wrote under the influence of alcohol and drugs. Another interpretation is that Tennessee Williams's gorgeous theatrical diction and imagination were in conflict with his increasing tendency to reduce his plays to a structure of monologues. For his supporters it was a pack of curs setting upon the old lion.

On the night of February 24, 1983, Tennessee Williams died of strangulation in his bedroom at the Elysée. James Laughlin, his lifelong friend and the publisher of all his works, told me that Tennessee Williams wished to be cremated and to have his ashes scattered over the Caribbean Sea, at the point where Hart Crane had committed suicide by leaping off the deck of a ship. But Tennessee Williams's surviving brother, Dakin, had him buried next to their parents in the family plot in St. Louis.

TW: I'm quite through with the kind of play that established my early and popular reputation. I am doing a different thing, which is altogether my own, not influenced at all by other playwrights at home or abroad, or by other schools of theatre. My thing is what it always was, to express my world and experience of it in whatever form seems suitable to the material.

CR: Were you conscious of this change, or was it something you experienced and understood in retrospect?

TW: My plays in the 1940s and 1950s were relatively conventional in their construction, because my mind was relatively balanced. You see, the dreadful period of almost clinical depression had not set in yet. But as my life became more desperate I had to change the style, because the conventional pattern of a play no longer could contain that kind of frenzy.

CR: Was it the pressures of your success or the attacks by the critics that brought on this crisis?

TW: It was the sudden change as much as anything. The public and the critics were both favorable for quite a while. That's usually the case with a playwright in America who breaks through at all. From about *Menagerie* through *Cat* I had only one or two failures, such as *Camino Real*, which was a commercial failure. Later it was recognized as an artistic success. It was too broad a canvas to work on, and neither I nor the director seemed to realize that it was really a romantic pageant. I'm hoping that in the opera we're making of it now, for production next year, the pageant quality will come through more clearly.

CR: Your love for that play continually comes up.

TW: Oh, yes, because it has such a free form, and I love that. I like breaking out of the conventional forms. Now, *Red Devil Battery Sign* is a return to the conventional pattern but with a most volatile subject matter.

CR: What other work failed?

TW: *Period of Adjustment*, although we thought it was going to be my most popular play. I called it a comedy. It really wasn't a comedy. It was funny, yes. So is *Streetcar* funny. Blanche is a scream in that thing. I would laugh like hell when I wrote both of them. But *Period of Adjustment* isn't. I began to go into areas of my own head which were not easily communicable to a large audience, but now are beginning to be.

CR: When did you begin to feel that you were losing your command over the theatre?

TW: With plays like *Camino Real*, which I thought most surely would be recognized for eloquence of language and certain passages but was simply dismissed by the critics, just laughed at. I remember in Philadelphia I was very angry on opening night. Great blocks of people would get up and start walking out, and I would get in the aisle and try to turn them back into their seats. I'd scream and peg things at them.

CR: Is there a critic or any criticism that you've found pertinent to your writing?

TW: I think the best thing you can do about the critics is never say a word. In the end you have the last say, and they know it.

They can close your play, but if it has vitality it will be done again. Sooner or later they will accept it.

CR: But as a leading playwright, surely you were prepared for the worst as well as the best.

TW: It didn't surprise me, to tell you the truth. It's the pattern in America. A writer has a period of success, and then there is something instinctive in the critical world; they create a figure which is somewhat larger than its actual size, and then they start trying to cut it down to what they think is its actual size. Sometimes they diminish it to the vanishing point.

CR: Did you write *Glass Menagerie* while working the graveyard shift at a factory in St. Louis?

TW: Well, no. A lot of people think I wrote *The Glass Menagerie* while I was employed by MGM. This is not true. I didn't write for films for more than three weeks. I was given the assignment of writing a film for Lana Turner—*Marriage Is a Private Affair*, it was called. The producer happened to have an attachment of a romantic nature to the lady, but he was realistic about her abilities as an actress. He would keep saying, "Oh, this is beautiful stuff, Mr. Williams, but she can't say it. She doesn't know how to read it. Now, why don't you just forget all about this Hollywood business, this screenwriting business, and just go out to Santa Monica. We're obliged to pay you two hundred forty dollars a week, so just come in and collect your check, go back out to Santa Monica Beach, and do your own work," he said, "because your own work is good." I saved enough money so that I could spend a summer free of harassment, and free of occupation, in Provincetown. I wrote *The Glass Menagerie* there, and also in the law school dormitory at Harvard, because I had a friend there.

CR: Perhaps I'll write the dorm suggesting they put up a plaque. Was that your first success as a playwright?

TW: Success is such a false word, really. I think perhaps Andy Warhol can define it: "Success is what sells," isn't it?

CR: It must give you some satisfaction to know that your plays are part of the international repertory.

TW: Yes, but as I said, they are usually the ones that were successful, the earlier ones. I get a good many letters from people who appreciate my work, but I don't get very good notices.

CR: Which play marks the transition in your writing?

TW: Let's say that the work has become darker. It began to become darker in the sixties and it became so dark that people find it painful. Now we're in a particularly escapist period. People want lighter and lighter things, and my work continues to get darker. *Camino Real* was a real departure from convention, yes, but *Suddenly Last Summer* was the first work that reflected the emotional trauma, that of my life, very deeply.

CR: The play introduces psychoanalysis to investigate the pathology beneath these privileged lives.

TW: Yes, quite true. I think mainly through the *tour de force* performance by Anne Meacham and Hortense Alden they broke through to the public, got the response to esoteric material on opening night.

CR: It's also the play that gives a definition of God.

TW: These people were total sybarites, creatures with no social conscience whatsoever, and consequently they're godless. They would conceive of God as being the predatory birds killing the newly hatched turtles. They would think that was the face of God. God exists in our understanding of each other, and in our acts based upon our understanding. This is what the doctor does at the end, when he accepts the girl's story. Now, Sebastian's death is treated realistically on the screen, which was deplorable. Actually, cannibalism was simply a dramatic metaphor. It's never been accepted as such because people have seen the picture and not the play.

CR: All of your plays were made into films. It's in *The Milk Train Doesn't Stop Here Anymore* that you have a central character who lives by sexually exploiting others.

TW: *Milk Train* is going to be recognized as an important film, some say, because it was much better written than the play version. It was somewhat damaged in the end by the foolish act of the man tossing a big diamond into the ocean. That wasn't in the script.

CR: I didn't know that you had written the screenplay.

TW: I wrote the screenplay. But I didn't write that scene, because the ambiguity is supposed to exist: there's the element of the con man in him, but there's also an element of the mystic. He has made a career out of attending very old women to the door but, I think, with real concern for them.

CR: The metaphor of cannibalism in *Suddenly Last Summer* is sex as one person consuming another.

TW: I think it's as old as time, as old as human history. I think people have always paid for the sexual favors of the younger. I'm very grateful that my sexual appetites are waning and that I look more for companionship now than for sexual excitement. I'm not free of Eros, but Eros may be free of me. There's a lot of comedy in that when you don't have to be heavy about it.

CR: Which play, then, establishes your changed viewpoint?

TW: I think it became pretty dark in *In the Bar of a Tokyo Hotel* and *A Slapstick Tragedy. The Gnädiges Fräulein* has a gothic quality to it, a grotesque comedy that was incomprehensible to people. They didn't even see the humor in it. They just saw what fears they have. Everyone has the fears that are expressed in these plays—death, confinement, and deprivation.

CR: Your characters have become isolated. Are they beyond forming relationships, or are they autonomous, if that's possible?

TW: There are people who are by nature autonomous, in that they are incapable of relating to other people. They do on the surface, but there's no inner commitment to another person, or other people, or to society.

CR: But that's a prevalent attitude nowadays.

TW: There's a particular withdrawal I've noticed in the seventies from social commitment, of feeling any responsibility to the society in which you live, and the time in which you live. I find it boring as hell. One of my best lines is "There's no such thing as an inescapable corner with two people in it." You have escaped into the other person, from your solitary self.

CR: In these plays, you present characters talking about themselves.

TW: Yes, people trying to be comprehended by other people, and talking almost compulsively about themselves. I find myself doing that. I become very garrulous about myself if I have an audience.

CR: On stage, in *Small Craft Warnings*, *Out Cry*, in *Tokyo Hotel* . . .

TW: Everybody is talking about himself. Actually, I think that's a fault. I saw a play in London that impressed me enormously, Harold Pinter's *No Man's Land*. The four characters—each had a scene in which he was the principal talker. There was a good interchange among them, although there was no real communication. One of the points he makes is that although they talk a great deal, and deliver long soliloquies, they don't really reach each other.

CR: Whereas your characters do, however briefly.

TW: Sometimes they do. I hope they do. Perhaps I'm a little less dark in my view of life than Pinter, although he writes more amusingly. He's very funny.

CR: *Out Cry* is an example of why you feel your later plays are misstaged.

TW: I had a number of references to sunflowers in the script; they had these huge projections of sunflowers on the back wall. They weren't necessary, unfortunately. I don't blame it on the gentleman who designed the set, because he was encouraged in this. Everything had to be literally shown. If they were in prison, there had to be bars, or trapped figures projected in huge size on the cyclorama of the set. It was put together by Mr. Peter Glenville, the director. He arbitrarily took out whatever he thought he wanted from all the versions. I had practically nothing to do with it. For instance, Genevieve Bujold came down from Canada twice to read for the part of the girl. I was not permitted to hear her. She would have been perfect opposite Michael York.

CR: Ordinarily, you rewrite your plays for each production?

TW: I rewrite more than most people.

CR: How many versions of *Out Cry* have there been?

TW: The first version was the one in London in '67. To tell you the truth, I was in no condition to notice much going on. I behaved abominably. I was introduced to the director and I said, "You know, plays have to be directed." To the designer I said, "Was that a set?" Well, I've had much happier experiences.

CR: You felt you were giving them what they deserved?

TW: No, I don't think so. I think a playwright should try to keep his cool under all circumstances. Even with Mr. Merrick—that's the acid test.

CR: Was the play rewritten for the Chicago production in '71?

TW: The text of the Chicago production was close to the current text, but it was not edited, it was not cut. One of the great improvements now is that the play has been reduced to its proper size. Between a third and a fourth has been cut out.

CR: Was it Mr. Glenville who re-edited the play for performance in New York?

TW: I'm being slightly unfair, because he did consult me to some extent about it. But I was so overawed by the prospect of having a Broadway production for this little play that I just let him go ahead. Things only got a bit uptight when we were on the road. I felt that I was not being allowed to cut and revise as I should. The time seemed wasted.

CR: It's surprising how the text of a play seems to have an autonomous existence.

TW: Autonomous existence apart from the writer?

CR: Yes, the way directors cut, change, and shape the text.

TW: Well, I'll tell you. People associate my name with successes. I've had a succession of failures. You have no idea of how it reduces your power. You have less and less say when you are dealing with people who are dominating and aggressive. You have less and less control over your productions.

CR: Are producers drawn to your plays chiefly because your earlier works were guaranteed box-office hits?

TW: I think that my new work is just baffling to them. They read it, and something intrigues them perhaps. Then, when they try to stage it, it eludes them.

CR: What do you think of experimental theatre groups which do not rely on the text for the performance?

TW: There's a great subtlety in interpretation by the director and the performers when they work as an ensemble with an exquisite sense of what each of them wanted, what they were working towards. There's a unity there, a concept.

CR: Even though you are a Broadway playwright, are you interested in experimental productions for your new plays?

TW: I find that my great happiness in the theatre now is not on Broadway, but off-Broadway and off-off-Broadway. There's not the financial responsibility hanging over your head. You don't feel there's three hundred sixty thousand dollars riding on something that you've written. I don't think that the money thing should be there at all, but it is there. That's what the producers are thinking about: "OK, we're making money here in Boston, but will we be making it in Washington for seven weeks?" Considerations of that nature impinge too much. I will never write for Broadway again. Except I made this one commitment to myself, which was to complete the play in which Anthony Quinn was so brilliant, *The Red Devil Battery Sign*. Quinn couldn't work off-Broadway. Certain big stars just can't work off-Broadway. A limousine has to pick them up and take them to the theatre, wait there all during the performance, and take them back to their Park Avenue hotel. That's part of their life style they cannot abandon because they feel they will be abandoning the prestige.

CR: You stated to the press that you felt that the demise of *Red Devil* before reaching Broadway was politically motivated.

TW: We had four producers. Bob Colby wanted to bring it in, but the other two sided with Merrick and decided not to bring it in, despite the fact that we were doing good business. But they did me a favor. I am glad this is on tape because I am going to say it: it made me so angry when they closed that I said, "God damn it, I'm going to show them I can write a fine play out of this." I worked like hell on it, and it is a fine play now, and it has a strong, straight story line. I used every trick of the craft I've learned to hold an audience. I've used sex—that's not a trick because I'm naturally sensual and like sexual scenes. The emphasis is no longer on sexuality. The emphasis now is on the inexorable story of two doomed people. He is doomed by a malignant growth on the brain, which is coming back after an operation. She is going to be faithful to her early heritage and testify before Congress in the McCarthy hearings. She has decoded documents in her possession which are seized when her godfather is murdered. The whole thing goes towards an inevitable conclusion.

CR: The events are set during the McCarthy hearings. Which aspect of that witch hunt did you find most upsetting?

TW: It's the moral decay of America, which really began with the Korean War, way before the Kennedy assassination. The main reason we were involved in Vietnam was so two hundred billion dollars worth of equipment could be destroyed and would have to be bought again. We're the death merchants of the world, this once great and beautiful democracy. People think I'm a communist [for saying this], but I hate all bureaucracy, all isms. I'm a revolutionary only in the sense that I want to see us escape from this sort of trap.

CR: Yet in your plays, many of your characters express a painful class consciousness rather than a social consciousness.

TW: All my plays have a social conscience. I don't think that any play, any playwright, or any work of art is going to make any difference in the course of history. History is inexorable in its flow, and I think the flow of history is towards some form of social upheaval. I'm giving you my viewpoint. I'm not stating fact, I'm telling you what I feel, what I intuit. Our country got into trouble when it ceased to be able to exist within its own frontiers. When it had to expand onto other continents, that was the beginning of our moral collapse.

CR: Do you see the possibility of change?

TW: I have a positive view of the future. I think we're going to go through almost total destruction, but not quite. I think we'll stop just short of it.

CR: What form of government do you foresee for this country? Is there a model you have in mind?

TW: I think England is fast approaching some kind of socialism, but they will retain their monarchy. They should, because a monarchy is an ornament. I met Princess Margaret recently at a party when some drunken Southern lady pushed me into a loveseat next to her. She said, "You two sit down and have a good giggle together." Princess Margaret was so startled, but so was I. I'm always impressed by the beauty of behavior of people trained in a certain way. The monarchy sets an example of good breeding and good manners for a whole nation. I believe that society can rectify any inequities without the shattering of gentle behavior. I find myself violating my own principles at times. It makes me angry when I'm forced to get angry.

CR: Is it the moral code attached to that behavior which you value?

TW: The moral way is the way of survival now. They become identical.

CR: Your characters fear social degradation. Is that the effect of the Depression? In your *Memoirs* you mention trying to join the WPA writers' project.

TW: In those days you had to prove your family was destitute or they wouldn't let you on. I had no way of proving that my father was destitute, because he was a sales manager of a branch of a big shoe company. He wouldn't give me a penny. Nevertheless, I wasn't eligible.

CR: Did that awaken a political awareness?

TW: Oh, I was a socialist from the time I started working for a shoe company. That will do it every time. Sixty-five dollars a month. Surrounded by all these lathes, my God!

CR: You write about Hart Crane, who influenced your own poetry.

TW: I never met Hart Crane. I read of his death in 1932, when he jumped off the stern of a ship called the *Esmeralda*. It was twenty-four hours north of Havana, and in my will there is a codicil that I should be buried at sea as close as possible to the point where he jumped overboard, because I had a great reverence for Hart Crane as an artist.

CR: In your *Memoirs* you've said that *In the Bar of a Tokyo Hotel* is the first full statement of your darker vision.

TW: That was the last play I wrote before I had my overdiscussed breakdown. You see, I was in a deep depression from 1963 till the breakdown occurred in 1969. At the time of *In the Bar of a Tokyo Hotel* I was just approaching the collapse. The producers, a very nice couple named Marks, were visiting in Key West, and I was seeing them daily. I didn't know they were in town. I was working slowly out of my own conscious mind. The one thing I rewrote during my confinement is *Tokyo Hotel*.

CR: What was your interpretation of the play?

TW: The theme of creation. I think the couple, the artist and his wife in that play, were two sides of one person. One side was a man driven mad by the passion to create, which was frustrated, and the woman, as he described her, was a compulsive bitch.

CR: What kind of changes did you make?

TW: Textual changes. I tried to remove some of the hysteria from the painter's talk about his work.

CR: Those are some of your most eloquent passages.

TW: I think the most beautiful passages were those of the woman. I also like the scene just before his death when he says, "One of those diaphanous August afternoons . . ." The music of the language is what I like.

CR: I found the description of the creative process beautiful.

TW: Of course that doesn't impress me because I'm so familiar with it. I was going through a bad time corresponding to what the painter was going through. But do you know who I thought I was writing about? Jackson Pollock, not myself. Tony Smith, a dear friend of mine, was also a close friend of Pollock's, and I knew towards the end that Jackson Pollock was crawling around naked on the floor with a spray gun, just spraying canvas and just streaking it over the canvas with his fingers.

CR: As the painter in *Tokyo Hotel* strips himself and nails the canvas to the floor. Were you aware of the suicidal drive in Pollock?

TW: Yes, yes. I realized that when he drove his car into a tree accidentally, but drunkenly. These things are not accidental. I know because I did the same thing with a car in Italy after a violent quarrel with a lover. I just filled a Thermos with martinis and I drove faster and faster, drinking the whole Thermos bottle. A truck came out of a side road and I just turned slightly, but I didn't control the car, and wrapped it around a tree. Well, this is a form of suicide. My typewriter flew out of the back seat and hit me on the head. It was amazing that I survived. I had a concussion. When I came to, I was surrounded by all these Italian farm people, *contadini,* they call them. Each had a little glass in his hand and was shaking like this. They thought I was dead.

CR: I wanted to ask you your thoughts on writer's block, and the idea of a writer having said all that he has to say, in the manner of E. M. Forster.

TW: All writers have periods of block, and some of them are blocked permanently. It seems to me around age forty-five it occurs, and it may be just a matter of their running out of material. They've said what they have to say. I've been blocked myself. The cause of it was a time of depleted energy after I had completed a piece of work. I just didn't have the strength to go on. The thing to do is rest, to take time off and let the energy rebuild. The desire to create is one of the strongest urges a human spirit can contain. It will always break through, I think.

CR: Aside from your plays and film scripts, you have written novels, poetry, as well as your *Memoirs*, so it's difficult to think of you as having any sort of block.

TW: Oh, I have, though, continually. I could have written much more and much better if I had not always been afraid of my inabilities to write. But I've learned to live with it. It's a bit late to start worrying that I won't be able to write at sixty-five. I haven't written half enough.

Marguerite Young

MARGUERITE YOUNG IS A WRITER who has always taken her own direction. In 1937 she published her first collection of verse, *Prismatic Ground*, written while she attended Indiana University. Next was the appearance in 1944 of *Moderate Fable*, her last volume of poetry, followed by *Angel in the Forest* (1945), the history of the two utopian communities established in New Harmony, Indiana, in the early nineteenth century. Through the forties and fifties, Marguerite Young was a regular contributor to *Vogue, Mademoiselle, The New York Times*, the Chicago *Sun, Harper's Bazaar, New World Writing*, the *Kenyon Review, New Directions*, etc. She was also fiction editor of *The Tiger's Eye*. Portions of the novel on which she was to work for eighteen years would appear in print periodically. *Miss MacIntosh, My Darling*, her novel, was brought out in its entirety by Scribner's in 1965. In its style and structure, *Miss MacIntosh, My Darling* turns away from all the conventions of the artistic milieu that produced it. Marguerite Young's novel is that rare phenomenon, a commercially published novel that experiments with all the conventions of the form. It is circular in construction and written in imagistic prose. The inquest is the thread connecting the four parts, each of which focuses primarily on one character. The first is Miss MacIntosh herself, the governess, who epitomizes the madness of common sense. The others are the Opium Lady, whose dream state encompasses a highly refined level of consciousness; Mr. Spitzer, whose life carries on that of

his deceased twin brother; and Esther Longtree, the barren waitress, who is perpetually pregnant. Each chapter is self-contained
yet repeats sentences and paragraphs from previous chapters—a
pattern that comes from Marguerite Young's own work in poetry
and the ballad form. Every step forward in the narrative conjures
up the past, and conventional time sequence is abandoned in favor
of the free flow of psychological association. The novel has imbed-
ded within it a speculation on history; but Western history, especially grass roots American history, is absorbed into the narrative
as image, metaphor, and emblem. The style as Marguerite Young
defines it derives from the Elizabethan: lush, elaborate, and ency-
clopedic in scope.

As a protest against the war in Vietnam, Marguerite Young
discontinued her work on the life of James Whitcomb Riley to
write a brief biography of Eugene Victor Debs, America's first socialist candidate for president. This work has grown into a two-
volume history of Debs and his times, tracing utopian and anti-
utopian quests, taking in the vast panorama of the cultural life of
the times.

Marguerite Young's daily routine and work habits take place
within the circumference of the West Village, with Sheridan
Square at its center. She is a predictable figure on the streets ra-
diating from that center. Yet someone unfamiliar with her remarked on seeing her, "She stood out as brilliantly and as
individually as a Florentine angel that had materialized on the
sidewalks of New York." She's of medium stature and wears her
long brownish-red hair straight, with bangs. Her clothes are worn
multi-layered in a variety of colors, with shades of red as her favorites. Over her long skirts and high black open-toed "Polish governess boots" she wears blouses, sweaters, jackets, ponchos, and capes
in layers accented with brooches and beads. Her pace is slow and
meditative as she walks, her expression abstracted, a preoccupied
state that separates her from the bustle of the streets. In the afternoon she comes out for coffee at one of three places where she is
always awaited and welcomed. There she seems most at home,
surrounded by the animation and talk of "the floating world," a
mixture of theatre people, writers, political activists, students, out-
of-towners, and down-and-outers of all occupations. It was in a

coffee house that we met and held several conversations until it was decided that the interview would take place at her home.

Marguerite Young lives on Bleecker Street where it transforms itself into a quiet tree-lined block of row houses. She admits no one into her apartment when working intensively, as she was now, on the life of Debs. I was the exception to the rule, she informed me. When she opened the door I entered the visible world of her imagination. The walls were painted red with white trim, and lined with bookcases holding her library of Americana and literature. On every shelf the room repeated itself in miniature sofas and easy chairs set on tiny rugs lit by minute lamps and chandeliers. On the walls and bookcases images of children, birds, angels, flowers, seashells were multiplied and repeated everywhere as pictures, prints, figurines, statues, and paintings. The room in which we sat was dominated by a merry-go-round horse with ribbons streaming from the brass pole that held it to the ceiling. Looking on this conversation with great blue glass eyes was a life-sized porcelain Victorian doll, exquisitely dressed in lace. Marguerite Young sat on a couch across from me. She placed the ashtray within easy reach on the coffee table. She smoked constantly during the interview. Her voice has a Midwestern flavor, sometimes slow, sometimes rapid, and even guffawing with laughter, in a rhythm of choice phrasing. With a sharp look of her brown eyes, she said, "So, just ask the first question."

CR: Where in Indiana were you born and brought up?

MY: I was born in Indianapolis, Indiana, "the Athens of the West," as it had been called in an earlier day. That was when Booth Tarkington, Meredith Nicholson, James Whitcomb Riley, various writers of the old Hoosier group lived there. We were always brought up to believe that to be born in Indiana was to be born a poet. That is a myth which I can't accept now but I did accept then. I remember telling my grandmother, when I was about seven years old, that I intended to be a poet.

CR: You were brought up by your grandmother? Did she shape your sensibilities?

MY: When I was three my parents went their separate ways. I have no memory of parental relationships at all. There were years in which I scarcely saw them. I lived with a grandmother who idealized me and projected upon me all her own dreams of artistry and poetry, the writer she would have been. She had a genius personality, according to all who knew her, and in my own recollections. She was a flamboyant, colorful, fantastic personality who spoke aloud in metaphors and similes, with proverbs and fairy tales, Biblical lore, all kinds of wonderful folk tales, and old Scottish border ballads. She believed in no inhibition whatever of a child's subjective life. No question in the realm of what might be dismissed by other people as fairy tale was ever dismissed by her as irrational.

CR: Did you know why you were so special to her?

MY: One reason that she was so drawn to me was that two weeks before I was born her little grandson Harry died suddenly of diphtheria. He was about seven or eight years old, my golden-haired cousin. She had his portrait hanging on the wall, wearing a white sailor suit, with long gold corkscrew curls of the Little Lord Fauntleroy era. She believed that I was God's gift to her, that little Harry had been born again in me. At times she seemed to believe this and at other times she would tell me that I was her favorite child on earth, but I had one competitor, little Harry, who had gone to heaven. She used to sing a wonderful old folk song of the nineties, "Little Harry's gone to Heaven / On a cold and Sunday night / With his Sunday cane beside him / In his little suit of white." I was interested in this sense of the dead child in my life, because when I read Dali's autobiography, he, too, was supposed to take the place of a brother who had died, and it was believed that he had returned to earth with the spirit of this other child. It contributed a great deal to his sense of the surreal, the imaginative, the dualities of life and the depths of dreams. Of course, you have this great relationship with an absolutely loving, much older person, who is preparing to leave the world and is attributing to you all the thoughts and dreams of her own, with the idea that you will be her vehicle in futurity. My grandmother believed what the Jesuits said, that if you have a child for the first eight years of his life, you have him forever. She always thought that everything about me would bear the impression of her dreams and her literary and artistic interests.

CR: Do you think she molded you towards fulfilling her idea of a destiny?

MY: She wanted me to be a writer. From the earliest infancy I memorized a verse or two of the Bible every day, the King James version, which she thought was important for a sense of imagery and music. It was the best training a writer could have, and she would always remind me that the translation was made under the aegis of one of my Stuart ancestors. She would tell me about the kings and queens of Scotland, France, and England from whom I was descended.

The first poem I wrote when I was about seventeen. It was

about my grandmother, the ballad-loving woman. "She was a ballad-loving woman / Who lived until she died; with a hey lillelu and a how-lo-lan / Her sorry tears were dried." When I was a very little girl my grandmother sang "Barbara Allen" or "There were three ravens set on a tree / They were black as black might be . . . " or that wonderful one about the girl who goes to meet her lover and gets up into the tree branches to wait for him. She sees him come and dig a grave, and she knows he's going to kill her. All those wonderful old ballads I would hear!

CR: Did she also make you write as a game or an exercise?

MY: Well, she praised my writing, and knew from the earliest time when I began to pick up a pencil that I would be a writer. She said I would be either a writer, or the first woman president of the United States, or that I would become a lawyer who would work to restore the lost family fortune. There were so many lost family fortunes that my little sister and I used to be afraid of kidnappers who would kidnap us for our golden crowns—although, of course, we were not rich. But we didn't know that.

CR: Was she as fond of your younger sister and her other grandchildren?

MY: She loved the others, but she thought her other grandchildren were exuberant, extroverted children who would not be writers. I have no idea of the earliest memory, nor of the earliest moment when she thought that I would be a writer. My sense of abandonment was very great. She would say to me, "And the stone that was rejected, shall be the foundation stone of the new creation. . . ." She felt that out of what might be considered a displacement, or what surely was a tragedy, some special good would come, something, somehow, which is almost the theme of *What Maisie Knew.* I would know, though I might have missed the normal things in life. So, rather than indicating to me that I should somehow envy the world of the middle class, the Main Street world, so to speak, she always acted as if there was a special beauty in this fate of missing the average way. It reminds me somewhat in later years of what Bertrand Russell's grandmother said to him—"How lucky you are that your parents died and you were left to me." They would have inhibited his development or killed him in some way, and she indulged all his fantasies.

CR: Since a parent's absence is such an open door to a child's imagination, did you make up an explanation for it? From a mature perspective, is it more understandable?

MY: This is something I've had to ponder on—why my mother was the rebel, the unconventional, beautiful, pluralistic person who had to have many loves. It may be simply the spirit of the time, because she was as beautiful as the Gish sisters in *Orphans of the Storm*. She had the same mothlike, beautiful face, and she wanted to be an actress or a dancer and was just too far removed from that possibility. She married my father almost as a wager, and the minute she said "I do," she was thinking "I don't." I heard that story from other women.

CR: Marguerite, when you were an adolescent, your grandmother began having hallucinations, but you continued to live with her.

MY: She was having cerebral hemorrhages, which were strokes, and she would be incapacitated for a few weeks and then be herself again, and on the fifth stroke she died. During the last year or two of her life she seemed to speak in a semi-hallucinated way to myself and my little sister. We were left to keep our sense of equilibrium, with no one's help. As I remember her now, it was like living with Lear on the heath, which I did not know was caused by her hemorrhages.

CR: When was her illness diagnosed?

MY: After her death. I did know that it was like living with some beautiful tragic actress, and I heard beautiful tales and Blakean visions. I have told a few psychiatrist friends of mine about her, and they always say that it sounds to them like a very rich personality but not someone who was mad. She was just in a state halfway between dream and reality, between life and death, knowing that she was going to die and speaking at the edge of the grave, dancing at the edge of the grave.

CR: You mentioned Lear. Was it a rage?

MY: Never! It was always poetic and cosmic. It had a great deal
to do with angels and unearthly creatures. I know there were
angels in the house. I had always been taught that there were
angels, and if you went to do anything wrong you were supposed
to say, "Get thee behind me, Satan." I was always whirling to try
to catch Satan as he was getting behind me.

    When my grandmother died my first thought was, Oh well,
now she can tell Anatole France that she has a little granddaughter on earth who adores him. I missed her so much. It was the
first death I ever knew. If I had been sure that I could find her
and Anatole France, I would have joined them. I would have
gone.

CR: Anaïs Nin tells the story of your attempting to commit suicide, but apparently you began writing a note and forgot all
about it.

MY: Which time? I used to think about committing suicide when
I was about eighteen. I had it worked out that I would do it in
multiple ways, all at once. I would stand upon a high tree house
overlooking the river, and I would put a rope around my neck
and take poison and shoot myself and fall into the river all at
once. I think I worked this out because of Dorothy Parker's
poem, "Ropes give . . ."—all the reasons you could not commit
suicide. At the age of eighteen all the young poets, all three or
four of us, we all thought we would be dead at twenty-one—of
old age.

CR: You have interesting antecedents. Does your family go back
to Brigham Young?

MY: Well, that was on my father's side. Brigham Young went to
school two weeks in his life and lived to found a university and a
great empire saved by the seagulls who ate the locusts.

CR: You mean Salt Lake City?

MY: Yes. I love Brigham Young and all things related to him, particularly Joseph Smith, who was the more poetic of that team.
The ancestry on which my maternal grandmother prided herself

was certainly not my father's people, Brigham Young or the Mormons, but rather, the family of the French Huguenot William Sublette, who discovered the Big Horn Glacier and was an explorer for the government. He was at the head of the expedition on which Audubon painted the birds. My grandmother was also a direct descendant of John Knox, the founder of the Presbyterian Church.

CR: In Scotland?

MY: Yes. He married the granddaughter of the King of Scotland who perished at Flodden Field. It was that side, the French and the Scottish, of which we were told a great deal more.

CR: Is that why you say the Scots consider you a Scottish writer?

MY: Well, I hope they do, since John Knox had the good luck of founding a family line that included some of the finest writers Scotland has ever produced, among them Lord Byron.

CR: Who else?

MY: James Boswell, David Hume . . .

CR: You're going to claim them all?

MY: I claim them all as relatives: Herman Melville, Jane Welsh Carlyle, Robert Louis Stevenson. So I hope I am a Scottish writer.

CR: If your grandmother was the great personal influence, the geographical impact was Indiana. Indiana is the center of all of your subsequent writing. But you are more interested in the psychology of your characters than you are in realistic landscape, aren't you? You do not have that love of the prairie grasses and the low horizon line of Willa Cather, for example.

MY: No. It was my fate to be born in Indiana. I probably would have chosen Edinburgh if you had asked me, or maybe Rome. But I believe that we start with what we are as writers, and Indiana is a land rich in legend. I tried to transmute this legend into a universal and cosmic statement of some kind and not to be strictly a regionalist. If you are asking me if I love nature, I could not really say that I do. I love the sea and the sand, but I am not a person who just loves nature. Yet I write about it continually, because I am interested in the birds and beasts for their symbolic value—their value as icons, as ways of saying things about people.

As a poet, I had been an expert in that realm, studying birds and beasts from Heraclitus onward, and I love the old bestiaries. I wrote my master's thesis at the University of Chicago on the birds and beasts of *Euphues and His England*—and for that I had to study the history of every bird and beast there ever was.

CR: Do you like the work of Cather and the regionalist writers?

MY: I like Willa Cather. I don't love her. I love Mark Twain, because he had this cosmic, dark, brooding pessimism. I love Theodore Dreiser. They were great thinkers, great dreamers, who happened to come from the Middle West.

CR: So you make a distinction between regionalist writers and writers who happen to be located in certain states in America, but who work in an international style.

MY: I have always said that Southern writers seem to be born to sing. They live in small towns where they hear the most beautiful balladry, every day, from their own people and from the black people. I have lived in Southern towns in the very heart of Kentucky and Tennessee. I have always envied Southern writers because experience is so directly accessible to them. But the Middle West is more prosperous and more middle-class. If you are going to be a writer from the Middle West, you have to become highly sophisticated, highly educated in order to interpret that land with reality. You cannot be just a natural-born singer—I could not imagine anything less possible. I think the Middle West begets bizarre, beautiful writers who have been dipped and dyed in traditions exceeding the parochial.

CR: Did you feel the need to go abroad to develop your talent, like other writers of your generation, such as Henry Miller, Anaïs Nin, Malcolm Lowry, and Paul Bowles, who went to Paris, North Africa, or Mexico?

MY: No. I felt the urge to go by mule's back to the mountains of Tennessee, collecting ballads, old Scottish ballads. I was very much an admirer of Stith Thompson, the great ballad authority who was a professor at Indiana University. But as it was the Depression—even that kind of adventure was impossible. Those people you mentioned were so far away. I never thought of them. They were like people of another planet. I was never a person who ever, then or now, watched what other writers do. During the depressed thirties, I was at the University of Chicago studying the Elizabethans and the Jacobeans, and then I became involved with utopias in *Angel in the Forest.* I had lived in and out of many Kentucky and Tennessee towns and was very fascinated by the individual history of each, such as Horse Cave, Kentucky, and the graveyard in Shelbyville. So you might say that I was a graveyard poetess at that time.

CR: Did you go to New Harmony specifically to research the town for *Angel in the Forest?*

MY: My mother and stepfather moved there, and they called me. They said, "You'll love this new town. It is the scene of two lost utopias, and it has in it the footprints of the Angel Gabriel. It has cruciform shapes on the doors, and a maze."

So when I went there, I simply lived there for seven years off and on and gradually began to write about it. There was no artificial research, except for the experience of living there and talking to the beautiful old-timers in that town. Some were believers in the party of Father Rapp, who was the founder of the first utopia. They loved him because he had left visible evidence of his place—the cruciform, the maze, the angel's footprints, the sundial painted on the wall. Before the railroad, the sundial was the way people told time; there was no watch in general evidence until the railroad came to the land.

CR: Can you recall how you worked then?

MY: Yes. I wrote *Angel in the Forest* at night, because I was teaching during the day. I would get home from my school at four o'clock, sleep from four to five, have dinner at the corner drugstore, and from about six to midnight I would write, every night. I did not write the book with any thought whatever of publication. I just thought that when I was finished with the book I would give a copy to the Library of Congress, for future scholars of utopias. I did want my poems to be published, but it was only through being at the University of Iowa that I met people who pointed the way toward publication.

CR: You were going to write a series of poems?

MY: The first version of *Angel in the Forest* was a series of sixty ballads, in a Robert Browning manner. After I did the ballads, I could see that while I had depicted the utopian town New Harmony and its personalities, the history was omitted. It was not what I wanted, so I tried blank verse in the Miltonic sense. I still couldn't get all those facts and figures in, so then I reluctantly decided to put it into prose. I was determined not to lose anything in the ballads or in the blank-verse version. So when I began to write for the first time in prose, I kept bringing into the text everything I had written in the two poetic versions. It was the prose variation that took me about three years. I used all those images. I wanted to write a poetic prose. I would never have written anything in plain prose then or at any time since then. It does not interest me.

CR: When you speak of poetic prose, do you mean an imagistic style rather than writing with the economy of poetry?

MY: Yes, the imagistic seventeenth-century tradition of Sir Thomas Browne, and Burton's *Anatomy of Melancholy*. I think they were the main influence upon *Angel in the Forest*. I always thought I would write lyric poetry, and I just got into *Angel in the Forest* through necessity. I wrote *Moderate Fable* simultaneously with *Angel in the Forest*. After I finished I wrote two more poems which appeared in *The Partisan Review*, and I have never written a lyric poem from that day to this. I have never really wanted to, because from the moment I began *Miss MacIntosh, My Darling* I knew that I was writing the novel as poem. It was the absolute incandescence of the poet's mind. One of the things that I remember in my first conversation with Carson McCullers at Bread Loaf, where I was an assistant to Louis

Untermeyer, is her telling me that she thought the novel was the epic of modernity. I had not yet written any prose at that time and I had no desire to do so—that came about a year later. But I agree with her; you can't write epics in blank verse very well now, or in rhyme.

CR: Weren't you tempted to follow the ideas of the day, to become involved in literary movements?

MY: In the Middle West we didn't know flocks of writers. Each writer was isolated, and thus he developed an inner vision. One read on a vast scale. It was not as if we were sitting around in cafés talking about literary movements. That would have been beyond imagination.

CR: How much influence or instruction can one expect from one's peers?

MY: I once visited Thornton Wilder's writing class at the University of Chicago. He had a habit of smoking in class, which one was not supposed to do, and when somebody approached he would put his cigarettes in the desk drawer . . . and I remember one time the desk's catching fire. I recall only one thing he said in that class . . . to remember above all things that the patient loves his malady.

I remember that when I began *Miss MacIntosh*, I fully thought it would take two years. If I had known it would take eighteen years I would have dropped in holy horror. Who could conceive spending eighteen years obsessed by one book and working from nine to five? I was pleased that when the book came out, a reviewer said, "When Miss Young finished her *Miss MacIntosh, My Darling*, she must have been as happy as when Sir Philip Sidney took the manuscript of *Arcadia* and threw it at his sister's feet and said, 'There it is, it's finished.' "

CR: But you did come to New York to begin your literary career here.

MY: Well, only because I received a fellowship from the American Association of University Women—fifteen hundred dollars, which was a fortune in those days. I remember that at the time I thought to myself, "Now or never. If I am going to find out about life in the East, this is the time." And within forty-eight hours, I had left.

Frank Taylor, the talent scout from Reynal and Hitchcock, had approached me in a snowstorm at midnight in Iowa City and said, "Are you the poet in this neighborhood?" I never know yet how he picked me out in that town. I said, "Yes, I am." He said, "Austin Warren said there was a poet loose." He took me to Smith's Café and I told him I had the manuscript of *Moderate Fable* and also *Angel in the Forest*. So he took them both with him that night to Madison, and he called me from there the next morning and said, "We will publish *Moderate Fable*, I am certain, and I'll let you know in a week or two about *Angel in the Forest*." Then I got the fellowship, and the day I arrived in New York I called him from a telephone booth in the drugstore on the corner of Eighth Street and Sixth Avenue. I was practically fainting with anxiety. They had taken it. The first reader, his adviser, was Mark Van Doren, who read it aloud all night to his wife, Dorothy, and accepted it the following morning. I had two books coming out, and they both came out together. I received the votes for best nonfiction of the year and also for best poetry from the National Academy of Arts and Letters. They give it only in one category to the same writer, so they decided to give it to me in poetry. When one of the judges, William Rose Benét, presented the award, he said it was given for "the preservation of rarity in modern poetry." I asked him afterwards, "Were you thinking of Elinor Wylie when you spoke of 'the spirit of rarity'?" And he said, "Yes." Elinor Wylie was my ideal writer among women in those days.

CR: Who dominated the New York literary scene when you first arrived?

MY: Well, when I first came to New York during the war, everybody was here. All the exiled writers and painters from Europe were here. The Americans came back, and numerous English and French artists were here, too. It was a time when every publisher was asking every man he met on the street, "Have you got a book?"; every cab driver, "Have you got a book?" So that you could pick up contracts, it seems to me now, like leaves from the trees. I am sure you couldn't in actuality, but by contrast with the tight situation now, it seems that way.

At the time, the literary world was really under the domination of the elitist critics, people like John Crowe Ransom, Allen Tate, Mark Van Doren, Lionel Trilling, Van Wyck Brooks, and Edmund Wilson. These people were people of great generosity towards young writers.

CR: You began writing professionally for magazines as soon as you arrived.

MY: The first person I met when I came to New York was George Davis. He was then the editor of *Mademoiselle*, and he had been formerly with *Harper's Bazaar*. This was before he married Lotte Lenya. It's always been surprising to me that fashion editors seem to be my best friends, and I never ever go to a beauty parlor. George had read *Angel in the Forest* and asked my editor if he could meet me. "Where is this woman who wrote it?" He imagined that I was in Timbuktu or some other far distant place. Frank Taylor said, "Well, that's perfectly simple. She lives right in the neighborhood and I'll bring her next Thursday at four o'clock." So I walked in and sat down and George was sitting there. And he said, "Well, where is she?" Frank said, "That's Marguerite Young." George said, "Oh, no, that's not Marguerite Young. You can't lie to me. That is not the author of *Angel in the Forest*." And Frank said, "Well, what do you mean?" He was taking this seriously, and so was I—I mean, to have my identity denied. George said, "The author of *Angel in the Forest* is an elderly woman who has spent her entire life writing one great book." I thought it was rather prophetic, because I could say that I was young when I began *Miss MacIntosh*, and old when I finished it, as George Eliot said about *Middlemarch*. But George Davis became the closest friend I had.

CR: Was he living in the House of Genius in Brooklyn Heights then?

MY: Yes. And I often went there just after the geniuses had departed. The previous year Auden and Carson and Richard

Wright and his wife and Colin McFee had lived there, each on a
different floor. An animal trainer was on the top floor with a
chimpanzee. The chimpanzee ate with the family and wore a
little dress suit and played the piano. George would always say,
"Don't make fun of the chimpanzee, he pays the highest income
tax of anyone in this house." One night George was in Sand
Street and met a couple of drunken sailors with a prostitute, who
had nowhere to stay. So he said, "Come on home with me, boys,
and I'll put you up." During the war he would always take anyone home who had nowhere to stay. The next morning, when the
prostitute came down to breakfast, she saw the chimpanzee sitting there drinking coffee and smoking a cigar, and she said, "Hi,
boys!" She didn't flick an eyelid. But when one of the sailors
came down, he took one look at the chimpanzee, put his hand
over his stomach, and screamed, "Oh, my God! What did I drink
last night?" He couldn't believe his eyes. I remember going to
parties when the chimpanzee would play the piano. That's when
I first met Kay Boyle, who was wearing a beautiful cowboy suit.
It was such a beautiful time because wherever you went you
would meet the ideals of your youth.

CR: Was it the critical success of your two books that established
your career in literary journalism?

MY: It was following the publication of my two books that I first
met Leo Lerman. I had seen him in the lobby of a hotel where I
was waiting for my editor. I saw this mysterious gentleman come
into the lobby, and I watched his every move. He was wearing a
large black cape and a black hat, and he carried a cane. He had
an air of such mystery about him, I thought maybe he was a
traveler who had just returned from Tibet. In those days you just
didn't know where anybody had been. Everything was so secre-
tive. About a week later I was at Yaddo. I looked up and there he
came strolling down the path of the rose garden. It was Leo
Lerman, I learned, and he became, at that instant, without further preliminaries, a friend. He was a Renaissance scholar,
deeply devoted to the theatre and to the arts. When I first knew
him he lived in the Eighties, and he would call people up to
come to a little party at his house. From the minute you got out

of the subway station you would hear a roar like from some great baseball field when the Red Sox were playing, or whatever. It was Leo's little party, and you could hear it for miles down the street. The place was always packed with people from every field of art. It was there that I first met Frederick Kiesler the architect, and Jane Bowles. I saw Marlene Dietrich, who used to come and light the stove for Leo when he was not well, because he does not like to be near a fire or a flame of any kind.

I used to go there sometimes on Sundays when there was no party. He would perhaps be indisposed and lying on his couch wearing his great red velvet dressing gown and a Turkish fez, and Truman Capote would be there, and we would play with nineteenth-century paper dolls, all of us. I've never seen anything like them. I loved Leo's house, because it was full of the most beautiful dolls, toys, rare antiques, and everything had a marvelous freedom of fantasy and joy.

CR: Was that also the summer when so many of your friends were at Yaddo?

MY: Truman was certainly there that summer, and lived in the finest of rooms, the tower where Mrs. [Katrina] Trask had written poems above the windows, on the walls. There was a harp which played music as you opened the door. I used that harp in my description of the Opium Lady in her bedroom for my novel. It was the way she had of telling whether the other person entering was living or dead, a dream or a reality. Truman was at that time writing *Other Voices, Other Rooms*. He used to frighten the guests by going through the rose garden at night with his long white shirttails flying. He would howl into the wind, "Katrina, tell Elizabeth the guests are to create, create under the trees. That's why she left the estate to them." I remember Leo was going to the rose garden one night with Agnes Smedley, who bumped into Ralph Bates. They had not seen each other since the Chinese Revolution, the time of Mao. Poor Agnes nearly fainted. I remember it was Truman who said, "I just knew this was 'blossom time'—reunion in that rose garden." We used to go to Agnes's farm and play murder. I remember Carson McCullers's wonderful speeches as a Georgia senator, defending the one accused. You were accused of murder when the game stopped if you were under a black umbrella, or somebody put the black umbrella over you.

Agnes was in a very nervous state of mind, because she was agitated about the progress of the Chinese Revolution. Truman and I were sitting on the bishop's chair in the main house when we overheard her talking about the Revolution quite openly, and some of the counterinsurgents—the movements of Russia. Agnes didn't mind that we heard them, because I think she thought we had not enough political sense to know what she was talking about. She used to go around saying, "Come the Revolution we're going to hang Truman from the trees!" And Truman said, "What did I ever do to you?" And she said, "I'm not talking about you, I'm talking about President Truman." It offended Truman that he wasn't important enough to hang. [*Laughs.*]

CR: You were such free spirits then.

MY: Also, I remember I was with Truman and Carson and Leo when we went to the American Hotel at Saratoga Springs, one of those beautiful old hotels. In the lobby we saw our first television set, and we looked at it with great skepticism. It was just a little ad for an automobile or something like that. In *Life* magazine people were saying that it was going to replace the world of books. Truman said, "Oh, this has no future." [*Laughs.*]

CR: So you had no intimations of change.

MY: I also remember putting Carson on the train the day of her thirtieth birthday, and it was as if, oh, old age was descending on her. She was just shivering and shaking from head to foot because she had reached thirty! It was horrible! And Truman and others were going down to console her, everybody taking roses to the train to help her not to feel that all was over. It was an enchanted summer. Truman and Carson were great friends in those days, but later feuded because Carson thought that Truman took a song that she had sung and had put it into one of his stories, "His Eye Is on the Sparrow." It's a very well known spiritual, so I don't think you can say he took it.

When I went to Rome and met Princess Marguerite Caetani,

the editor of *Botteghe Oscura*, she said, "Word comes that Truman Capote and his forces are waiting on the outskirts of Rome for the withdrawal of Mrs. McCullers's forces before he enters the city, lest there be some new, terrible war in Rome." I do remember that Truman took me in his car when we were invited to have dinner with Dennis Devlin, the Irish ambassador. When we saw Carson leaning on her silver-headed cane on a traffic island, Truman said, "There she is. I can get her now." He swerved to get her. I said, "Don't do it, Truman! Everybody will know you did it on purpose, just because you don't like her." So he didn't do it. He was not serious, 1 hasten to add. But they never did settle their differences, though at Yaddo he had been at her feet and she had robbed him of his shirt and his tennis shoes. Anything he had on that she wanted, he would take off and give to her to wear. She could wear his shirts and shoes—she had to have little feet, I guess. But after that pleasant episode was over, I must say that I sympathized with him then.

CR: You traveled over to Italy on the same boat with Carson?

MY: Just by accident. I went to Rome on the *Queen Mary*, and by coincidence she and Reeves were going on the same journey. The editor of *Mademoiselle* wanted to give a little farewell party for both of us, but she was in a horrible dilemma. She called me and said, "What shall I do?" She was just about hysterical. "Sister is in second class and you're in first class. It would kill Sister to have anyone in first class when she's only in second." So I said, "Let's have the party in her room. She doesn't need to know where I am." All the way across the Atlantic she was reading Proust for the first time and reading him with black glasses on.
     She refused to look at Gibraltar because it was in an insurance ad. She turned deliberately away from it, and I was rushing from side to side—"What's become of Carson?"—she gave us all the slip. Remember Browning's beautiful poem of a would-be poet who disappears and becomes a diver for pennies at Gibraltar?

CR: You were very close friends with Reeves as well. To think that this journey would eventually become the end of the line for him!

MY: Everyone seemed to sympathize with Carson in any troubles she had with Reeves. He was a very lonely person, but he had a wonderful knowledge of folklore. He could tell marvelous Southern tales. He came from near Plains, Georgia. I never really understood Carson, how such a sheltered person knew so much about the underside of life, until I met Reeves and heard him talk. Now, I'm sure her work was absolutely her own, but she could not have been so much the glassy-eyed child. She wasn't. Part of it may have been her relationship with him. I felt it was a creative relationship. She told me that the reason she was in second class going over was that she had to pay for her automobile, her dog, and her husband, in that order. And it was just that way. He really sacrificed for her the years when she had nothing. But when she became so celebrated and well off financially, he didn't seem to share the glory with her. When I heard of the suicide, I was terribly sad. It put a different light on suicide for me. I always thought that the difference between murder and suicide was just whether you turned the gun out or inward. But I began to see what the stoic meant when he advised that if you don't like this life, flee to the cool tombs. Because he was just wrecked. That goes back to early childhood, and it had nothing to do with his marriage, which was probably the only important thing that had happened to him or ever could have happened.

CR: For everything you have said about regional writers, Marguerite, one of your closest friends was Mari Sandoz, who wrote about the Indians and the West. How did you originally meet?

MY: I used to go to a café on Sheridan Square for coffee in the mornings. It was full of people rattling and reading newspapers. I was very naïve, you must remember. I would see this peculiar-looking red-headed woman sitting there, passionately writing on yellow notebooks in the midst of all that chaos. I thought, She must be absolutely mad. Then I was walking along Sheridan Square in the worst snowstorm, and I saw her strolling along with her coat wide open, no hat on. You would think it was a summer's day. I said, "Oh, that poor madwoman, she doesn't even know it's snowing. The birds are singing and the flowers are blooming for her." And she said to me in the shrill wind, "I read your chapter in *Harper's Bazaar*. I used to write like that." I thought, Oh, God, this is really getting worse. She's absolutely mad! Almost a year passed. I was sitting in Bloom's Drugstore, which was a central place for everyone who wrote in the neighborhood, and there she was, sitting next to me. I was lonely, and she smiled, and I thought, "Oh well, poor soul." I said, "I don't believe I ever caught your name." She said, "Mari Sandoz." I said, "What?" She said, "I wrote *Old Jules*, you know." I said, "Why, you're one of my favorite writers. That's a book I love. My God, I thought you were crazy, writing in that café. What were you doing there?" She said, "What were *you* doing there?" That was her idea of an answer. And we became fast friends from that moment. We lived to call the previous year the lost year of our friendship because we could have been friends for a whole year.

CR: You followed her work, since you wrote a profile of her and articles about her home, Sandozia, the great ranch. And you still speak about her.

MY: I would love to write a book about Mari and Nebraska in the Cheyenne autumn. But I don't have eight years to go on and learn Indian language and lore, so it's something I will never do. When she was dying, the governor of Nebraska had a session of the legislature, both houses, to swear out a resolution that, with God's help, they would not permit Mari Sandoz to die. The governor flew here to show it to her. She said, "Ah, my dear governor, this is New York State and you have no jurisdiction here, nor does God." She was such a charming person. She is buried in Sandozia.

   She is buried in the sand hills of Nebraska alone. The Indians called her the Sand Hills Kid, after the crane, because they thought she looked like a crane with her beautiful red-gold hair, her fabulous body, which was that of a dancer. She was a very independent, proud, lonely person. I think she felt that to have left the sand hills was to be alienated from her own land. And yet she couldn't have lived there. This was the place for her. She had a Henry Jamesian culture. She was very intellectual, a brilliant woman.

CR: Anaïs Nin studies you in her diaries. Do you recall when you became aware of her interest?

MY: I saw her at the Gotham book parties. She always wore purple in those days. There were acres of young men around her, and most of them on their knees. It was not the girls who worshipped her in those days, but the boys. She didn't have a large audience of readers at all. Then I saw her a few years later at a party as I was first going to Europe and she was going to California. I had been editor of *The Tiger's Eye* and had published one of her short stories. When I got back to New York, after being away for two years in Rome and then having taught at the University of Iowa, the telephone rang in my new apartment, and it was Anaïs Nin. She had been looking for me for years, because she loved *Miss MacIntosh*.

CR: What was the basis of your friendship? You were such opposites.

MY: It was my work, and she was also sure that I would attract the large audience that she never would. What surprised me was that, unlike most people who achieve sudden and unexpected great fame, she remembered those who had not and who had been generous to her and whom she admired. As you might *not* guess from just reading her journals, she was very objective and very analytical and almost selfless in her relationships with other writers. I was startled to see that she had written many pages on my work and that she spoke about *Miss MacIntosh* all over the United States. So she was just an absolutely wonderful friend.

CR: Yet her sensibility and her style were the exact reverse of yours.

MY: What she found in me was what she had in Henry Miller, she told me. She found something of the American consciousness, and she was fascinated by American folklore and mythology and history. She wanted to write about American themes. She intended to write outside herself.

CR: By contrast, it is interesting that her fame came out of her diaries, and that's basically her persona.

MY: She knew that and she resented it. The fame came to her too late and for the wrong things. She had just begun to reconcile herself to that fame and to enjoy it when she received her death warrant, that is, word of her cancer. She told a friend when she was dying that it was difficult for her to believe in God because God had given her the death warrant the very day He gave her that for which He made her work all her life in absolute obscurity.

CR: Were you ever tempted to keep diaries?

MY: Anaïs kept the journals, and I had never had any inclination to keep a diary at all. But I decided I would, and I kept it for about six weeks. Every entry was either what Ruth Stephan or Anaïs was doing—where they were, who they saw. Maybe what Mari was doing if she was on a trip with the Indians, going up-country towards some faraway Indian camp. So I thought, Why should I keep a diary when I don't put a thing about myself in it? Not one word. I don't have an introspective tendency, and I asked Dr. Erica Freeman if that surprised her. She said, "Not at all. It's all in your writing, and you don't have a moment left for introspection."

CR: John Gardner often mentioned that you were his teacher at Iowa at a crucial moment of his development. What was your impression of him then?

MY: Well, when I went to the University of Iowa to teach, he was my student among many who had just come out of the Korean War. Some of them had seen terrible things and had no language in which to write about them. There were two teachers who shared the fiction seminar, both ex-Marines and with a very hard-boiled approach to literature. They encouraged bad imitations of Hemingway. John was brilliant; he had a remarkable education in philosophy and theology. He could not make up his mind whether to write in that hard-boiled style, very bad imitations of Kerouac's *On the Road*, or to try and plow the deeper resources of his cultivated mind. He told me of this conflict and invited me to dinner to discuss his future. "Well," I said, "I think you're too gifted to write in this bald way—'Get on with the narrative' and 'Hi, man, what are you doing tonight, kid.' " Somebody throws a cup of coffee into somebody's face, grinds a cigar into a prostitute's bosom, and all kinds of crazy things. I said, "If you follow my guidance, you can become a major writer." He said, "Do you mean that?" I said, "Yes, let's sign a contract." So we signed a contract, a Faustian contract in blood, like signing a pact with the devil. He cut some blood out of his finger and mine and wrote on a piece of paper, "I, John Gardner, will follow Marguerite's advice and pursue the interest of style and substance that she believes in. She has promised me that if I will, I'll become a famous writer." And we signed it in our blood. He wrote his first two novels in my class; both were published. At that time, he told me that he was going to write a novel on Beowulf, because he was an Anglo-Saxon scholar. I thought, "Oh, kid stuff, he'll get over that!" You see, he knew his future better than I did, because he wrote that wonderful novel *Grendel*. That other group was the motorcycle crowd—the Beats were just coming in then. When John died in that motorcycle accident on the highway, I was terribly grieved. I said, "I kept him from becoming a motorcycle *writer* but not from becoming a motorcycle *rider*."

CR: You and Henry Miller were coeditors of the *Conscientious Objector*. Were you ever an editor on a literary magazine?

MY: I was the fiction editor of *The Tiger's Eye*, which was an avant-garde magazine of which Horace Gregory was poetry editor. Brom Weber and I were the fiction editors, and the editor-in-chief was Ruth Stephan, who with her husband, John, was the founder, and who herself was a beautiful poet. She used to marvel at the fact that Brom and I never quarreled; the reason we never did, although we didn't like the same things at all, was that we had a meeting the first day we were appointed and we agreed that I would never challenge his tastes if he never challenged mine.

CR: If *The Tiger's Eye* was an avant-garde magazine, did Gertrude Stein's work influence your thoughts on writing? Gertrude Stein was a disciple of William James, and you have used William James as your text in teaching. Do you feel there is a sympathy between your work and her work?

MY: I knew Gertrude Stein when she was a visitor at the University of Chicago, with Thornton Wilder as her host. I think she was a beautiful, fabulous human being. I enjoy some of her writing, but I feel no empathy with her as a writer. I don't engage in automatic writing. I know I am controlled by intellectual ideas; ideas about—or should I say, the obsession with—certain pathologies. I would say I have almost a medical imagination; I have that kind of reading background. The writers I feel close to are Sterne, Gogol, Dickens, Mark Twain. I do not feel close to Gertrude Stein.

CR: You are interested in psychology, but you are not interested in the novel of personal autobiography. You have often said that.

MY: My friends could have deep secrets and I would never ask them to tell me. As a writer, I would never write a novel dealing with the love of one character. I am always interested in many people. I have a muralist's imagination. I like to see the epic swing of the thing, the many as opposed to the one. I am a pluralist in that sense.

CR: Is that also a principle in the way you live?

MY: I'm a pluralistic person, and I know thousands of people not well. People come and go in my life. I've always said that I am a shoreline, the waves come and the waves go, I do nothing to invite them, and I do nothing to cause them to withdraw, I am just there. But the shoreline continually changes. I have a very restricted life caused by work.

CR: That is very much William James's concept of the imagination.

MY: Yes, and it is also my temperament. It was true of *Angel in the Forest* when I was writing of the utopian society, true of *Miss MacIntosh* when I had surrounded her with every kind of individual pathology of which I had ever heard or known, and true in my present biographies, where the central figures are surrounded by vast numbers of characters. Through them, you see the character unfolding, everything unfolding, in relation to society as a whole.

CR: Do you have a concept of portrayal of character?

MY: Yes. According to the logic of a vision working itself out in strange, unusual, and ultimate ways, which are recognizable, true to life, and are always based on people whom either I have known or, more likely, have read about in the daily newspapers.

CR: You get your images from the newspapers?

MY: I get my characters from the newspapers and from biographies and medical histories and a thousand sources. I believe, like Browning, that the poet is a reporter. I can understand his writing, for instance, that beautiful long poem *The Ring and the Book*, which was based on a real murder in Rome. I do not believe in inventing characters.

CR: Is the Opium Lady a real person? Is she based on your mother?

MY: Well, fortunately, I am not an autobiographical writer. I started the book projecting the entire matter of the Opium Lady as my recollection of an opium lady I knew while I was a student at the University of Chicago and with whom I spent much time, reading aloud the works of Shakespeare. That is how I worked my way through school.

CR: Who was she?

MY: She was a fabulous lady who had been under opium for about fifteen or twenty years and had not walked for at least ten years. She was one of the original patronesses of Harriet Monroe's *Poetry: A Magazine of Verse*, and of Jane Addams's Hull House. She was also a friend of Thornton Wilder and many of the great intellectuals of that day.

I was with her during her opium dreams. I was with her when the golden bird who was the spirit of Heraclitus perched upon the bedpost. I was literally with her when she had a long conversation with the head of John the Baptist.

CR: After decapitation?

MY: After decapitation. I was there when she spoke with a little rabbit. I was with her when she entertained an imaginary elephant and when balloon fish would be floating over her bed. So that when I began to write my novel quite unexpectedly—I had planned to write a biography of Toussaint L'Ouverture, the Haitian rebel, but my publisher wanted me to write a novel— she was the most fabulous single person I had ever known. I was interested in her for her dreams and her beautiful personality and surroundings.

CR: And the problems of opium addiction?

MY: The doctors in her household were always rushing about with Elizabeth Barrett Browning's letters to try to explain to themselves this beautiful opium lady who was their patient. Of course I had read Elizabeth Barrett Browning and De Quincey's *Confessions of an English Opium Eater.* I had read Coleridge, too.

CR: So that you would understand her?

MY: I had De Quincey in my background before I ever arrived at her house. It was just right for a young poet. There couldn't have been a better place. I was offered opium every evening, but I always said, "No, thanks." She used to call me the prosaic sprite, because I didn't need drugs to dream.

I stayed with her most of the time, because I was offered the bed in which Edna St. Vincent Millay had slept when she was a visitor in Chicago; and the idea of sleeping in Millay's bed seemed to be the most marvelous thing that could ever happen to any young person. On the bedside table, near the Opium Lady, was a silver drinking cup which had belonged to John Keats, a little mosaic Persian letter set, and a beautiful bird with a seashell. I have all these things at my bedside now. Her daughter gave them to me when she died.

CR: You did not enter the Opium Lady's dreams?

MY: I do not think she dreamed about people. She dreamed about Mandarins and beautiful human-size blackbirds standing in the hallways, or the invisible elephants in the hallway. Adlai Stevenson—he may have known her, by the way—when he was running for office, talked about the invisible elephant. I don't know if he ever got a letter I wrote him, telling him about the invisible elephant in the Opium Lady's dreams. He had the same idea: that the thing you think is not there may be there.

CR: Here you are talking about an individual, and yet you have said you are not interested in individual personality.

MY: I met Thornton Wilder several years later at a Gotham Book Mart party, and he asked me what I had been doing. I said that I was writing a novel in which the Opium Lady was one of the leading characters. He said, "Oh! As a way of revealing the unconscious." He knew exactly what the theme would be. It is the unconscious that interested me. I am interested in the bizarre and in people at an edge. I am interested in extreme statements about people because that is where drama is most apparent: in human character. And I am a Scot. I am economical about my working so hard, so I begin with what I know is easy—with something strange and beautiful—and then it starts to activate itself. It is when you start with the normal or the neutral or the average that it is so difficult. I imagine it is, anyway—I have never tried it and I never will.

CR: Did you have to do research for the other characters, such as the nursemaid?

MY: No. Not for Miss MacIntosh, because I knew all these things, or had observed them; also, I would be drawn to examples of this while I was writing. There is a book of novellas that I left out which has been asked for but has been deferred by me until my next book comes out. I wrote a section which I did not include in the novel, about the window peeper, who was a rather mystical character in the novel. At the very moment I was writing it, a window peeper came to my window. You meet people who are like what you write.

CR: What about the love story with the deaf man?

MY: Well, I know this wonderful stone-deaf man in Greenwich Village, and in fact he is a very close friend of mine. Howard Mitcham was one of the most interesting people I know because of his brilliant mind and a missing sense. He is a painter, and I put him in my novel because he was such a sensual contrast to some of the other characters. I thought he was the perfect lover for Vera Cartwheel in the end, because I figured that she could not marry a man who was absolutely normal—she would be bored to death after all she had been through. So she ends up by marrying a man whose hearing is missing.

Then, of course, I was also getting beautiful, stimulating ideas about a character from what was actually happening in the world. I always read the newspapers a great deal—I do now, too. I had Miss MacIntosh walk into the sea, stark naked except for wearing a pair of black gloves which she had carefully darned the night before, as if she were going to her wedding, and leave all her clothes along the beach, including her red wig on the back of a horseshoe crab and her Admiral Dewey corset and her sea boots and her plaid mackintosh. After she walked into the sea at dawn, when both sun and moon were in the sky, carrying her black umbrella until her bald head reached sea level, I read about a boy in northern Long Island who, stark naked except for black gloves, walked into the black sea. The fact that such a bizarre thing had happened after I wrote about it made me feel that I was psychologically correct in the kind of death I had imagined for Miss MacIntosh. Now, that death was based in part upon the death of Virginia Woolf, who had walked into the River Ouse in England.

CR: What is the psychological significance of that "gloved" death?

MY: Well, I wondered about that myself. I thought I knew what I meant, and then I consulted with Dr. Ernst Hammerschlag, a friend who was a psychiatrist from Vienna. I used to distrust my imagination for fear that I was simply fantasizing, and that is the one thing I believe I have never done. He explained the entire case—all the meanings of the word "black," and gloves, in relation to psychology and guilt, and why it was the correct image.

Similarly, when I had the detective in the novel who would not handle a case in which anything black appears—even a black rooster or the ace of spades—I thought, Well, I must have gone mad at this point to imagine such a character. I asked him again and he said, "Well, that is a classic case of schizophrenia," and he gave me a long series of case histories like that. He was a very close friend throughout all these years, with whom I spoke about psychological matters.

You asked me if I did research upon *Miss MacIntosh*. No. Because this came from my observations of reality. Evenings I spent reading biographies of the period from 1870 to 1926, which is covered in the two biographies I am now writing; so that I accumulated a rich knowledge of all the characters who appear in the next books, but not in that book.

CR: Scribners commissioned *Miss MacIntosh* but it took you eighteen years to finish it. Did you lose yourself in the writing of the book?

MY: No. They gave me a contract in 1945 to write it. I submitted about fifteen pages of it, that is all. I think that mainly they gave me a contract for it on the basis of *Angel in the Forest* and my poetry book *Moderate Fable*. I did not know when I began that it would be a long novel. I had all the major characters in my mind the first day, as a direction in the themes of the book. I knew it would be an inquest into all the illusions individuals suffer from. I had already written a book about the illusions society suffers from in utopian states, and then I wanted to transfer from society to the individual. I thought it would take two years and that it would be about two hundred pages. But the book started expanding because these characters became more and more lively, more and more interesting to me on many levels. I had chosen very vivid characters to begin with, who were capable of development, and I had the patience to allow them to develop. Also, I was enchanted by the whole project, and the music of it all. I never stopped. I was never bored. If I had been bored, I would have stopped. I realized somewhere along the line, early, that it would take a long time. I wanted it to be a book about my view of total consciousness and also a book of books. Dr. Hammerschlag said that it was the Song of Songs of schizophrenia. I knew for sure that nothing else in life was going to interfere. I would not easily marry, I would not easily travel. I wanted to write—and I don't regret it.

CR: Was *Miss MacIntosh* written and rewritten in layers?

MY: No. Well, I wrote it straight through, or almost through, once, and then I discovered that something was wrong with it in my mind. Mr. Spitzer was playing a trick and pretending he was his twin brother. He seemed to assume more and more grandeur as he got the two-way ticket across the River Styx—the man who could come back. When I realized that he wasn't sure which twin he was, I went back and rewrote. And that's where I think the book took on its cosmic magnitude. Before, it was almost a kind of de Maupassant joke, when he knew and he pretended. When he ceased to be so sure, you realized that it was the dead soul, which was his own as a living soul, the dead in you, the dead who lived, the living who died—that kind of split. It cost me months and months of my life to make that clear. And once in a while I would come across a character who would make me think, think, think, and write, write, write, to get to the quality of sincerity. I could be clever, but I don't want to be clever. I want to be real, as I want to be sincere and profound. I know that I probably have a sense of comedy, but it's based upon a greater tragic sense. During the years in which I was writing *Miss MacIntosh*, I never went to other novelists for inspiration but, rather, to biographies. For instance, when you had that musician who plays the violin in the Philadelphia Orchestra for twenty years, with his bow never touching the strings. One day his bow touched the string and made one note and he was fired. You hit reality once and die. There is not one single invented moment in all of *Miss MacIntosh*. If you tell the truth everybody thinks it's a dream or an illusion beyond ordinary belief.

CR: Do you think that in going from *Miss MacIntosh* to the biography of Eugene Debs there is a progression from fiction to history parallel to the progression from poetry to prose?

MY: No, I think that, through fate, I just happened to become involved with biography, and I happen to love it. I would rather read a mediocre biography, any day of the year, than a mediocre novel. I don't mind if I read a biography of Marilyn Monroe or Tallulah Bankhead that isn't one of the great classics on earth: I learn something about these people. I may read some beautiful biographies of Marilyn Monroe, and then I may read something in the *Daily News* about her. I don't care where it is, I just like to follow the people. I read biographies by the ton. It's the metaphor, it's really the human comedy in the Balzacian sense that I get out of it. These characters in Debs's life, for example, are the kind of characters Shakespeare would sit up all night and look at—this can't be that this happened, but it did. It cannot be that there was such a person as Susan B. Anthony, one of the most fantastically interesting women who ever lived, or Mrs. Stanton, or Dr. Mary Walker, or Victoria Woodhull. Victoria Woodhull ran naked for president. She would strip herself naked, or almost. She did tear off all her clothes once at a rally when her male adorers were tossing red roses at her. She was the one who told on Henry Ward Beecher, because he was a male hypocrite who made love to his favorite parishioner's wife while she was making doll clothes. All these little things are so interesting, and they just don't appear. They were and are madly beautiful people.

CR: Marguerite, when you began the biography of Eugene Debs, did you know it was going to be a long effort?

MY: Not really. I was going to do a very short book on Debs, because of the Vietnamese War. It just grew like Topsy, because it was such fantastically rich material that it would seem to me insane not to have pursued it.

CR: Is there a difference between writing fiction and history?

MY: No. I often have to hold myself back in writing nonfiction, because it is stranger than fiction. You can never assume that you know the logic of a character in nonfiction. You may think you do, but there are surprises. You have to double-check and triple-check everything. The beautiful thing is that as the research piles up, it begins to assert a life of its own. You can have the same thematic relationships to that research—the flood, the ebb, the flow of history. But the river is a dream—imagination. You have the same relation to it as you do to the unconscious. It takes over, and you can do the same artistic writing. The fact is that all these people, no matter who they were, of which political party or whether they were opposed to utopia or not, all had a lingua franca which all understood and which was based upon poetry, like Whitman, Melville, Longfellow, or Lowell—they all spoke in metaphors. It's about myth, the architect of heaven on earth, the earthly paradise, the lost Atlantis, Noah's Ark—it was for many, many socialists. So they have these dream boats, these enchanted birds speaking, savants coming down through all the millennia. So transcendental socialism preceded Marx. And I go into all of that.

CR: We're back at an idea that you mentioned before, which is the psychology of contact. Which we should define.

MY: There are great personalities who are phenomenal in themselves. There are so many beautiful people who have conveyed ideas and dreams. I find that I'm fascinated by them all. I'm doing it through people and what they said and did in their quest for utopia, of which Debs said, "If we are not right in our quest for Utopia, it all seems very Pickwickian indeed."

CR: What is your daily work routine?

MY: I used to start at eight and stop at maybe three or four. Now I start at nine or ten and hopefully stop at four or five. Every day I write. If there is ever any interruption, like an electric-meter man or a doorbell ringing, it drives me crazy. I don't care how many people call me up, but I don't want anyone near me physically. I don't want to see anyone. I'm just absolutely closed in, and I get more so as the years go by, more and more loving of privacy.

CR: How do you get started in the morning?

MY: I always leave off the day before. As Thomas Mann advised, when the going is good, when you know exactly where you are and you are in a moment of exuberance, you stop. When I hook on the next morning, if the going was good I just go. I feel it emotionally, almost in the blood, the pulse, the excitement.

CR: Dreams are also a strong influence, aren't they?

MY: I once dreamed I was in Iowa City at a party in my house. Henry James was there, and he was sitting in a corner, pouring whisky into his high silk hat. Two weeks later I came to New York, and on Seventh Avenue I found a book, *Memories, by a Publisher's Wife*, in which I read, "Henry James was here the other evening, and was so drunk that he sat in a corner, pouring whisky into his high silk hat." It was a very obscure little memoir, and I had never read it or heard of it, or known that Henry in actuality would take a drink. I believe that there are visitations in dreams. He would come to me in my dreams, night after night, during the writing of *Miss MacIntosh*, and read what I had done. I sometimes was typing and sometimes writing in longhand, beautiful pages which of course faded from my mind. He used to say, "That's beautiful. . . . Go right ahead. . . . Go right ahead. . . . You're the late-twentieth-century development of what I was doing" and things like that. Which I don't think I am, but in my dreams I thought so.

CR: You've often said that you feel the presence of other writers.

MY: When I'm teaching, I'll say, "Come in, Mr. James." . . . My students love this. I will stop—"Oh, how do you do, Henry James, won't you be seated?" Oh, they all look, they believe he's really there. Boswell will come. Cervantes—I spend a great deal of time with him. I entertain: I see Emily Dickinson quite often, Virginia Woolf, and Dickens. Poe . . . oh, all the time, I see him on misty nights at Sheridan Square when the raindrops are falling. He's going into that little cigar store to get a cigar. I am on very close terms with Poe. Now, I don't believe all this, but in an irrational way, I live it all, so what can we say?

CR: Well, I know you have this theory that individuals speak through many voices. Do you see most people as possible writers?

MY: No. Most people are not, though I think talent is fairly common. I see innumerable talents in my teaching of fiction writing at Fordham University and the New School. I see much talent. But many of them will be lawyers or bridge builders. Many of them will think they are going to write but will be turned aside by fate. Who needs to be a writer, of course, is the answer.

CR: In your teaching and in your work, you stress the concept of multiple voices in writing. Do you make a distinction between multiplicity within the work and multiple aspects of the writer?

MY: I do not write about myself, consciously, at all.

CR: You are after the archetype.

MY: Yes. I project into the heightened individual character all that I think that character is, that towards which he tends; that which he might become at any moment if he splits into one or more personalities: his relationship with others. And I interweave him throughout with many other obsessed characters. Even a very minor character would have to have a problem in my book, or in anything that would interest me. I do not have just a name on a page, because it is not a character. Only toward the end of the book do I ever realize—and maybe that is because I have been so busy writing it and also because I do not think of myself consciously—that, after all, it is my own project, and that I am really writing an autobiographical novel. Naturally, I met these people, knew them, or someone like them. You asked if the Opium Lady was my mother: yes, but I did not know that until almost the end of the book, since my mother was a kind of Titania-like dreamer and irrational; in a way, it was my mother. But if I had known that at the beginning, I would not have written the book, since I am not interested in autobiographical literature at all.

CR: One must have incredible staying power in addition to the talent. When the book came out, you were compared to Norman Mailer.

MY: I met Norman Mailer at a cocktail party after *Miss MacIntosh* was published. I had never seen him before. He came up to me and said, "Were there any fighters in your family?" I answered, "Why, yes. My half-brother was a champion in the ring." "I knew it," he said. "I knew you had a fighter in the family." "Well, what made you think that?" I asked. He said, "Because it took a lot of strength, hanging out in the sawdust ring like that, punching away for eighteen years the way you did."

Then he wrote to my publisher to say I was a gentle Hercules in high heels. My publisher's publicity department gave that letter to the cartoonist Dick Schaaf at the *Herald Tribune*, who drew a cartoon of me punching it out with Norman Mailer, with that caption—"A gentle Hercules in high heels." I suppose it took stamina in a way, but it takes stamina to write anything for eighteen minutes.

CR: It's been eighteen years since the publication of *Miss MacIntosh* and you're finishing volume one of the life of Debs.

MY: I'm not running a race with anyone. I don't think that anyone can do a literary and imagistic portrait of the nineteenth-century utopian dreamers and anti-dreamers at speed level and evolve in it the political metaphors, not only of that day, but of previous days, and the political cartoons and the actual labor histories and statistics, as well as the individual personalities. I think that I could do a factual book on Debs in a short time, a year or two, but it wouldn't make any difference. I'm not in any hurry. I'm not interested in just getting my name into print. I was brought up religiously regarding literature and the sacredness of the word. I may not be any good as a writer at all, I recognize that. I think anyone who tries anything real—think of Proust or Dostoevsky—risks being an absolute fool. This is what Freud said, too. But if you're mistaken, be *terribly* mistaken! Melville died thinking he was an absolute failure. He said, "No man ever hitched his wagon higher to a star or fell so low." You can't tell, you know that. Leonard Woolf used to grab the manuscripts from Virginia before she could read them, because she would want to tear them up. I don't think anybody can be sure what he's doing, especially if he's really trying.

CR: And now, what's next?

MY: Well, I really want to write short pieces, stories or novellas. I want to go around the world, even if I have to be carried on a stretcher. It's actually the strangest thing, I tell all the young people I know, including yourself. This is what William James said: you go on doing your little bit day by day, week by week, and you gradually accumulate vast resources. My artistic consciousness, unless I'm sadly mistaken, is at a supreme height now. And Henry James said, "How can it be, alas, that this consciousness which I have so worked to make rich, is alas rich, just when I face extinction." But it's really the most joyous thing, this age, when you do know so much and you have your power. But as long as you can go on "creating, creating under the trees," as Mrs. Trask said of Yaddo, you're happy.

PART TWO

William Burroughs

WILLIAM BURROUGHS COULD ONLY BE published in this country in opposition to official censorship by the government and the policy of self-censorship among publishers during the fifties and early sixties. The participants of this round-table discussion are Maurice Girodias, founder of Olympia Press in Paris; William Burroughs; Allen Ginsberg, poet, who acted as Burroughs's agent and placed his first book, *Junkie* (1953), written under the pseudonym William Lee, as a pulp paperback with A. A. Wynn Company; and James Grauerholz, who is Burroughs's present agent. Maurice Girodias discusses the function of Olympia Press and how the Traveler's Companion Series included literary works by writers who would dominate the literary climate of this country at the end of the fifties and the early sixties: Vladimir Nabokov, Samuel Beckett, Lawrence Durrell, J. P. Donleavy, Henry Miller, William Burroughs, and Terry Southern. These authors were published in the United States only after a long, systematic campaign fought against censorship in the courts by Grove Press and other publishers. The legal restrictions that created Olympia Press in the first place cast Girodias into the limbo of running a clandestine press with his copyrights voided before the law. Within this context, William Burroughs and Allen Ginsberg recount the events leading to the publication of *Naked Lunch* by Olympia Press in 1959, followed by *The Soft Machine* (1961) and *The Ticket That Exploded* (1962). The

demise of Olympia Press and the republication in the United States of the major writers from its list delineates the shift of focus in the cultural consciousness to a complete preoccupation with American writing.

Grove Press first published William Burroughs's *Naked Lunch* in 1962, followed by *Yage Letters* (with Allen Ginsberg, 1963), *Nova Express* (1964), *The Soft Machine* (1966), *The Ticket That Exploded* (1967), *The Wild Boys* (1971), *Exterminator* (1973), *The Last Words of Dutch Schultz* (a film script, 1975), *Port of Saints* (1980), and *Cities of the Red Night* (1981). This conversation was recorded in 1975, the year that William Burroughs returned to live in the United States. By then, through the enormous influence of his work, he had become a cult writer.

William (Seward) Burroughs was born on February 5, 1914, in St. Louis; he attended Harvard, graduating in the class of 1936, and he continued his graduate studies in ethnology and archeology there. At the University of Vienna he began medical studies which he did not complete. He tells of working at jobs as varied as being a reporter, an advertising copywriter, a private detective, and an exterminator, all of which enter as subjects of his writing.

William Burroughs's loft is in a massive dilapidated red brick warehouse on the Bowery. To pass through the ornate wrought-iron grills to reach the front door means avoiding derelicts panhandling or passed out on the steps. James Grauerholz cheerfully opens the door and leads the way upstairs to the enormous loft known as "the Bunkers," occupied by William Burroughs. The fireproof concrete walls are painted white, the floor gray, and the space is in a half-light because all of the windows have been blocked off to secure the place after a series of burglaries.

William Burroughs is sitting under a bare bulb at the plain kitchen table, a tall, thin man of colorless complexion, dressed in his habitual colored jackets and thin neckties. His greeting is dour, delivered in the strong Midwestern twang that makes his deadpan readings from his own works such a subtle, dramatic, and riotously comic experience. In reviewing this text he checks the names, dates, and places against those in his own records, kept filed way in another room. I am again astonished at how conscientiously he and Allen Ginsberg have maintained thorough archives on the "Beat" generation.

MG: It was Allen who first brought the manuscript of *Naked Lunch* to me, in '58, in Paris. I was publishing books in the English language at the time, books which were unpublishable in America. The prose was scintillating, but the typing was pretty horrendous. I don't know what happened to that manuscript before it reached me.

AG: Kerouac had typed part of it in '57 in Tangiers, and Allen Ansen had typed part of it, and I typed part of it. It was a composite of different typings.

MG: It was dazzling, but it was difficult to make out. So I must say that I reacted very badly. I remember saying, "This is great but I can't even get a straight judgment on this book. Can you do something about it?" That was our first conversation. I also remember your looking like a dapper young American, extremely businesslike. You were doing your job as an agent, I suppose. A month later, Allen came back with a retyped, rearranged manuscript which was published in 1959.

WB: The point is that the manuscript which you saw in 1958 was not even approximately similar to the manuscript published in 1959. As I remember the story, you became interested after publication of excerpts in *Chicago Review* and then in *Big Table*. One morning, Sinclair Beiles came to see me and said you did want to publish the manuscript and that you wanted it in two weeks. So we all got busy and reorganized the material. The book was out on the stands one month later. I think that's a record. We had made the selections from about a thousand pages of material, which overflowed into *The Soft Machine*, into *The Ticket That Exploded*, and into *Nova Express* as well. I was producing it in pieces, and as soon as you got it, it was sent to the printer. When it came back from the printer, instead of rearranging the proofs, Brion Gysin, myself, and Sinclair Beiles took one look and said, "This is the order, just leave it the way it is."

AG: It was all happening about one block from the Seine River, within a few streets from each other, from Rue Gît-le-Coeur to Rue Saint-Séverin. It was a very short walk back and forth, and everybody was seeing each other for coffee in the morning anyway. That's one reason why it was possible to do it so fast. We wanted to take advantage of the publicity that was emanating from Chicago. Maurice, what other books were you publishing that year?

MG: I had run through a number of pretty fantastic books in the mid-fifties. I started Olympia Press in 1953. My first list had a book by Samuel Beckett, *Watt*, and a book by de Sade, I think *The Bedroom Philosophers* or *Justine*, and a book by Henry Miller, *Plexus*. It was a great start for a completely new imprint and a new publishing firm with no money in the bank. We were very lucky. We really had a nice literary list to start with.

AG: And you also had a long series of books written by young Americans in Paris.

MG: Yes. Mason Hoffenberg was one of them, Iris Owens was another. Chester Himes was published under his own name. All the others had pseudonyms, and we invented colorful names for everybody such as Ayataullah Mardaan, Akbar Del Piombo— that was Norman Rubington and Harriet Daimler, who was Iris Owens.

WB: Yes, people still ask me if I'm Akbar Del Piombo.

MG: I never understood why so many people thought that William Burroughs had written *Fuzz Against Junk*. Years later, I was asked for the first time whether Burroughs had written *Fuzz Against Junk*. I discovered that there was once a mistake by which you were credited on the copyright page because it had been misplaced by the printers. I think it was all my fault.

AG: Norman Rubington was the author of *Fuzz Against Junk*.

JG: Didn't he also write *Diary of a Beatnik*?

MG: That was published in America when I was trying to re-establish Olympia Press in the late sixties.

WB: Maurice, didn't you publish *Zazie in the Metro* in '59?

MG: Yes. After the mid-fifties, when I published *Lolita, The Ginger Man, Candy*, which came out in '58, and a number of books by Beckett—my list was fluid and bizarre in those days—then the last important thing I did in those days was *Naked Lunch* in 1959. After that, it was a downhill evolution. I had been harassed by the French administration to the point where I was almost out of business. Also, censorship had started to recede in America and it became possible, partly thanks to Grove Press, to publish, in America, some of the books I had first published in France. Unfortunately, this happened years after their publication in French, and because of the American copyright regulations most of those books were out of copyright and were pirated by American publishers. But that was not the case with *Naked Lunch* and *Lolita*, the only two that escaped being pirated. So, after '59, there were two other books that we published by William Burroughs. The first one was *The Soft Machine*, and after that, *The Ticket That Exploded*. I don't know which one had the dust jacket by Brion Gysin.

WB: That was *The Soft Machine. The Ticket That Exploded* had a collage jacket that was made by Ian Sommerville.

MG: Well, the next step was the publication, in America, of *Naked Lunch* by Grove Press in '62. There was a long interval, and you must realize that in '59 there were still incredible problems that most American citizens have completely forgotten about. For example, the fact that in '59 *Lady Chatterley's Lover* was published for the first time, by Grove Press. It was a breakthrough and a very daring thing to do. That was only a short time ago. It's a hard thing to believe.

AG: The point I'd like to make is that most of the American literary establishment, the publishers and the editors, adopted a party line which said that the reason "obscene" books were not published in America was that there were not very many of literary merit anyway. They were claiming that they were not leading any kind of fight, because there were no real manuscripts of great importance.

MG: That's a very devious cover.

WB: I remember the correspondence between Barney Rosset and Maurice Girodias. Barney was saying, very emphatically, "Do you really think *Naked Lunch* could be published? You're absolutely out of your mind. It is impossible. It must be done in a series of steps, starting with *Lady Chatterley's Lover* and then Miller. Perhaps after that, depending on how the litigation goes . . . "

MG: Yes. That's what Rosset did, and I see that it was a rational approach. It worked very well. He slipped in Jean Genet and Frank Harris. It had to be that way. It's very interesting to see that, in fact, it's the publication of a number of books like that which really changed the rules of an entire generation and made things possible that were impossible before. What happened by way of books was extended to all our forms of expression.

AG: By the time *Naked Lunch* was published, that was precisely the time of the great battle in New York over Lenny Bruce, and of the battle in the movies over Jack Smith's *Flaming Creatures* with New York filmmakers. There had been a meeting of district attorneys in New York, somewhere in the early sixties, to take concerted action against one or another of Grove's items, to see if they could break the house.

MG: The first step, before Grove Press did anything, was the publication of *Lolita* in 1958 by Putnam. I think it was the first event of this sort, an open challenge to censorship, which Putnam did not follow up. The district attorneys had to let go of *Lolita* because of a completely stupid, irrelevant incident of a copy sent to a literary critic in New York which had been stopped by the customs people and which had been released. I wrote a letter to this customs officer after hearing about this incident and asked him if indeed he had stopped a copy of *Lolita*, examined that book, and released it after examining it. He answered in the affirmative. Therefore one copy of *Lolita* had been processed through customs. Since customs was one of the two bodies which were actively in charge of censorship, the other being the post office, this created a legal situation whereby an American publisher could then publish *Lolita* and have a precedent strong enough to defeat the effort to suppress the book in court. It's very weird, but this is really what started the whole thing going.

AG: I remember the battle about *Lady Chatterley*, which involved Arthur Summerfield, who was the postmaster general. He put a copy of *Lady Chatterley* on President Eisenhower's desk with the dirty words and passages underlined. Eisenhower was quoted, in *Time* or *Newsweek*, as saying, "Terrible, we can't have that." He gave Summerfield the green light, "Go ahead and prosecute anywhere possible against *Lady Chatterley!*" That involved a couple of hundred thousand dollars in legal fees expended by Grove Press to defend it.

MG: *Lady Chatterley's Lover* didn't get as much opposition as *Tropic of Cancer*, which was the next one on the list and published by Grove Press in 1960. That's where they really had trouble with local police and cases being started against them all around the country. They fought, and finally won all the cases when the whole thing was reviewed by the court.

AG: The other thing that should be pointed out is that when Grove went over the barbed wire and got *Lady Chatterley* legalized, immediately all the other publishing companies in New York jumped in, Putnam's among others, and printed their own editions of *Lady Chatterley*.

MG: That's when the issue of public domain and copyright came out.

AG: All the other publishers were too chicken, or too cowardly or conservative, to actually fight for their own rights in regard to the earlier classic texts. As soon as Grove established the classic legal nature of *Lady Chatterley*, they began pirating it. The government's attitude in those years was in some way expressed by J. Edgar Hoover, who made a public statement in the early sixties saying that the three greatest threats to America were the communists, the beatniks, and the eggheads.

MG: There were editorials in the New York *Daily News* attacking either the new culture, or literary publishing, or freedom of letters. So there was, to some extent, a concerted government conspiracy which involved the FBI, who officially had started its counterintelligence program back in 1956. There may have been illegal manipulations by the FBI to discredit the literary community that far back, to say nothing of the activities of the CIA. An international literary atmosphere which was a big wet blanket was created to discredit any literary breakthrough of either the old or the new classics that would have been considered obscene.

WB: Yes. It's true that *Encounter* magazine, which definitely turned out to be partially subsidized by the CIA, was among the bitterest critics of my work and also of Maurice Girodias. There was an article against Maurice and Olympia Press written by George Steiner.

AG: Yes. We sent early chapters of *Naked Lunch* to Stephen Spender when he was working on *Encounter.* That was in '58, when manuscripts were being solicited by Grove Press for *Evergreen* and *Big Table* in Chicago. Spender wrote back that it might be of interest to a psychoanalyst but had no general literary merit.

WB: Yes, he said, "Having waded through the yards and yards of entrails . . . " Maurice, you were the first to publish Genet in English, were you not?

MG: Well, there had been a privately printed edition of *Our Lady of the Flowers,* published by a Cocteau protégé whose name was Maurian and who shortly after that started the Club Méditerranée and made a fortune, which he didn't do as a publisher. He was trying to run a very interesting bookstore and publishing firm, and he was the first one to publish the book in English. But that was only a few hundred copies and it was never put for sale in bookstores.

AG: It's funny, Genet made such an impression here, too, just at that time. At least, in our small circle of people.

MG: I suppose the first shocker the French had was Céline, before the war, but there was nothing else which was that provocative and that intense in French letters until Genet came out. I published two of his books, *Our Lady of the Flowers* and *The Thief's Journal.* I got into serious trouble because of Genet. At the same time, the French versions of his books were published by Gallimard, who was a great importer and a wealthy literary publisher.

AG: Didn't Gallimard publish edited versions of Genet?

MG: No. They were the complete texts. My English versions were banned, and I was prosecuted for it, which doesn't make much sense. But that was another illustration of what we were saying earlier: that it was really not just an American effort to stop the liberation of writing and thinking, but it was really an international effort. My problems in Paris started with the British government's bringing pressure through Interpol and the French government to stop me from publishing those horrible books in English.

AG: The Traveler's Companion, which tourists were carrying across the Channel.

MG: Right, they were a mixed bag, in which I had some amusing pornography written by very good writers who were doing this as a lark.

AG: And to make some money.

MG: Yes. These were interspersed with books like *Lolita*, which I could only sell because I was selling them as if they were dirty books. It was the only way to get the nice tourists to grab a copy and pay the nine francs that we were charging for them. Of course, we had to take the position that we were publishers of pornography, which we were to a very large extent—and very proud to be that at that time. But there was also a counter-effort to stop us and to completely wipe me out of existence, because I was the only publisher in the world who was able to publish these books in English and who made an effort to select them and to try to give an audience to good writers. So this is how, after weeks and weeks of litigation, I was completely run out of business by the French administration.

AG: In the Western world, what was the reason for such concerted action that would have stretched through Interpol, through Arthur Summerfield the postmaster, through President Eisenhower, through the British; what was their motive?

MG: I think that their motive was the suppression of any free discussion of sex. Remember the problems Freud himself had before those years. He was fighting the same fight. I think that an arbitrary system was imposed, and the way to impose this was by sexual repression and by forbidding people to read certain books. So you had the British society in the Victorian era split in two: the working classes were not allowed to read anything and the upper classes were having a good time, quite deviously.

AG: Enjoying privately printed, deluxe editions of *Fanny Hill.*

MG: But this was not the French attitude at all. Before World War II, France was probably the only free country in the entire world. Then it was knocked out of existence by Germany and was subjected to the rule of the German Army for the four years of Occupation, during which the French middle class got a taste of censorship and found out what it could do with censorship. In my case, it was pretty atrocious. Even recently, English was an unknown language in France. I was being prosecuted and sentenced for books in English that the judges could not read. The French police willingly let me see some of the files denouncing me, and in particular right before *Lolita* was banned, which was my first big brush with the French authorities. I saw a big file and letter from the British police, addressed through Interpol to the French police, asking them to do something about stopping the crazy activities I was engaged in in Paris. I'm sure that Hoover was playing a role in all that. He was the great fighter against pornography, obscenity, and any kind of leniency.

AG: Well, the conclusion that I would derive from all of our experiences is that there is a great fluctuation back and forth in this question of liberty, and the old American saying "Eternal vigilance is the price of liberty." It would be a good thing for later generations to bear in mind that you can't take it for granted that the ruling classes will allow questionable works to circulate freely. You always have to fight for them, and probably we'll still have to continue battling for them for the next decade or so. Especially as there will be greater and greater repression.

MG: I've been through the experience of the French Occupation, the war in France, and the Occupation by the Germans, and I can assure you that it is absolutely devastating to see how a completely free country, educated and raised in the culture of freedom and in the respect for absolute freedom, individual freedom, can turn around and in a few months become a nation of slaves and idiots. I mean it's dazzling.

Joseph Heller

ON A WARM, SUNNY DAY during the Thanksgiving weekend I turned off the Montauk Highway onto a road leading to the beach. The brilliant yellow and orange autumn foliage had fallen in great masses on the road, leaving red berries, bronzed privets, and curled brown leaves on the trees.

The driveway curved by the garage to the front door of Joseph Heller's old white house, with all of its windows sparkling in the sun. It's nestled among trees and shrubs that were now without leaves, so I could see through the house to the terrace out in the back. Joseph Heller came out to greet me, smiling a boyish, crinkle-eyed smile, his face framed in a halo of thick white curls. He's tall, with strong shoulders, and conscious of his physical presence. His voice has the unexpected charm of blending the rhythm of his native Brooklyn speech with that pungent and elegant sense of language that's in his written style.

Joseph Heller was born in Coney Island in 1923 and attended local schools until he joined the air force as a cadet. During the Second World War he flew a total of sixty missions in the Italian Campaign. After the war Joseph Heller attended NYU on the GI Bill of Rights and began publishing his short stories in *Esquire, The Atlantic, Harper's*, and numerous other magazines. His story "Castle of Snow" was collected in Martha Foley's anthology of the best stories of 1948.

Joseph Heller published his first novel, *Catch-22*, in 1961. The title has entered the language to signify a no-win situation, and his satire of the war made the novel a major inspiration for the public protest again the war in Vietnam during the sixties and early seventies.

Something Happened (1974) portrayed in a first-person narrative the psychic dislocation of a conventional corporate career and suburban family life.

Good as Gold (1979) is a parody of the Jewish family experience as Gold sets his sights on a career in Washington to rival that of a Kissinger.

Published in 1984, *God Knows* is a historical first-person narrative told by King David in his feeble old age.

Joseph Heller and I sat on the terrace at the back of the house, enjoying the sun. At our feet, the empty swimming pool's aquamarine walls were dabbled with golden leaves. Joseph Heller has been living here in East Hampton since his recovery from Guillain-Barré syndrome, in 1982, for which he had been hospitalized for a year. He became ill in the course of divorce proceedings from his wife.

The feeling of having just completed his novel made him welcome a conversation about his work. And in the course of our discussion his mood ranged from the satirical to the nostalgic, withholding nothing, and he was clear about his work and what he wanted from it.

Even though Joseph Heller has recovered completely, he had to conserve his strength, and these conversations were recorded during one-hour sessions on several consecutive days. After each conversation we went for a long walk for exercise in the beautiful weather.

CR: I wanted to ask you about your childhood, because I read that you lived in Coney Island during the heyday of the amusement park, and I wondered if you had grown up in the atmosphere of a constant festival.

JH: In my piece called "Growing Up in Coney Island" I've written that there was something almost unreal about it. At that time there were two very large amusement parks in Coney Island, neither of which exists now. One was called Luna Park and the other was called Steeplechase. There were also scores of different amusements and food stands, all within walking distance. In addition, Coney Island then was an extremely safe neighborhood. The idea of a safe neighborhood is almost incomprehensible to somebody living in New York today. But I cannot remember a single crime taking place there the first nineteen years of my life. Consequently, children were allowed a tremendous amount of freedom. Also, it was in the Depression, and there were very few automobiles. In the summer cars would come in, but in the spring and fall you could play in the streets all day long and seldom have to interrupt any games to let an automobile pass by. And I was allowed to stay out very late. I think when I was nine years old I could stay out till nine at night, when my brother or sister would come looking for me. I thought nothing of wandering to the amusement area to watch people. There was the Coney Island boardwalk—it was very long, about four miles. And the beach was there as a playground. That was kind of exciting. My own children grew up in Manhattan and had nothing of the freedom that I had. At an early age, from kindergarten to first grade, I was allowed to walk to school myself—about a quarter of a mile away, without even crossing streets. It's inconceivable now. At that time Coney Island—it was about two miles—almost half was Italian and half Jewish. There was a slight overlap. And there were two elementary schools, one in the Italian section and the other in the Jewish section. And there was never friction between them. When the weather was nice, there were always parents sitting out in front of the houses, talking. If my own mother wasn't watching me, she'd know someone else was. There was a lot of conversation out of the windows.

CR: As a child, did you have a keen sense of observation?

JH: No. I don't even have it now. I'm not a visual person to the extent that descriptions enter my books. It's always conscious, I feel I *have* to say whether a person is tall or short or pretty or not. Had we not been talking about this, after you left I would not remember the colors you were wearing. I have a nephew who was about twenty-five or thirty years old before my wife pointed out to me that he had blue eyes. I was always more conscious of food. I love the smell of food. And, as I said, there was a tremendous sense of freedom.

CR: So, you went from that cozy freedom and plunged straight into the military.

JH: I went into the military and enjoyed what I thought was even a greater sense of freedom. In that period after high school, when I was looking around for various jobs, my sense of responsibility became kind of oppressive. There was not much money in the family, and it was very hard to find an interesting job that paid more than fifteen or sixteen dollars a week. And when I did find it, it meant traveling an hour and a half into the city and back. The thing is, most people lived their whole lives that way, traveling three hours a day, back and forth, to work. When I got into the army there was a sense of being sprung—it was like going away to camp. The sense of protection was great there; it was a substitute for the family. Also, I was very young and did not know what war was. That particular war was unique because the whole country was in support of it after Pearl Harbor. Just by being in the service you were loved by every American. I made more money as a private—the army was paying sixty or seventy dollars a month, and room and board as well. I had a good time in the military, even in combat, except towards the end, when a man in my plane was wounded. It was only then that I realized that the war was for real. Otherwise I was living in a fantasy world in which I pretty much saw myself as a character in a movie, every once in a while pretending to be shot down. I would watch the parachutes come out. Until one time when we almost were shot down.

CR: You actually flew sixty missions?

JH: My sixty missions would be equal to maybe two that the Eighth Air Force was flying over Germany. There were never any German fighter planes, and on half the missions, there was no anti-aircraft fire at all. They were short missions, seldom as long as four hours. When I read about the missions the Eighth Air Force flew, it's still perfectly horrible to me. They were under constant attack by German fighters. They flew eight- or nine-hour missions. I can't imagine myself doing that, although I suppose if I had been assigned to the Eighth Air Force I would have flown in those missions.

CR: When you said you felt as if you were a character, was there also a narrative going on in your head?

JH: No. I was just having a great time. I was nineteen or twenty years old, an officer, making what was then an unimaginable sum of money. I was getting flight pay, which was 50 percent more than base pay, and then overseas or combat pay, so I was getting between four hundred and four hundred fifty dollars a month. That's over a hundred dollars a week. When I was growing up, the idea of someday making a hundred dollars a week—that was riches! There I was in the army, making more than that and having a good time doing it. There's a line in *Something Happened* which touches on this. Slocum says that it was after the war the struggle began. A good many people have spoken about this experience. I believe it was Kurt Vonnegut who said World War II was the longest-running war in history. If you were in World War II and weren't taken prisoner or wounded or killed, I think most people would regard it as an extremely salutary experience. I benefited from it tremendously. I never would have gone to college otherwise, even if I had wanted to.

CR: So after the military, what made you decide to go to college?

JH: It was easier than going to work. Also, I wanted to be a writer. I wrote a few short stories while I was overseas waiting to come back. The first one was accepted for publication by *Story Magazine*, shortly after I was back from overseas. I believe now it was an awful story, but it was accepted. And by the age of twenty-two I couldn't deny to myself that I really had an imagination and a real appetite for knowledge, for reading, particularly about literature, philosophy, history. And the government made it possible for me to go to college.

CR: But you wrote as a child.

JH: Yes. I even submitted stories to the *Daily News, Liberty* magazine, and *Collier's.* They all published short, short stories. The *Daily News* used to publish one story every day, and on weekends they ran a serial.

CR: As an adult, was there a moment when you decided to take that direction?

JH: Just before I came back from overseas, I really had nothing to do—the missions were finished—so I began writing short stories. I did a lot of reading, more good literature than I had before, because the army was sending certain paperback editions of novels and short stories overseas. When I went to college, in my freshman year I wrote a humorous theme and got an A on it. I erased the teacher's mark and sent it to *Esquire,* which accepted it for publication, and then I had good reason to expect that I could succeed as a writer. In Creative Writing, I wrote three or four short stories that were accepted for publication, by *Esquire* again and the *Atlantic Monthly.* I didn't have any concept of what I should write—almost everything I wrote was imitative. I would read a story in a magazine like *Good Housekeeping* or *Woman's Home Companion,* and I would then try to write a story for them. I was not good at it. The ones I thought were successful were in *Esquire* or *Atlantic Monthly.* By the time I finished college I had a critical sense, and I was intelligent enough to know that what I was writing was not much good. I wasn't even writing out of my own experiences as much as writing out of my experience of reading other people's work. There was an unintentional hiatus of perhaps two or three years in which I did virtually no writing without even knowing I was not doing it. I stopped and didn't begin again until I was about thirty years old, when I decided I ought to try writing a novel. I felt I knew enough. And I started writing *Catch-22,* which was my first novel.

CR: What was the relationship of the stories to *Catch-22?* Had you tried to put some of the material in short-story form?

JH: No, not at all. The one published in *Story Magazine* was a complete fabrication, in dialogue similar to Ernest Hemingway. Another story *Esquire* published was set in a Coney Island pool-room, and afterwards I realized it was a variation on Heming-way's "The Killers." The one called "The Girl from Greenwich" was about a literary party, and I had never been to a literary party in my life. The element that several had in common was, I think, a propensity towards the imaginative or surrealistic. It could take the form of a farcical situation or a surrealistic situation. There's a story published in *Gentlemen's Quarterly* in which the main character begins living in his imagination. Steamships were the way to travel then, and he would pretend to be seeing someone off on a trip. The one good story was "Castle of Snow." It's set in Coney Island, and it's about an el-derly Jewish guy who has lost his job. He thinks he has found a job, but his wife sees him playing in the snow with children and is embarrassed. He explains to her that when he went to the job he was expected to be a scab, and he couldn't bring himself to do it. His imagining he's a child and building a castle of snow— that's the element that has always been appealing to me, along with the farcical. I think that shows up and is present in all my books. It's there in *Catch-22,* and it's in *Something Happened,* where it takes the form of the psychological. My ambition in high school was to write farces, plays like Moss Hart and George S. Kaufman were writing. Of course, they didn't need me, be-cause they already had Moss Hart and George S. Kaufman.

CR: In 1948, when your story was published in *The Atlantic* and you were very proud, that's when Mailer came out with *The Naked and the Dead.*

JH: Yes. And Truman Capote was already famous at that time. He published *Other Voices, Other Rooms* maybe a year or two before Mailer.

CR: What was your reaction to the war novels?

JH: It was to make me feel inept and immature. I still have trouble with literary language. And I am not naturally a fiction writer, in the sense that I don't have a literary vocabulary. Dialogue comes easily to me. The plot and situations come very easily to me, almost cinematically. Putting it down on paper is, I feel, the hardest part. And I am surprised every once in a while when I talk to somebody who professes his own surprise about what I'm saying to you. It could be that other writers struggle as much to get the sentences as I do. But certainly when you read them you don't get that impression. When I was trying to teach creative writing, one of the few points that I made that I thought would be valuable to the students was to tell them that every writer I know has trouble writing and that all books are rewritten. They must free themselves from the idea that when they read a book it's printed exactly the way it occurred to the author. Which is the way I used to feel. In reading Mailer's work I saw for myself years and years of arduous application, requiring more education than I felt I had. So it had a very prohibiting effect on me. I suppose I did have a fear that if I did write a novel it would be based on the war. War novels were coming into vogue then, even before Mailer. The first war book that made a big sensation, although it was not comparable to Mailer's, was John Horne Burns's *The Gallery*, which came out in 1947, a year before Mailer. Then a stream of war books came out. Mailer's, in terms of size, was the tome, the masterwork, the book with tremendous breadth and scope. It wouldn't surprise me if it had a similar effect on James Jones, who was probably well into *From Here to Eternity*.

CR: Did you feel that they were also mining war experiences you wanted to write about?

JH: No. I thought I had better stay away from that subject until I had something different to write about the war. My memory of *The Naked and the Dead* is that Mailer was very good as an illusionist. He gave the impression that he had experienced the actions he wrote about. And then with *From Here to Eternity* it was the same kind of thing. I felt that my own war experiences were very limited—I was only overseas for nine or ten months. Going to war was like walking down Coney Island, going to the amusement park. It had an inhibiting effect on me that I think was beneficial in the long run. My strength as a writer is not as a realist. It's also not particularly with plots. I recognize that in myself. Had I started to write a novel then, it would have been, again, derivative in all respects, including form. Despite my education, I did not really know that there was more than one way to tell a story. And it was when I was teaching at Penn State that I read, within a short period of time, the comic novels of Evelyn Waugh, and Céline's *Journey to the End of the Night*, and Nathanael West's *Miss Lonelyhearts*, and I remember Nabokov's *Laughter in the Dark* particularly. I was comprehending for the first time that there were different ways to tell a story, and the methods these people used were much more compatible with my own technical ability—but, even more than my technical ability, with my own imagination. My imagination is fertile in that direction. It is not too fertile in telling a straight scene.

CR: Yet your work is grounded in reality. If you speak of illusion, the most surreal aspect of your work conveys a grasp of reality.

JH: I'm no good at nonfiction writing, at journalistic reporting. The few times I tried it, a couple of book reviews, articles, I realized that I'm less than mediocre. Whatever is best in me is not called upon if I'm dealing with facts. Very small parts of my novels rely on research. It's good for me to have some foundation, where the place is and what takes place there, but beyond that I feel that if I'm dealing with factual matter my imagination is inert.

CR: Did the time lapse give you a sense of detachment about the war when you began writing about it?

JH: Oh, yes. When I was writing *Catch-22*, so much of it I saw as being related not to World War II but to the domestic situation here, the political situation. It was the Korean War, and the cold war. And I did not have a feeling that I was writing about World War II. Very little was said about World War II in *Catch-22*, other than that fascists are bad, and that's it. Most of the polemic that is there, and the topical humor, relates to events occurring after World War II, during the McCarthy period. Deliberate anachronisms. There, too, I was intentionally fusing or confusing two completely different time periods, two different eras. I also found out something else about myself. Even in *Good as Gold*, I don't like to keep track of time. I have no idea of how many weeks or months it takes for different episodes to evolve in my book.

CR: In *Catch-22* the drama of the war isn't presented with that sincerity which I think characterizes all the novels that came out of the actual war experience.

JH: It's the absence of specific details which I think gives it that sense of application for today. One is always at war with one's own superiors. I think events work in my favor also. You can always count on a Gerald Ford or a Ronald Reagan coming along.

CR: Were you surprised that *Catch-22* spoke so immediately to another political situation and climate, the protest against the Vietnam War?

JH: I was surprised that it was as successful as it was, but that was the objective. Neither I nor my editor expected it would have as large a readership as it did have after the first year. It's a novel that intentionally reverses the convention of storytelling, which is to familiarize the reader with the essential facts of the narrative, the location, the character, what it's about; whereas I deliberately inverted, created confusion, for about sixty, eighty pages. And knowing what I was doing. It's like picking up the work of Marcel Proust or James Joyce or William Faulkner, all of which I think I did, without knowing anything about it, without having any idea what's inside, and expecting the usual narrative form, without some guidance, even if it's in the form of some recommendation from somebody. I think what happened to a great extent with *Catch-22* was that most people just put it aside. They had no reason to believe it was worth the effort. I did not want it to be that obscure, that much of a chore. It was women and young people who would pick it up and have no trouble with it from the beginning. They would be the ones to tell the others to stay with it.

CR: I was thinking of the role it played during the whole Vietnam protests. It was a basic text of the movement.

JH: Not only the people opposed to war, but people in war; and not just enlisted men, but high-ranking officers. I've heard from them. By the time the paperback came out, a year after, nobody complained about its being difficult reading. Whoever was picking it up had heard enough about it to know it was an unusual book.

CR: How were you affected by the fact that your novel eventually found its own historical moment?

JH: I think every novelist writing a book hopes to achieve certain things, and the hopes exaggerate themselves as the indications of success or fame begin to appear, even if they're all auspicious. It enlarges the magnitude of the possibility. *Catch-22* was never on the best-seller list. Therefore, what did happen exceeded my expectations. I think every daydream I had about that book did come true within two or three years. And so it's a more gratifying experience than I will ever have again. Another thing it did do was make it safe for me to write a book like *Something Happened*, knowing that because of *Catch-22* and my own reputation, the book would be at least read by reviewers. *Catch-22* did make it possible to do that—to feel I could take as long as I wanted to write the book, keep it as inert as I intended to do. It would be approached respectfully.

CR: Had you ever expected an imaginative work of yours to have social impact?

JH: I don't think books do that. I think books verify feelings that people have, confirm people who are already leaning in that direction. I didn't expect *Catch-22* to have that effect. You see, I don't think that a novel or any book is particularly useful as propaganda, for several reasons. They take too long to write, and they take another year to publish, and then they have such a small audience. Even *Catch-22*, with eight or nine million paperbacks sold, reached an infinitesimally small audience in terms of the number of people who turn on the television. In 1964 the involvement in Vietnam began, and there was a resurgence in the paperback sales, which had declined. It achieved its widest popularity between '64 and '68.

CR: I'm thinking of the moral authority of a novelist who knows that his work has affected the reader.

JH: I suppose this is part of the gift, or luck, incorporated in my imagination of creating certain characters, certain phrases, which would apply to a situation even if the book itself was forgotten. *Catch-22* has been mentioned in a Supreme Court decision. It's when the chaplain is taken down to be interrogated. And they say, "We accuse you of crimes we don't know about. How do you plead?" And he says, "How can I plead if you don't tell me what they are?" And they say, "How can we tell you if we don't know about them?" That was quoted by Justice Powell in a decision.

CR: Do you believe that the artist reflects the currents of his time?

JH: It's maybe an instinct people have for timeliness. In my case, *Something Happened* was published at a time when very respected, conservative people were writing about the disillusionment of people who were successful in business. Not people who were failures—people who were successful, reaching a point where nothing was paying off the way they hoped it would. The realization that ambition was merely a substitute for some other drive. When the goal is achieved, the initial drive is still there. The initial hunger is there, it is not appeased. I was lucky in having that coincide with the book.

CR: I recall those were the issues of the Me Generation. Did *Catch-22* give you a sense that your work had an autonomous life and that it addressed a particular consciousness?

JH: I think the ingredient is the aesthetic one. I don't think there's an idea in *Catch-22* that's surprisingly subversive or even radical.

CR: So that when you began writing *Catch-22*, you set out to put everything into one major work.

JH: I thought it might be the only novel I would ever write, because it takes me so long to write.

CR: So that the very decision to start a novel was a major event?

JH: It was a moment, a definite time. I had spent two years in Pennsylvania teaching freshman English to students who had no more interest in learning than I had in teaching. Then I came back to New York, found an apartment, found a job in a small advertising agency, where I was very happy And the nice thing about advertising is that for hours at a time there is no work to do. I kept running into people who were getting contracts for novels, and I thought, I can do as well as they can. Why not start a book? The first idea for a novel that came was *Catch-22*. I didn't pick war as a subject—I just decided I was going to write a novel. The opening line of *Catch-22* has the first words that came to me. *Something Happened* came to me in a line I used in the second chapter. *Good as Gold* came to me the same way. The book I'm doing now—I don't know where it comes from; that's what's frightening about my imagination. If I were a journalistic writer I could pick a subject, as James Michener does. "I've got the best story in the Bible, better than Moses or Genesis." And then, as I kept thinking, it became the story of King David. Those lines are in *God Knows*. It doesn't open that way—the lines come later.

CR: When you have the first line, you say that you don't start writing until you have the last line.

JH: Oh, yes. I spent a year making notes. With *Catch-22* I wrote the first chapter and then typed it at the office. I have a beginning, and I sometimes have an end, and I work towards that pattern, but in between there has to be something. And that's why I think all my novels—*Good as Gold* could be an exception—but most of my other novels are retrospective. In *Catch-22*, almost all the action has taken place before the time.

CR: You said that *Catch-22* gave you the freedom to do what you wanted in your second novel, and yet *Something Happened* is a book you worked on over a long period of time. By contrast,

Good as Gold was written quickly. I was wondering what is the rhythm of your writing?

JH: *Good as Gold* is exceptional among the three because it's the only book of the three I was able to work on exclusively, without doing other work in order to earn money. All through *Catch-22* I was holding regular full-time jobs. *Catch-22* didn't give me economic freedom. In the course of writing *Something Happened* I had to continue working, so I did some screen work, a television script which didn't take much time, and then the play *We Bombed in New Haven*, which started almost as a novel. Once the producer got interested in it, I earned perhaps sixty or seventy thousand dollars from it over a two-year period. I taught four years at City College, during which I did work exclusively on finishing *Something Happened.* But teaching, as you know, despite the small number of hours you put into the classroom, eats away at time in preparations and in reading manuscripts. So it's really like a full-time job. When *Something Happened* was published, I did earn a lump sum and was able to make a resolution not to do any other type of work. With *Good as Gold*, I worked on only that. Nothing else impeded, and there was no more distraction. I've pretty much stuck to that rule on the book I'm doing now. Until I got ill and couldn't work, that was the only work I was doing. I am able to write every day because there's now nothing else on which I have to work.

A second consideration would be the nature of *Something Happened* as contrasted with *Good as Gold* or even *Catch-22.* The text has less dialogue. If anybody wanted to take the trouble to count the average number of words per page, they would probably find that in *Something Happened* there's maybe twice the number of words. The number of pages may be the same, but there's more writing in *Something Happened.*

As far as the rhythm goes, I used to become infuriated at myself in *Catch-22*—it would go so slowly; I would be fortunate if I could do as much as a page a night. Usually I worked about two hours after coming home from work. It made no sense to me then that somebody with a college degree and the gift for writing, as I had, couldn't just sit down and write four or five pages at a session. By the time the book was finished, I came to terms with my own pace and my own method of working. I don't choose to work the way I do because it's more efficacious and productive. I realize it's the only way I can work. With *Catch-22* sometimes I'd set myself a goal of doing ten pages a week. But they'd all have to be rewritten so many times that it would average out to perhaps a page a session.

CR: Generally it's the first novel that's written in the first person, and as the writer becomes more confident of his craft, he turns towards the third-person narrative.

JH: Oh, I didn't know that. I didn't notice any difference. *Something Happened* was born in my imagination as a first-person novel, told in the present tense. With me there's very little that I do actively in choosing the subject or choosing the person or point of view. The novel comes to me as it's written. I did not sit down to write a book about World War II, and I didn't decide to put it in the third person rather than the first person. The same thing is true of all my books. The idea occurs to me as a novel, rather than as a subject, and the novel already encompasses a point of view, a tempo, a voice. I don't begin with the subject, I begin with the idea of doing a story.

The paragraph in *Something Happened* that occurred to me first included a large number of presumptions about what would happen. That was the paragraph with which the second section opens: "In the office in which I work there are five people of whom I am afraid." If he is an executive on a middle-echelon level, which you knew before that paragraph, the chances are good that he's married, he lives in the suburbs, and he would be fairly successful within the corporate structure. That also implies a certain age—he's not going to be under twenty-five or over sixty-five. The book *Something Happened* came to me with those sentences. You see the tense is present tense. I never asked myself whether this should be done in the third person. I can't imagine it in the third person, as I can't imagine Yossarian in the first person. If *Catch-22* were in the first person, I would have had to expose much more of Yossarian's thoughts and psychology and past than I do or did. A decision I did make with *Something*

Happened was that he not be Jewish, yet I was aware that in his ruminations he could very easily have been Jewish. Had I made him Jewish, he would have had to dwell an enormous amount of time on the sense of his own Jewishness and to what extent that affected his marriage and his job, and I didn't want it to be a book about that.

CR: But that's the subject of *Good as Gold.*

JH: The books are different from each other. I would not have wanted to emulate *Catch-22.* So much of *Catch-22* is stylistically conspicuous, and I felt that appropriate for that book about that subject. It would not be as appropriate for either of the other two books. Even apart from that, I would have felt I was imitating myself, and using many similar devices which, while organically useful in *Catch-22,* would be only ornamental, like showing off, in *Something Happened.*

CR: *Something Happened* was written in a sober style. In *Good as Gold* your style becomes again much more exuberant, satirical.

JH: In *Good as Gold* there is a chronological plot. It's farcical in conception and description, but it is a story, it has a beginning, a middle, and an end. There's a character who is moving towards an objective, and, in correspondence with conventional storytelling technique, the reader is notified very early what the objective is. That's not true in *Something Happened.* What he wants in *Something Happened* is to be allowed to make a speech, which is deliberately trivial.

CR: But the title *Something Happened* leads straight to the conclusion of the novel, the next-to-the-last chapter.

JH: *Something Happened* is taken from idiomatic speech. I knew what the ending was going to be before I began writing, but the title was given to me fortuitously. I was on Fifth Avenue and there was the sound of two automobiles colliding. Two kids who were there said, "Come on, something happened." As soon as I heard it I thought, That's a good title. Then I began using the phrase, which is what happened with *Catch-22*—once I decided on the title, then I began using it in the text a good deal.

CR: Idle curiosity—how did you coin that expression, since it's entered into the language?

JH: It just came out of the idiomatic expression used in the first chapter. I put down that there was a catch to it. I can't explain the idea of giving it a number. I cannot explain how my imagination works. Since I'm almost solely at the mercy of my imagination, I often dread that thoughts and notions like that will cease coming to me. I don't know where the notion came of giving it a number and institutionalizing it as a statute or regulation. When I got to that point about signing other people's names, where there was a catch to it, at that moment the idea of giving it a number came to me. Why or how? Those are mysterious processes of an individual's imagination.

CR: In *Something Happened*, there are major sections which are portraits of each member of his family. In the course of describing each of the characters, the narrator goes through a full circle of possible emotional attitudes. In reading the portraits, I wondered if you wrote them in layers.

JH: There's a swing to his ambivalence—he's as much afraid of his tender emotions towards each of these people as he is aware of his hostility to these people. That was indeed part of the plan. If you ask me how it's executed, I don't know. I do know that it's part of the full circle. In the last two sections, preceding the end, I did have in mind a man having a breakdown. And there, too, the syntax, the language, is intended to correspond to that. So whereas in the earlier portions he was punctilious about grammar and sentence structure, in those last sections he does have run-on sentences, the use of parentheses, he loses his logic, and he even begins having what amount to auditory hallucinations. He imagines dialogues taking place, and he knows he is imagining them. And many of the things he thought, which he would experience as internal fantasizing earlier, are presented with quotation marks as actual dialogue, corresponding to an auditory hallucination. He's out of emotional control. He can't even direct his obsessive thoughts, his free associations, and they go back more and more to the gross, to the sensual. Then I pull him out of it. And I wanted to do that without his having to go see a psychiatrist, or without the reader's being told this is a man having a breakdown. I wanted to put that loss of control into the normal operations of a person. People normally experience states of mind in which control is gone. With each of the characters, particularly his children, there is an ambivalence which he tries very hard to conceal from himself. So with the son who's a favorite, he begins by talking obsessively. Then gradually it comes out—the tremendous amount of resentment, disappointment, and anger. With the retarded son, he begins in a very callous way, but he can't deal with it. What I was trying to suggest there is that he's avoiding discussing it, it's very unpleasant for him, and he does digress, but eventually has to come back to face it. Facing it is almost literary—talking about it, telling the reader that this is the way he is and this is what they went through with him. In the course of that his resistance, his defenses to all the people in his family, just begin crumbling. His mind races on.

CR: I was moved by the intimacy of the observations of character, as well as the analysis of his ambivalent reactions.

JH: The present tense was chosen to give that effect, to justify certain exclamations and emotional stress. Usually in a first-person novel, the narrator is talking in retrospect. You would not expect him to react reflexively in retrospect, as you would with Slocum talking about it as though it's going on while he's talking. It was meant to be a first-person, present-tense, uncomfortably intimate book.

CR: Yet there's a clinically detached observation of these characters.

JH: At certain times Slocum can look at them and look at himself, as if almost in a schizophrenic state, where he's watching himself accurately in relation to these people. At other times he can't; he loses that ability to distance himself from them. The emotions he is talking about and in which he is involved take hold. Then at the end there was also a psychiatric model I had in mind, which I thought was consistent with him, which is to deny and forget, and very quickly he recovers from that accident. That last section was deliberately terse and controlled to show he's back in authority, not so much in the company, but trying very hard to control himself.

CR: Is your technique one of building on the narrator's ambivalence, taking him from one extreme to another?

JH: The specific techniques used in the places where I shift and let certain things happen come from intuition or a sense of taste. Also, keep in mind that what you're reading was rewritten and edited considerably. Most of the rewriting was done in sections, and a tremendous amount of cutting takes place. This has been true for all three books. It's usually not taking out episodes, but repetitions of language, parallels, long descriptions. The manuscript usually runs between eight hundred and nine hundred typewritten pages, and after the deletions are made and it's retyped, it's usually one hundred fifty to two hundred pages shorter.

CR: Is *God Knows*, the novel about King David you just finished, a historical novel?

JH: It's set in the past, but it would not be called a historical novel. Historical novels, like biographies or autobiographies, presuppose an intention to re-create accurately events that took place at a certain time, whereas in the first few pages of this there are anachronisms—an allusion to Mexican food, an allusion to the state of Maine. That's a way of informing a reader of what a book is about and how to interpret it. But it would not be a historical novel. About the time I got the idea of writing a book about David, I didn't know enough about him. What was delightful for me was to go to the Bible and discover how rich it really was in melodramatic episodes, much more than I imagined. The events in the novel are based almost entirely on those that appears in the Books of Samuel, 1 and II, and the opening of Kings. David has to make the choice between giving the kingdom to Solomon or to his other son, Adonijah, who has the right to it. David decides to make Solomon king. And also the fact that he's so old and he's cold and they give him the most beautiful virgin they can find to sleep with him. Even though I had taken a course in the Bible, I had not known that David was Saul's son-in-law. Did you know that?

CR: No, I didn't, and I taught the Bible.

JH: David was married to Saul's daughter; Saul arranged the marriage to ensnare David. For the bridal gift, he had David go out and get a hundred foreskins from the Philistines. Saul's intention was that David would be killed. But, David being David, he brought back two hundred foreskins. David was talking about in-law troubles: You think you have in-law troubles? How would you like a father-in-law who spent his life trying to kill you? Saul did remorselessly try to kill David. First he tried to have him killed by others, figuring he wanted his own hands kept clean. He did everything to try to get him killed by the Philistines. He sent him on the most dangerous missions. But then, when he couldn't stand it any more—he believed that David had a charmed life—he himself tried to kill him. He turned David into a bandit, like Jesse James, and came out every year with three thousand men, trying to trap David and kill him. I had not known that David, to escape Saul, went over to the Philistines and joined their army of mercenaries. And he was going to war against the Israelites in the battle in which Saul was killed. The only reason he didn't go was that the Philistines didn't trust him. And he begins to think that maybe God does exist after all. Because had he gone, had Saul been killed at that battle, they never would have accepted him as king.

CR: Wasn't David's eldest son Absalom?

JH: Absalom was killed ten or twenty years back before the time of my novel's beginning. There is a recurrence, a repetitive pattern in many of the Bible stories. What happened with Absalom and David was very close to what happened with David and Saul. And what happened with Solomon and Adonijah. That is fratricide. Absalom killed his brother, who had raped his sister. After David's death, Solomon does have Adonijah killed. So there is that pattern. And one of David's boasts throughout is that he had taken a country the size of Vermont and built an empire the size of the state of Maine. From what I've read, the land of Canaan was the size of Vermont, and if you add Jordan and Syria, it became the size of the state of Maine.

CR: Do you know why you were drawn to this Biblical figure?

JH: No. I don't know why my imagination takes me where it does. I just feel so lucky to get a single idea for a novel that I can write about. When I get one, my ruminations and daydreaming grow and lead to other things, and I feel that there is a book there. I'm just so fortunate that I want to write it. I've never had more than one idea for a book at a time. I don't begin writing until I've thought about it, and I feel it's a book I can write, one that's particularly suitable for me to write. There's none that I started right in on.

CR: I was thinking of the recurrence of the family drama in both *Something Happened* and *Good as Gold,* in another tone altogether, and I was wondering if that's what interested you in the story of David also.

JH: I don't know whether it interested me, other than the fact that I began to perceive possibilities that entertained me or excited me, comic scenes or dramatic potential. In the play and in the three novels, the climax does deal with the death of a person. In *Something Happened* it's a child. In *We Bombed in New Haven* it's a child. In *Catch-22* it's the death of Snowden, which has taken place in retrospect, but in the organization of the book that is the critical moment, the climax. And the reference to David and Absalom is in the climactic scene in *We Bombed in New Haven* and now in my book on King David. But somebody other than myself can point to these things and talk about them, death as a climax, and death of children.

CR: In *Something Happened,* death is a smothering. . . .

JH: Both actual and symbolic. Shortly after the book came out, Bruno Bettelheim wrote my editor a letter about the validity of the death—the father willfully, deliberately killed his son because he had no choice. When I read that I started getting chills, because I had not thought of that. He won't kill his retarded son, because that's for convenience; but a person will kill to keep from losing the one person he loves. His attachment to his favorite son is such that they were virtually the same person. As the son was going away, rather than lose him he would kill him. I had not gone into it that deeply. Slocum used the phrase "I could kill him," but he used it idiomatically. Now, it could be that in terms of drawing on recesses of my mind, with which I'm not in touch, what Bruno Bettelheim said was there. I was not aware that I was aware of it.

CR: That's like the contrast between the family structure and the corporate structure, even though there is that total fear that animates his perception of the corporate structure.

JH: The fear of the corporate structure is probably an extension of the anxieties he suffers from his family. He is safe in the corporate structure because there are tables of organization and he knows where he stands and what his functions are. Nothing requires him to respond with emotions. He is well paid and there is really nothing wrong with the company he works for. The danger is when he comes home. He doesn't know where he is within the family structure. He does not know his relation to his daughter or sons.

CR: At the end, there is a total break-up of the family. I was wondering if some of the narrative was based on an experience.

JH: A few people told me that they didn't know that I had a retarded child. It was not based on experience. I never lived in the suburbs. I did not have a retarded child. I never had that kind of tragedy in my life. I don't have a large family as in *Good as Gold.* The family dinners that made such a big impression on so many people were things I heard about from other people.

CR: In *Good as Gold,* the corporate structure is replaced by the government.

JH: The government is an object of satire. His own ambitions, his own view of the government is more the subject than the nature of the government.

CR: That's what made so many reviewers see it as a satire of Kissinger.

JH: Well, it's not so much a satire of Kissinger. It's the nature of government, the inevitable mediocrity which you have. But, again, I think I'm kind of fortunate in timing, because the presidents continue to get worse. Ford was president while I was writing the book. Then Carter came in. And now you have Reagan. It is a subject for comedy—Ronald and Nancy Reagan, the people around them. I do think that if I go back to giving readings, I can read the same sections of *Good as Gold* and there'd be as much laughter in relation to *this* administration.

CR: By contrast, the patriarch of the family despises his son's ambition.

JH: He's about the only one with principles towards the end. He calls Roosevelt "that bastard," and he's furious when he finds out that his son is courting the favor of this well-known anti-Semite. The old man is interesting, too, because he's obnoxious, he's authoritarian, he's impossible, and yet he's sympathetic. He clings to the family because he doesn't want to die alone. And then he goes and makes that speech. In the old days you didn't send aging people off to nursing homes or to Florida; people died at home.

CR: The comedy comes from the children's suggestion that he buy a condominium in Florida, and his constant avoidance of the question, which creates a comedy of death.

JH: With *Gold* you have the ambivalence of a man who wants to shake off his family associations because he's snobbish, and yet realizes that his ties to them are ineradicably strong. And that many of the people in the family are much better than he is, ethically and morally. I do think that in *Good as Gold* those thematic points we're talking about, the moralistic polemic, are less important than they are in the other books. I think in *Good as Gold* it's mainly the farcical actions. The satire in *Good as Gold* is the main objective. And then the principal color in the palette

I'm using is death. It's death there, because people do get old and die.

CR: In *Good as Gold*, the drive to power is related to the subject of King David. Yet at the same time, your comedy is always based on the fact that the characters are trapped.

JH: Yes, they are usually trapped by their intelligence. In *Good as Gold*, power is only important to social status. Gold just wants to be socially accepted, to be invited to theatre openings, to benefits he reads about. And it's a good way to get girls. There's a tremendous amount of social envy, but what he hates about Kissinger is not so much his actions as the fact that the man is such a celebrity. I satirized it because it's reprehensible, it's current, and it's socially acceptable.

CR: Are you pursuing this again in the new novel, *God Knows?* Because David is more than a figure of power, he is heroic.

JH: He's not heroic in my book. It's based on fact, and a few commentaries I read. He was not particularly successful as a ruler. Whereas his son Absalom, who succeeded in winning the support of the people, made the mistake of going out to battle against David, who had the army. The image that we have of David as the ideal ruler, a heroic ruler, is not justified by his story. It is interesting that I discovered that another character in the Bible is given credit for killing Goliath. Long after it happens you read about other battles, and a man is mentioned in the Hebrew text who killed a Philistine named Goliath. In the King James version, in order to avoid that they put in the word "brother" of Goliath. I didn't realize this, either: whenever you see anything in italics in the King James version, it was to cover an ellipsis in the Hebrew text, and the ellipsis here was that they didn't want Goliath being killed twice, and the second time by somebody other than David. The same way in the Song of Solomon—the translation would be almost obscenely erotic. In the Song of Solomon, the female voice is talking about "last night he put his hand in the hole of my door and I felt my bowels move." "Of the door" was in italics. I think that was put in just to clean it up a little bit. In Hebrew it's "he put his hand in my hole."

Being vain, and also a heroic soldier who knew his popularity among the people, perhaps David realizes all the time that he is unconsciously plotting against Saul.

CR: David is one of the few characters in the Old Testament whose erotic life was an integral part of his legend.

JH: I didn't know that David was the second king. Saul was the first king. There was a civil war after Saul's death. David made himself King of Judea, which was like being King of Mississippi. And it took him seven years of civil war before he became King of Israel. But Israel never liked him. So David was the second king, and the first one to have a harem. I didn't know that, but I knew the story about Bathsheba. The consequence was that a curse was put on him. I made many allusions to things that happened. But as a result of that prophecy—the sword will never leave your house, your neighbor will take your wives—the one that really hits in my book is not the death of Absalom. It's that the baby that was born to Bathsheba would surely die. God told Nathan to tell David this. And in seven days the baby falls sick and does die. So there again you have the death of a child. He can never forgive God for that. My David's at war with God. Even though he's convinced God is dead and God doesn't exist, he still wants to be talking to Him again.

CR: Is the historical canvas one that gives you greater scope?

JH: I don't know. I think if you have five or ten American novelists choosing the same subject, we'd all come up with different books. Some of the things Styron writes about, or O'Hara, would leave me with nowhere to go. I would not be able to find enough material to make a short story. John Updike chooses subject matter in the three books on Rabbit—his imagination produced it and it's interesting to him. Given that character and that occupation, I couldn't go on; I couldn't get a second paragraph. I could work with a good deal of Philip Roth's subject matter and probably do it in much the same spirit, but his interest in the aesthetic and literary problems of writing—my mind wouldn't tell me anything about that. The subject I took in *Something Happened*—there's virtually little narrative action in it. And what little there is is concealed, subordinated, it's done indirectly. Other authors would take that subject matter and focus probably on the corporate lives and the effect of it on the executive. Maybe John O'Hara has done it, maybe Updike hasn't, but they would be completely different books. And I would not have thought that any subject in the Bible would capture my interest. But what happens is that my interest is reactive, my imagination works, and I begin thinking of certain scenes. And it happens. I think the novel has become such an individual, vital form. Given the novelists we are talking about, I do believe you can give them the same subject, and half of them would not be able to write any book at all, and the other half would write books that would have very little similarity to each other.

CR: You have an organic sense of how your imagination works, and you have a sense of when it stops, where your interest ends.

JH: Either my interest ends or I feel my talent ends. And I cannot go on with this in this way in any particularly inventive or original fashion. I do notice in myself—and again, a psychoanalyst might give a better reason—a preference for indirection. I have a preference for dealing with the more dramatic scenes in retrospect, after they've already taken place, rather than telling a straightforward narrative and building to a climax to keep the reader in suspense. My tendency is to announce; to let the reader know—such as the day Milo bombed the squadron, or Snowden's dying. And then, two hundred or three hundred pages later, only then do I get to Milo's bombing the squadron. That's the technique Faulkner uses, particularly in *Absalom, Absalom!* I have a preference for that which I cannot justify except with the feeling that, the way I work, the way I write, the way I perceive, it would be better done that way than to have the actions proceed chronologically.

CR: The first time you mention Milo bombing the squadron it comes as such a shock, and then you move on.

JH: If I were going to do that with a straight narrative form, it would not be believable. And not only would that not be believable, the absence of severe consequences would not be credible.

It's irrational. As bad as society sometimes becomes, certain things are not condoned that easily. Whereas if I present and talk about something as having already taken place, the reader assumes it has taken place, and does not question its plausibility.

CR: When you speak about where your interest stops, you are also talking about the density that you want in the work, the exploration of the material by your imagination.

JH: I don't know why, but it has to do with the nature of an individual's imagination in relation to his limited range of talents. If we have twelve possible ways of writing a novel, I think most writers would have a strong command of maybe three or four, then a somewhat weak command of another two, and the others would be alien to them. Certain things I admire in others, I cannot do. It's as though it's a different form entirely. And I cannot explain why I use the combinations that I use, except that I feel that I can use them more effectively than other writers can, and would use different combinations to a very poor effect. I know intuitively that it's true, and I tend very hard to avoid those areas in which I have no particular techniques or talent. And I will choke off a scene because I feel I've already done the most I can with it, whereas another author could elaborate on it, extend it, and make it as interesting as or more interesting than what I did with my method. But I cannot do it. And I don't think that many other authors can do what I do.

CR: In terms of the nature of your talent and what you can do, is there a sense of narrative qualities which dictates the direction you take?

JH: Oh, the sense of quality is there. I have a feeling it would be more effective for me to do it the way I do do it than the way I don't do it, or the way other writers would do it. And even though we're talking about handling specific episodes, I'm not only referring to that, I'm referring to the whole Gestalt. The whole work itself has an organizational personality, in which I will usually have a number of straightforward scenes. But they are part of a distinct personality that is my literary personality. I may change the time, the pace, the combination of those things.

But even though there are infinite possibilities in a novel, I don't think that any writer has the infinite talent to explore them all. What I'm telling you I'm doing, I think any writer would tell you. I'm trying to write what I'm writing most effectively. I occasionally choose the wrong subject, I occasionally choose a subject and have to deal with scenes that I'd rather not deal with. And perhaps I cannot hide them; they have to be mentioned, they have to be dealt with in a confrontational way, and so then I have to do that. So I'm alert to that; that's one of the reasons why I don't begin a book until I know there's a middle and an ending, so that with my sense and my judgment, it will have an organic justification. I remember the first time I met Philip Roth. We were talking, and he was telling me that he tried to write every day, and often he began a book or a story without knowing where he was going, and after going thirty or forty pages, realizing perhaps that he was not going anywhere, he might just stop. I can't work that way.

CR: Your comedic sense is one of the rarest talents.

JH: It cannot be taught. I can be funny, and given enough time with any dialogue I write, I can have somebody make a remark which will produce a response. And it will be funny. I know that I have that ability, whereas I have almost no natural affinity for metaphor or descriptive writing. Comedy for me is something to use, and because I do it easily, I don't do it sparingly. I will shift very abruptly from a scene that is very emotional, perhaps almost painfully so, into something really flippant. If you ask me to justify doing it in literary terms, I can't. I just have a feeling it's right. Other authors also work in the same vein. I'll never forget the dialogue that takes place in an Evelyn Waugh novel. A woman's son has been killed on a horse—the son has the same name as her lover. Maybe it's John. Anyway, she's at a numerologist's and getting her fortune told by having her feet read. Somebody comes in and says to her, "I've got terrible news. John has been killed." She thinks it's her lover, but the person says it's not the lover, it's her son. And she says, "Thank God." There is so much acid in that portrayal, and it's also funny to read it that way. As in *Laughter in the Dark*, the tricks they play on the blind husband. In the books I'm writing I feel the flippancy, the switch in tone is good in context or I wouldn't do it. I'm not doing it just to be sacrilegious.

All my books have come dangerously close to being sentimental. It's one of the things I'm very much on guard against. If I let myself go, I would become maudlin. Slocum lets himself go and often does become maudlin, because he has these defects or weaknesses of nature or character. He's not that different from me. Yossarian can become that way and knows it; he fights against letting himself feel emotion. Even though all my books seem to be iconoclastic, there's a sense that my characters may not be decent, but they do know what decency is. I may justify rebellion and protest, but I don't think I ever justified evil. I use flippant humor as a way of expressing certain attitudes without being pontifical or moralistic.

CR: There's a basic assumption in speaking about your talents that in your comedy there is a looking into the abyss. That's evident in the first two novels.

JH: Oh, sure. Gold is as astonished by some of the things he hears and sees in Washington as I want the reader to be. He says, "I have no qualifications, so what difference does it make." And Gold is astonished by the fact that it may even be true. It makes no difference in the government if there's intelligence or morality. What we see, and what we can write about, is a direct projection of morality and of sentiments, which would include the imagination. A person's political tune might change on a single point, but even that change would be consistent with that person's behavior. What you find in Catch-22, you will find in all my books. And as frivolous as they are or might be—Good as Gold is not a book with that much depth—the basic attitudes would be the same. Comedy's present in all three.

CR: And the extraordinary cruelty—does that come out of a fundamental pessimism?

JH: I'm a pretty cheerful guy. All I'm trying to do is write good novels. Basically, my objective is to be successful in writing what I and other people would consider a serious work. But the objective is aesthetic. And I think the educational aspect of fiction, if it exists at all, is extremely faint. I don't think that any novelist that I know has any new message to bring to people. What they may have new to bring is the use of a fictional form, practices and techniques which would incorporate ideas. If I were going to write a serious book, it would have to deal with the imminence and inevitability of death, the possibility of disease, the fact of cruelty, social neglect—those are the subjects I respond to. I love Malamud's short stories, but I couldn't write one. Every once in a while I can imitate his diction. I can't write short stories like anybody's. My imagination likes long, long books. I can take a simple subject and through certain distortions I process it, enlarge it, extend it. And I think a good part of *Catch-22* was so simple, and, put in chronological order, it's not worth writing about. A bombardier whose commanding officer wants his men to fly more missions than others—that's pretty much what it is. And I didn't even know that was a story. I felt I'd better keep moving things along. I have no choice—I cannot write the books Saul Bellow does, I cannot write the books William Styron writes. I could come a little closer to writing the comic books that Evelyn Waugh wrote, but only close in terms of the humor. I don't have his language, and I don't have his ability to write concentrated stories. My books get very long. But also I feel a need to put things in which he doesn't. Which goes beyond the satirical implications. I'm doing what I can, and luckily what I can do is interesting to people.

CR: You've said that you don't know what your next novel will be until it comes to you and you start writing it. But I was wondering, do you ever foresee a body of work?

JH: I'm beginning to see it now. I have four novels, and in them there are similarities which indicate the mentality or the soul or the personality that produced them. I think the personality, the viewpoints, including the aesthetic viewpoints, the desire for innovation, and the forms which the innovations take in each book are specific and limited. If it surprises you, it's because I've been successful. There are really only four or five ways of being funny—the wisecrack, the surprise, the unexpected, etc. And when I'm being funny, I'm aware that I'm doing something similar to the surprise that I used back there. There are not that many ways.

What I take seriously is this: I'm very pleased with *Catch-22*, as it remains popular, it remains a classic. I'm very pleased to run into people who tell me *Something Happened* is the book they think is the best, and I run into more and more people who do that. But what I'm mainly concerned about is this novel that I'm doing now. I write it and read it as though I'd never written a book before. I want this book to be extraordinary—at least, extraordinary in the year it's published. I want to be successful, and every novelist wants this, including some as reclusive as Samuel Beckett—I'm sure he'd rather be successful than not. When the book is out, I want to be able to get an idea and do another book. Even though I confess to you a feeling that subjects choose me and techniques choose me, I've never been long without an idea for another book. It was probably one year after *Catch-22* was published that I was making notes on *Something Happened*. And in less than a year after *Something Happened* was published, I was making notes on *Good as Gold*, and less than a year after *Good as Gold* was published, I was making notes on *God Knows*. So I'm never very long without an idea for a book. And I expect that that will happen again. And I'm sure these things don't happen completely accidentally, but unconsciously I'm thinking about what I'm going to write about, thoughts go through and I have to make a decision, or stop to think a little longer about something. And maybe that's when it will happen, and an idea for a book will come to me. And then the form will take shape.

But I really and truly could not write a book about a man who has a house on one acre in East Hampton. I have a friend I knew when I was a copywriter and he was a salesman for an art studio, and now he is rich. His name is Marvin Green. When I got sick, he wrote out a check for three or four hundred thousand dollars for a 25 percent share in a novel I would write about my experience. He would give me the money right then. What he was doing was finding a way to help me out, while making what he felt was a sound investment. And I said, "Marvin, you'd be wasting your money. It's true I probably can get a million-dollar advance on a novel, but I'll only get that much if I do it. I don't know if I could write a book of fiction on my illness."

CR: I heard that you and Marvin Hefferman were writing a book on your illness.

JH: But that's a nonfiction book. I'm going to start on it in another two, three weeks. Speed's got a house out here, too, and he's already written his parts of it. He has a sense of humor. I haven't read them. I know the subject matter, and I'm going to write from my point of view. He was with me the day I got the first symptoms, and he moved into my apartment and began taking care of everything for me. He and Valerie and I came directly here from the hospital and spent the summer and much of the winter, went to St. Croix together and came back, and spent this summer together, too.

CR: Will the book be a record of your struggle with Guillain-Barré syndrome?

JH: It would be my record as a patient, and what happened, and coinciding in certain areas with my divorce. And for a couple of reasons I agreed to do it. One was that I was out of cash, and the second reason was that I wanted Speed to have a reason to stay other than the altruistic. As soon as we moved out here, Speed wrote a piece on taking care of me in the Hamptons which was published in the *Times*, and it was funny. Someone at Bantam Books said, "Why don't you do a book?" Speed asked me and I said I thought we could do it together. I began getting things— collecting letters from other people who had this disease, and I got my hospital records.

CR: Do you ever worry that this book might infringe on your own material?

JH: I will stick to my intention, to deal with the facts, the nature of the illness itself, the rarity of Guillain-Barré syndrome and the very severe effects it has.

CR: Did that experience leave you with a residue of anxiety? Is it something that can come back?

JH: They say it never comes back. The only person I've run into who has had a recurrence was a person who was treated with cortisone. It inhibited the severity by arresting the progress. But he told me the potential is there and still active. When he stopped taking cortisone, it returned. He told me he would be on cortisone the rest of his life.

CR: I remember hearing that as soon as you developed the illness you were rushed into the hospital. Do they know how to treat Guillain-Barré syndrome?

JH: The only thing they can do is keep you from dying of asphyxiation, as the breathing muscles fail, and give you anticoagulants so you won't develop bloodclots, which people die of. And keep me from starving to death because I couldn't swallow. But once the disease reaches what they call the plateau (I know this now, but they didn't tell me then), there's no way of knowing that there will be any recovery at all. Many of the nerve tissues could be destroyed. And the majority of people do make a significant recovery—I think the statistics are 80–85 percent do make what's called a 100 percent recovery. I'm considered a 100 percent recovery. But nothing determines who will be in the 15 percent who don't make a full recovery. I think 5 percent of the people still die from the disease itself.

CR: That must leave a residue.

JH: What frightened me most was the possibility of a stroke. There are no strokes in my family. But half or more than half of the patients at the rehabilitation center were stroke patients. With my morbid imagination, as I was recovering very slowly— I was there almost four months—it occurred to me one day there was nothing to stop me from having a stroke as well, even while I was there.

CR: Is this the disease that was mistaken for a form of polio that struck adults?

JH: The medical profession became familiar with the disease during the swine-flu epidemic. Because patients developed very bad side effects from the swine-flu inoculation, and the government had to discontinue it. If they're not familiar with it, the symptoms are very similar to polio. The differences are, with polio you generally have symptoms of a virus, which would include fever. And usually polio is not bilateral; it will attack one side more severely than the other. Whereas this is bilateral, and there usually is no fever, or any other signs of a virus infection. The disease is going to run its course. It's not a virus—it's a body producing antibodies which have an affinity for tissues of the nervous system. The effects would be like polio, with the exception that with polio you experience viral symptoms immediately. With my disease there is usually a viral infection maybe two or three weeks before. In my case it was so mild, I just felt tired. And my case was remarkable because they diagnosed it quickly. I was talking to other people who had it. There was a piece on me in a magazine, and I got loads of letters. They almost all had trouble being diagnosed. Women are often sent to psychiatrists.

But you can recover from it. "Spontaneous" is hardly the word, because it doesn't happen that quickly, but a person recovers on his own. When I asked the doctor in the rehabilitation hospital what else could it have been, he could not find anything else. He said it could have been a bloodclot in the brain stem, but by now we would know it. It would be more serious. My laboratory test, a particularly painful test called the EMG, did not confirm it. It didn't exclude it. Certain results would make it impossible to establish it as myasthenia gravis. In the spinal tap, you usually get a high elevation of protein.

CR: Had you started working on *God Knows* before this illness struck you?

JH: Oh, yes. In fact, I had just given the second section to a typist. I write longhand and I type and I rewrite on the typed pages. I called her up and said to bring it over to Mt. Sinai. And I didn't know what it was to be sick. I'd never been sick. I mean, I didn't know what the word "weak" meant. I thought it meant being tired, listless. About three days later I couldn't hold a page, couldn't close my fingers.

CR: Were you able to get back to work soon after you left the hospital last year?

JH: When I got back that summer it went very slowly. I had the attention span to read and write. Valerie, who used to be a typist, had gone through that whole section, about two hundred pages, and, me being me, I added about seventy-five pages. My fingers would tremble when I was trying to put a page in. I couldn't turn the rollers. And when I was trying to use Ko-Rec-Type, I would have to hold one hand with the other. Last summer I had no strength in my hands or fingers.

CR: Did your illness change the tone of the narrative? Is it still a comic novel?

JH: Given the fact that I was going to continue with this novel, that I had thought it through and had written a few hundred index cards, and it was set in the time when it was, there was very little that I could introduce. I was fortunate to this extent—I'm dealing with a character who is so weak he can't get out of bed. David has chills all the time. And they give him this virgin, not because he wants sex, but because he hoped she would keep him warm by lying with him. He got no heat from this, so she didn't succeed. You have this guy who is so weak and so old, and sleeping with this beautiful girl but sexually impotent, and he is very conscious of his weakness. I began putting in certain things which I will probably take out, because they won't fit in with the rest, such as the fact that his hands are so weak that he can't hold a bowl of food.

CR: You started working again last year and you finished the novel a few weeks ago.

JH: We haven't started the editing. This is the first draft—there'll be changing sentences, a good deal of cutting. What surprises me is how much work I have done since last summer. Usually with my books, when I get to the last third, the speed with which I write increases tremendously the closer I get to the end.

It's not hard to explain—it's because I've used up most of the material that I've had in mind. So I don't have to decide where I have to put anything. It's out of the way. That's a load off my mind.

CR: Then, when you started writing again, you had regained your strength?

JH: Yes. Towards the end of the summer, I began to work on the whole manuscript. I went back to page one and began reading it and making what I felt were improvements. Then I went on to the second section, which required a great deal more work, because the first section I'd gone over several times but the second section I was seeing for the first time after my illness. I can be a fairly prolific writer if I don't have distractions, because there is very little else that I want to do with my spare time. I'm fortunate in that I have no interest in athletics—tennis, fishing, skiing—and a limited interest in travel. And I like what I'm doing now. If I retired, I would live exactly the way I live now, assuming my health was good. Sleep as late as I want to, which is about eight in the morning, have a leisurely breakfast, and begin writing fiction. That's what I want to do.

Susan Sontag

SUSAN SONTAG IS A VERSATILE writer who has worked in many genres. Her primary concern is that each work surpass her previous work. Therefore, there's a duality in her discussion of her writing. Her sense of beginning anew with each piece, as opposed to having a body of work behind her, is the preoccupation of the essayist who uses her faculties for criticism and synthesis, and therefore does begin anew with each subject. Yet her main concern in writing, as exemplified by her discussion of her novels, is a constant striving to give fuller expression to a personal source of material. It is this concept of artistic development that informs all of her work.

She was born in New York City in 1933, but spent her childhood in Arizona and California, where she began her university studies at Berkeley. She transferred to the University of Chicago, where she obtained her B.A. in 1951, and did graduate work in philosophy at Harvard and at Oxford. Her first book was the novel *The Benefactor*, published in 1963, a first-person narrative by an anonymous young man studying at a major university in the capital of an unspecified country, who recounts a dream life more vivid than his outward involvements. By contrast, her second novel, *Death Kit* (1967), portrays an amiable young man who falls out of his life. After an attempted suicide, he begins to act out a drama of unknowing. Alternating with these novels, Susan Sontag published collections of essays which immediately drew her into the public arena: *Against Interpretation* (1966) and *Styles of Radical Will* (1969).

That same year Susan Sontag went to Europe, where she made two feature films in Sweden, *Duet for Cannibals* in 1969 and *Brother Carl* in 1971, and the documentary *Promised Lands* in 1974, on the Arab-Israeli war. She returned to writing with the essays *On Photography*, published in 1977, and the collected short stories of *I, etcetera*, in 1978. *Illness as Metaphor* was written in 1978, after her own hospitalization for cancer. The essays collected in *Under the Sign of Saturn* in 1980 focus on the particular temperament of the artist in determining the concept of the works. In 1982 she published a selection of her most important and representative works in *A Susan Sontag Reader*.

In 1983 Susan Sontag made a film for Italian TV, *Unguided Tour*, which was set in Venice and freely adapted from her story with the same title. In early 1984 she will direct the first American production of Milan Kundera's play, *Jacques and His Master*, for the American Repertory Theatre in Cambridge, Massachusetts.

Susan Sontag lives on a tree-shaded street of row houses within walking distance of her publisher, Farrar, Straus and Giroux. Her library occupies the top floor of her brownstone duplex. The sparse white book-lined room is lit to an even glow by the skylight, and now, in the late afternoon, from the front windows, shafts of sunlight randomly illuminate the table and the books on the shelves. We're seated facing each other across the library table she uses as a desk. It is completely covered with stacks of books, manuscripts, and publications, which threaten to bury her typewriter under a constantly impending avalanche. Coffee cups, pens, clippings are on top of, and in between, these piles.

Tired at the end of the day, she wears a dark sweater and slacks. Her straight dark-brown hair is swept back from her forehead and cut shoulder-length. As she speaks, her eyes deepen almost to black in their intensity, against the matte white complexion of her high-cheekboned, oval face.

Only when she pauses does it become evident how completely

her attention is given to each topic. In her clear, resonant voice, words race with her thoughts as she takes up each subject. Her philosophical training is evident in the way she states her position, develops her ideas from several perspectives, anticipates objections, makes her defense, and draws the implications of her ideas. Running through everything that she says there's a tone of passionate concern. Her openness to inquiry gives the distinct impression that there's nothing that can be asked that she has not thought about before.

The first conversation occurred in the spring of 1981, and the second a year later.

PART I

CR: Many people ask you about your critical work simply because your last novel appeared at the end of the sixties. People assume that your imagination's been taken up with your essays.

SS: I've always gone back and forth between the two. My first book was a novel, *The Benefactor,* which came out in 1963. There were all those essays, and another novel, *Death Kit.* In 1968 I went to Vietnam, and my anguish about the war made it very hard for me to write. I couldn't get it out of the forefront of my consciousness. I had been thinking about movies throughout the 1960s and living more and more in the film world in Paris and Rome, so I went to Rome with an idea for a film that I wanted to direct. While I was looking there for a producer, I got an invitation from a producer in Stockholm, and I lived in Sweden the better part of two years doing two movies. In 1972 came a great crisis. *Under the Sign of Saturn* opens with this situation. I'm in a tiny room in Paris thinking, Where am I? What have I done? I seem to have become an expatriate, but I didn't mean to become an expatriate. I don't seem to be a writer any more, but I wanted most of all to be a writer. So I gave up a film project in Paris—I'd written a script and had the go-ahead from a small independent producer there—and began to write again.

There was a second crisis in 1975, when I got cancer. I tried to respond to those crises. To my illness, with *Illness as Metaphor.* To my semi-expatriation, with the essays in *Under the Sign of Saturn.* Having discharged my debts to these obsessions, I feel a tremendous liberation.

CR: You speak of purging yourself, and yet there's a loving quality in your essays about these writers.

SS: Yes, I would much rather write about what I like. That's why I'm not a critic. An important job of the critic is to savage what is mediocre or meretricious. The essay that was written most quickly was the one on Leni Riefenstahl, because it's easier to write from anger than from love.

CR: Was the Paul Goodman essay the most difficult to write, since it's the most personal?

SS: No, the hardest to write was the essay on Syberberg. The essay on Goodman was the easiest. I read in the *Herald Tribune* in Paris that Goodman had died, wrote the essay in an afternoon. Grief made me rapid. Normally, I write very slowly.

CR: Was your illness the decisive event that changed so many of your attitudes? In your essay "Approaching Artaud," you write about his gnostic concept of the body as mind turned into matter, and the physical thoughts of the body.

SS: Becoming ill, facing one's own death, being in the company of people who are suffering terribly—many of them dying—for several years is, of course, a watershed experience. One is not the same person afterwards. I was told that very likely I would die. I didn't die. I had excellent medical care—better than what most cancer patients get, for many fewer people would die of their cancers if they had proper treatment. That horrifies and enrages me—the needless suffering and deaths—and that's why I wrote *Illness as Metaphor.* Writing the book was part of my way of not giving up, not accepting the sentence of death. And, as Nietzsche said, whatever doesn't kill you makes you stronger. But also—as someone quipped—whatever doesn't kill you leaves scars. Having been brought so close to death, you can never come all the way back. I have a different, less innocent relation to time. And a more anxious relation to my work.

CR: You said that you think of films as part of your own creative work.

SS: I write the script, I conceive the shots, which determine how it will look. I work with the composer to make the music, I direct the actors, and I edit the film. I do all those things myself from beginning to end, so that filmmaking is as much the creation of a work in terms of images and sound as the writing of fiction is a creation of a work in language. Directing in the theatre means taking a play or an opera that already exists and trying to make it wonderful for the audience—even better than it is, if possible.

CR: What attracts you to directing?

SS: First, that directing is a way of seeing, of visualizing. It's tangible, concrete, artisanal. And then the fact that there are other people—writing is a wholly solitary activity, but directing is always a collaboration. By directing, I mean directing for the stage as well as making films. In some respects, these are similar activities with the same pleasures—thinking visually, musically; working with actors. But there is a large difference—at least for me. A film is an original creation, but when I think of directing in the theatre or in opera, I think always of directing some work which I admire, not of writing an opera libretto or a play. Therefore, in terms of intention and passion, directing in the theatre is related to my consciousness as an essayist. Directing a play by Pirandello, as I did in Italy last year, or an opera by Strauss or Janáček, as I would like to do, would serve the same purpose as writing an essay about them. I care about these bodies of work. I want to keep them alive and make them interesting to people, and directing on a stage is another way of dramatizing consciousness. My aim is not unrelated to that of the essays, which are portraits or dramatizations of consciousness.

CR: You are thinking of your critical faculties as serving the function of translating and dramatizing the work? Your critical faculty is directive because it interprets rather than controls?

SS: Yes, communicating love and passion. The essays come out of extremely passionate relationships to the works described. I am learned but I am not particularly cerebral—in fact, very little so.

CR: How do you view the essays in *Under the Sign of Saturn* in relation to your other work?

SS: *Under the Sign of Saturn* is the book on my relationship to Europe, my identification and my perceptions—an autobiographical act. The essays are stories about minds, filtered through my mind. The portrait that I give of Elias Canetti has at least as much to do with my concerns as it does with Canetti. The vast private library, for instance—that's my library I'm talking about as much as it is Canetti's.

CR: Do you find that there is a burden of consciousness because of your critical faculties? Does the superego clamp down on the creative and imaginative faculties?

SS: No, I don't think so, but I'm perhaps not the best person to answer this question. I'm not aware of it at all, as a matter of fact. Do you mean in writing fiction and in making films, on the one hand, as opposed to essay writing and directing on the other?

CR: When you're basically with yourself, in the range of writing from critical to imaginative, it would be clear whether there would be a conflict there.

SS: Not only am I not aware of a conflict, I'm not even aware of any relation between the two. When I write fiction, it is the only thing that interests me. I feel that I have the usual naïve relationship to my own fantasy that everyone has to start with, and then I struggle with verbs, adjectives, and commas. I don't have any preconceptions of how it ought to be, and I've certainly never written fiction in order to illustrate any idea that I had as an essayist.

CR: When you've completed a page of fiction, the critical consciousness doesn't start rewriting or criticizing or ordering what you have done?

SS: Only in the sense that every writer has to be both the idiot who goes in there and takes out handfuls of raw whatever it is, fantasy, and also the tough editor who decides that's self-indulgent, that doesn't work, that's boring, that part should go here. I don't write easily or rapidly. My first draft usually has only a few elements worth keeping. I have to find what those are and build from them and throw out what doesn't work, or what simply is not alive. So there is a process of rewriting, of accumulation. In that sense, the critical faculty *is* active; but I don't dignify it by calling it the critical factor—it's me, functioning as an editor of my work. It's a very artisanal kind of consciousness. It is not theoretical, but practical and intuitive.

CR: What contemporary American writers do you think are seriously trying to do something literary?

SS: There are many. William Gass, Elizabeth Hardwick, and E. L. Doctorow are writers who have nourished me, given me pleasure, and taught me something. I don't know what I've learned; maybe the pleasure was the learning. And John Updike is certainly a first-rate writer, though I don't think he has written a first-rate novel. I feel similar exasperated admiration for Philip Roth, who is a thrilling sentence-by-sentence writer. Recently, and belatedly, I've discovered the stories of John Cheever.

CR: It dawns on me that your interest is in the process, rather than the content, because these are all formalist writers.

SS: My interest is in the quality of the prose. I want to be enchanted and delighted, I have other standards for writers I read in a language other than English, or in translation into English—for the great European writers who sit in my head. That's another way of reading, another way of being inspired.

CR: But, on the other hand, you deplore the fact that there is no American novelist who faces up to American society.

SS: In American letters there is a notion that writing is above all an expression of the unrestrained expansive self. The temptations of egotism and of commercialism are such that you have to be very eccentric to be a good writer in this country, to love literature above all and not be mainly concerned with self-promotion. The writers who are going to last are those who care about language, and it may be that the best writers that we have right now are those who are working in fragmented narrative forms. I'm thinking of Hardwick's *Sleepless Nights* or Doctorow's *Loon Lake.*

CR: In fiction, is your own material something you've always had, and wanted to write down?

SS: I suppose I'm stuck with my basic pool of fantasy, but I want the stories I am working on to be as different from the ones I published in the sixties as they are from each other. Maybe because, like everybody else, I am profoundly uncertain about how to write. I know what I love or what I like, because it's a direct, passionate response. But when I write I'm very uncertain whether it's good enough. That is, of course, the writer's agony.

PART II

CR: Over this period you were reviewing all of your work to compile *A Susan Sontag Reader.* Is this a project you've thought about for a long time?

SS: The *Reader* was my publisher's idea, and he had to persuade me that it was something desirable. My first reaction was: "I'd like to have another show but I don't think I'd like to have a retrospective." The convention of a Reader is, after all, for writers whose work is finished, or after they are dead. I'm more interested in my recent work than in past work, and above all interested in the work I'm now doing or in the work to come. I made the selections for the *Reader* on the basis of a number of considerations, one being what I couldn't leave out because it would be disavowing something.

CR: Does your perspective always shift according to your current interest?

SS: Absolutely. I react to my work as something that I am trying to go beyond. So, by definition, if I've done it I'm not so interested in it. I'm least fond of some of the essays in *Against Interpretation.* I do like "Notes on 'Camp,'" which I think is original as an argument and a *tour de force.* In "Against Interpretation," however, I think the argument is too assertively stated. But I forget the literary climate against which that essay reacted, the often reductive philistine way books were talked about in the late fifties and early sixties.

CR: Did Roger Straus, your publisher, provide an objective point of view you could refer to?

SS: Once. I said, "What if I include just four essays?" and he asked, "Which ones are you leaving out?" I said, "I thought I'd leave out 'Against Interpretation.'" He said, "You must be out of your mind." I laughed and he laughed and that was the end of it.

CR: What made you want to omit that piece?

SS: Perhaps it was because I couldn't imagine writing it now. But all the early pieces have that "first voice" from which I have since evolved. Then there are other moments when I think that I'm always writing the same thing. I'm in flight from my past work, and I know that my task is to open my writing to new themes, themes that obsess me which I haven't yet had access to as a writer. These themes are my capital. But I hope to enlarge the repertoire.

CR: Feeling this contradiction, on what basis did you make your choice?

SS: I tried not to be too self-conscious, and to put in as much as I could of my best work. In particular, I wanted to give a good idea of my fiction. The first book I published was a novel, and I'm quite fond of my two novels—*The Benefactor* and *Death Kit.*

CR: What is the development you saw in your essays? "Against Interpretation" and "Notes on 'Camp'" are written as concentrated fragments or notes, whereas your later essays are integrated.

SS: It's much easier to write notes. You say something, you explore it, you contradict it. You work with it and around it, and then you cut and go on to another sequence. These units—their ideal form is aphoristic—are more interesting if they play off each other. Since that is the easiest kind of essay writing, for me, I decided to make it harder for myself. The later essays in *Under the Sign of Saturn* each took an embarrassingly long time to write—many, many months.

CR: Have you looked at the Sylvia Plath diaries? You were speaking of the fifties and the temper of the times, and when I read her diaries I was struck by the sterility of the cultural climate as she perceived it.

SS: I find it distressing to remember that this writer of genius regularly compared herself with writers who were in no way her peers and was upset by their success and longed for a certain kind of commercial success which was so much less than what she deserved.

CR: You both published first novels at the same time: *The Benefactor* and *The Bell Jar* came out in 1963.

SS: We are of the same generation. But commercial standards didn't have the same hold on me, because I remained in the university world until 1965. She came to New York as a guest editor on *Mademoiselle,* and she was already published by 1953. When I was a university student in the 1950s, I have to admit, I'd never heard of *Mademoiselle.*

CR: How do you understand the conventionality of her aspirations, not only artistic but also emotional—a husband and publication in *Mademoiselle,* then a child, next a novel? Nothing in the culture broke through her narcissistic concentration.

SS: It's a great handicap to grow up thinking, What is life going to give me? or Am I going to be allowed to write what I want to write? The tone of the diaries does remind me of women I knew in the fifties. The idea was that life had to present you with a package: the perfect spouse, children, and the admiration of your peers. I too thought I would have a so-called normal life. My earliest model was Madame Curie and her husband working together in the laboratory and having children who became scientists too. Then, also, I married when I was seventeen, so that I didn't think about it, I did it.

CR: You married at seventeen, then, right after high school?

SS: No, I graduated from high school when I was fifteen. I was in my third year of college.

CR: Was rebellion against these conventions, or breaking away from them, an aspect of your writing?

SS: No, I have been writing since I was seven years old. I always wanted to be a writer. I also wanted passionately to become a doctor, but I talked myself out of it in my mid-teens. It seemed unrealistic to hope to do both well. What I've written has been in no sense a rebellion against anything that I know of. I never felt, consciously or unconsciously, that there was any conflict between my vocation and being a woman. Writing is the one art where there are a great many first-rate women.

CR: Did you also have a great woman writer as a model?

SS: I didn't think I was going to be a woman writer. Nor did I have a woman model. My models when I was in my early teens were Gide, Mann, Kafka. I never thought: There are women writers, so this is something I can be. I thought: There are writers; this is something I want to be. I learned to read very early, and the very first writers who enthralled me were Edgar Allan Poe, Jack London, Victor Hugo, and then the Brontës.

CR: At what point did you decide to get your work out into the world?

SS: When I did finally finish something I thought publishable, which was *The Benefactor,* I made a list of publishers. Farrar, Straus was my first choice, because they had just published *The Selected Works of Djuna Barnes.* New Directions was my second choice, because they published many more writers I admired, but somehow I had the impression that they were more inaccessible. Third was Grove Press, because they were publishing Beckett. I put the manuscript of *The Benefactor* in a box and left it at Farrar, Straus and Giroux. Two weeks later I got a call, was asked to lunch by Robert Giroux, who offered me an option that turned into a contract. I spent several months reworking the book and they published it. I am now in the unique position of having published nine books with the same publisher, and that publisher is the first one to whom I took my first book. Close to twenty years have gone by, and I have dedicated the *Reader* to Roger Straus.

CR: Was he your first editor?

SS: Well, Roger is the president of the firm and is a bit everybody's editor. My first editor—that was for *The Benefactor*—was Cecil Hemley. Starting with *Against Interpretation,* my editor was Robert Giroux. With my last book, *Under the Sign of Saturn,* my editor was David Rieff, who also happens to be my son. I have great confidence in his judgment. But Roger Straus is central to everything I do.

CR: By contrast to your fictional work, your essays, such as "Against Interpretation" and "Notes on 'Camp,' " immediately drew you into a public dialogue that's a continuing process.

SS: One of the blessed aspects of fiction is that it doesn't invite a certain kind of dialogue. I suppose one could be in a dialogue with a novel like Saul Bellow's *The Dean's December*—which seems to be the vehicle of his opinions. But, generally speaking, there is something autonomous or sealed-off about fiction, which is not true of essays. I feel very ambivalent about this dialogue. Of course I want readers and I want the work to matter. I do want to contribute to some kind of dialogue, but I also don't want to get caught in it.

The essays in *On Photography* are a good example. I've been thinking about photographs for many years. Then, finally, I thought I had something to say. I wrote those essays, which took me something like five years. *On Photography* is an account of several different ways in which one can think about the presence of photographic images. Ultimately it's about the modern world, about consumerist consciousness and capitalism—about many modern moral and aesthetic attitudes of which photography seems such an extraordinarily rich example. That's all I ever want to say about photography.

CR: Do you feel, then, that the public response invites you to continue adding to what you've already said?

SS: Yes, adding, defending, explaining, perhaps even changing. But I don't think I should *have* to respond, because I don't feel the work belongs only to me once I've published it. I have the "message in a bottle" ideal of publication.

CR: Why did you leave out *Illness as Metaphor* and *Trip to Hanoi?* Or your film scripts?

SS: Because I couldn't cut them and including them would have made the *Reader* too long. Both *Illness as Metaphor* and *Trip to Hanoi* are extended essays—and it doesn't make sense to me to give an excerpt from an essay. Or a film script. Or a story. The only excerpts are from the novels. Everything else is complete.

CR: After you finished the selection of essays for the *Reader,* I wonder whether you had a sense of your development?

SS: The ordering, which is chronological, suggests a certain evolution, and that's why I included the *Salmagundi* interview, where the notion of my development as a writer is discussed. I see two distinct periods in my writing. The first, from 1963 to 1968, ends with the publication of *Trip to Hanoi.* It includes the two novels and the first two collections of essays. The second period begins in 1973 with a story, "Project for a Trip to China," and more new fiction writing. I got sick in 1975, just after I did the *Salmagundi* interview, and when I was well enough to be able to work again, I completed the essays in *On Photography,* which I'd started in 1973. I wrote *Illness as Metaphor* very quickly, in about two months, but I had already written it in my head when I was in the hospital. I then wrote several more stories and the essays that went into *Under the Sign of Saturn,* and that takes me up to the present.

The *Reader* is about the first two periods of my work—since there was the big break for filmmaking, and the crisis and feelings of doubt that often occur, or should occur, perhaps, after you've been writing for a while. Now I feel that I am at the beginning of another period. Although I was a precocious child, I'm really a slow developer and my best is still to come.

CR: Is that based on the sense of work that you've always wanted to accomplish?

SS: No, I think I understand better what writing is now.

CR: Which is the theme of the last essay in the *Reader*, on Roland Barthes, called "Writing Itself."

SS: That essay is the expression of things that I feel profoundly, and it addresses the part of Barthes which I can identify with. But it is also a farewell to certain ideas. I have been thinking all my writing life about what is implied by the aesthetic way of looking at the world. It's in *The Benefactor*, it's in "Notes on 'Camp.'" The Barthes essay is a restatement, at a much deeper level, of themes in "Notes on 'Camp,'" a sort of "Notes on 'Camp'" revisited, but with far more subtleties and complexities. At the time I was writing "Notes on 'Camp'" I felt the deepest ambivalence towards the subject. Yes, I understand the sensibility, which is partly mine. And I repudiate it, too. The Barthes essay is also steeped in ambivalence, though I love and honor his work. I'm arguing with myself in this essay, making the best case for these ideas and trying to go beyond them. The essay is not the herald of something new but, I think, the end of something.

CR: In the essay on Barthes you see the structure of his development where his untimely death stopped it.

SS: It all makes sense, as if he died just when his work was completed.

CR: Unless he was going elsewhere altogether . . .

SS: Well, yes, he wanted to go elsewhere, but I don't think he could have. Who knows? Death always confers a retroactive structure. Mozart died after finishing the *Requiem*, Beethoven died after the late quartets, so these works seem like an ending. Who knows what could have happened? In my own work I tend to see what extends and coheres, though usually in the form of a

paradox or a contradiction. If the subject of an essay is somebody's work, the work is usually interesting to me as something
to write about because of the problems that it raises and the
larger themes that can be discussed using this work as an example. The essay on Barthes is really about what writing is and
about what the aesthete sensibility is.

CR: Your concern is expressed through the subject.

SS: The essay on Walter Benjamin is about the melancholic temperament in a writer; the essay on Syberberg is about the Wag-
nerian notion of the masterpiece, of which Syberberg's film
Hitler is an example. The energy of the essay comes from the os-
tensible subject's being the platform for discussing the larger
theme. That's what made those essays so hard to write. The obitu-
ary essay on Barthes was written very rapidly under the shock of
his death, and it is a brief account of the general climate or range
of his work. When I had agreed to do the introduction to
the *Barthes Reader* I had a month of agony in which I felt that I
had nothing more to say. Only when I realized that I had the
larger subject could I start work on it.

CR: The metasubject, then, is the area of synthesis with your own
concern.

SS: That's right, and that's why those essays start to become almost portraits. I felt that the Benjamin and the Canetti were like
stories.

CR: Is there a similar transformation in your ideas about fiction?

SS: I want to write fiction which is not solipsistic, in which there
is a real world, but I'm not drawn to the conventions of realism,
what Barthes called "the reality-effect." Still, the novel is far
from being dead or exhausted. On the contrary, many possibilities remain unexplored.

CR: When you speak about the next phase of your work, is it the
novel you're thinking about?

SS: A lot of my fiction has been different ways of expressing distress, perplexity, and alienation. It assumes too much about the

world, and devalues the world in a certain way. One is always inside a head, but I think I can get the world into that head now—and not just in the form of an attitude about the world, such as anguish or stoical perseverance.

CR: Is part of your exploration of form a synthesis of the different genres you work in?

SS: In the novel I am now working on there are letters and journal excerpts, and dialogues and anecdotes. I like this kind of free form.

CR: Roland Barthes towards the end was turning away from criticism to speak about his own writing, his journals and especially the final synthesis he wanted to make, a work of art. This is a tradition in France. Do you feel an affinity with him in that?

SS: I'm very different from Barthes. His connection with the university world was profound, and mine is not. I am in part a product of the university culture. Most books that I read are scholarly books. Most books that I own are published by university presses. But I don't operate within the bounds of the university. I don't have that kind of language and I don't have that view of the writer. Barthes was a university writer, which in part is maybe why he couldn't free himself to do other kinds of work. Although he longed to make this jump, I doubt he was capable of making it. I think he had gone too far in the other direction, because fiction demands a different kind of consciousness, a different way of letting go, a different kind of rigor.

E. L. Doctorow

DRIVING DOWN A RESIDENTIAL side street of the village of Sag Harbor to E. L. Doctorow's summer home, passing the deeply shaded homes of colonial, federal, and Victorian styles, I thought this village with its layers of time seemed an apt place for him. Each of his novels, in language and form, concerns a different period of American history.

E. L. Doctorow is a native New Yorker, born Edgar Lawrence Doctorow in 1931. Prior to turning to fiction, he was a notable editor at Dial Press and a celebrated teacher of creative writing, a career he continues at Sarah Lawrence. His works experiment with the genres of fiction as well as with qualities of language and form. His first novel, *Welcome to Hard Times* (1960), was a Western, followed by *Big as Life* (1966), which is a science-fiction fantasy. *The Book of Daniel* (1971) has as its subject the impact of the Rosenbergs' trial for treason and subsequent execution on their children. This was followed by the historical panorama of the year 1906 in *Ragtime* (1975), and *Loon Lake* (1980). In between he presented a play off-Broadway in 1979, *Drinks Before Dinner.* His short stories and a novella were collected in the volume *Lives of the Poets* (1984).

The Doctorow home is an ample, comfortable Victorian house with a wraparound porch painted a blue-gray with white trim. In

the backyard, where we settle to speak, the flower beds, neatly mulched, circle the lawn to an arched trellis, and steps lead down to the water. E. L. Doctorow is a tall, stocky man, dressed casually. His neatly clipped beard and thinning hair give him the air of an intellectual quite bemused by what he observes.

I remind him that exactly five years ago we had taped a conversation on *Ragtime* in New York City, just after publication, when there was a storm of praise and curiosity about the author. His manner is relaxed and open, his voice is soft, thoughtful, and he often muses over his choice of words.

PART I: *RAGTIME*

CR: "Do not play this piece fast. It is never right to play ragtime fast." This quote from Scott Joplin and the title of your novel, *Ragtime*, comes from a musical technique, syncopation. Is there a literary equivalent in the novel?

ELD: Well, the book is in four parts. A rag customarily has four themes. Beyond that, a number of critics have found something in the rhythm of the prose which would suggest ragtime, a syncopated right hand against a marching left, but if that's so, it's not something I knew I was doing. I wouldn't know about that. I was interested in writing narrative, the kind of prose that would recover the spirit that existed in fiction before it became modern, as in the stories of Kleist, or Poe, or in the exemplary novels of Cervantes. Aside from the intention to write a relentless narrative, I had no scheme for the rhythm of the prose.

CR: You published selections in *The American Review* much earlier. Were they from a first version of the novel?

ELD: Of the excerpts for the two issues of *The American Review*, the second one was lifted whole from three chapters in the book, dealing with Ford and Morgan. The first excerpt involved a bit of editing, for purposes of self-sufficiency. I used the opening page of the *first* draft of the novel to get it started. I wanted that in print somewhere because it is the embryo of the book: it has the images which got me going. The first line, "I live in a house that was built in 1906," is not in the finished book because when I wrote it, *I* was talking. But it suggested the era. Images sprang to mind. Teddy Roosevelt was president. People wore white clothes in the summer. Women carried parasols. I think history lives in people as imagery.

CR: These images evoke language in your imagination, since the statement "I live in a house that was built in 1906" started the writing.

ELD: Before I wrote that line I had become fairly desperate. One of the things I've discovered about writing is that you have to sink way down to a level of hopelessness and desperation to find the book that you can write. The same thing happened to me with the previous novel, *The Book of Daniel,* when I wrote one hundred fifty pages and threw them out in despair before I broke through to that book. I think many novelists have this experience. For about a year before I wrote the page beginning "I live in a house that was built in 1906," I wrote a lot and nothing yielded to me; nothing set me off. This set of images did.

CR: You mention images, yet the title suggests something that evolves in time.

ELD: For me, the title has meanings beside the musical one. There's a sense of satire in the word "rag." Also an idea of impoverishment, of something sewn together from bits and pieces of colored cloth. And so on. A title is of practical use to an author. You'll find a title and it'll have a certain excitement for you; it will evoke the book, it will push you along. Eventually, you will use it up and you will have to choose another title. When you find one that doesn't get used up, that's the title you go with. I was about a third of the way through the novel and Ted Solotaroff of *The American Review* said, "Well, we've got to put a title to this excerpt." I said, "How about *Ragtime*," which had been on my mind. He said, "great," and I kept working, and *Ragtime* carried me to the end.

CR: Once you had this key, then how did you select the material for the panorama of the period?

ELD: There are certain things that I was very receptive to, for example, the names of machines and their look—the characteristic technology of that age. I happen to love trolley cars. It occurred to me that trolley cars were very new and exciting at this time. The most systematic research that I did for the whole book was to find, in the New York Public Library, a rather technical volume on the history of interurban street rail transportation in America. It felt good just holding that book. Do you know what I mean? I didn't really read it. I looked at the maps in it and discovered that it was possible for someone with enough nickels in his pocket to go from New York to Boston by trolley car. As a matter of fact, it was possible to go as far as Chicago that way. My idea of research is to discover that some instinct or intuition of mine is, in fact, corroborated by a responsible source. My first novel, *Welcome to Hard Times*, took place in the West in the nineteenth century, and when I wrote it I'd never been west of Chicago. But I had in my mind an image of a treeless plain. Eventually I found a marvelous geography of the West—a book by Walter Prescott Webb called *The Great Plains*—and it told me what I wanted to hear: I could write about this place as having no trees.

CR: If the title is an impetus for writing, do you believe, as Borges would have it, that a concept uses the writer as a vehicle?

ELD: I think authors, in order to get their work done, have all sorts of private rituals of self-hypnosis. So I would agree with Borges.

CR: The title *Ragtime* came out of a clear concept of the novel you wanted to write, a narrative with the qualities of a Poe tale. I have two ideas of the nineteenth-century novel, historical as opposed to romantic.

ELD: The realistic nineteenth-century novel is not the model for this book. Think of *Robinson Crusoe*. Or *Journal of the Plague Year*. The things Defoe was doing, mixing fact and fiction, are really as disreputable and irresponsible as anything any of us have done since. [*Laughs*.]

CR:　Many critics have questioned the mixing of fiction and history in your portrayal of the era.

ELD:　I think that's inescapable. The principle of selection of the events in the book, the inclusion of certain characters whom I think of as historical imagery, was totally unpremeditated and uncalculated. I don't know why it was Houdini who drove up the Broadview Avenue hill, but there he was. Certain historical images have names like Pierpont Morgan and Henry Ford, that I enjoyed thinking and writing about. Others did not evoke any strong feeling, and so I neglected them. There were certain facts that seemed to me necessary to put down exactly as I had read them or had found them, and others that demanded to be changed. There's some kind of aesthetic involved, although not at the level of conscious thought. But there is a principle, too: imagination is a form of knowledge. In any event, it's probably naïve to think that there is an always clear distinction between fact and fiction. We all compose the world we live in every moment of our lives.

CR:　Would you extend that and apply it to the writing of history itself?

ELD:　Of course. I don't think any professional historian would claim he's achieved objectivity. History writing is creative. Time is conceptualized. Events occur but, until the historian determines their moral nature, their history can't be written.

CR:　The example of invented history always cited is the bringing together of Emma Goldman and Evelyn Nesbitt, two women who are so antithetical—an anarchist, and the ultimate luxurious woman. Were you playing with the irony of the political versus the feminine consciousness?

ELD:　In that scene, Goldman addresses herself to just that question and analyzes Nesbitt's function in American society, and I think her analysis is good. But I think Goldman blunders quite a bit, and in her application of political beliefs to every moment of her experience, she hurts people. I think that's part of the humor, as in the conversation when she says things Nesbitt finds so shocking.

CR: I can understand that Emma Goldman would speak to your imagination the way your own created characters would. But was your imagination as fascinated by Pierpont Morgan?

ELD: Absolutely. I love all the characters in the book. I'm talking about author love, you understand.

CR: But it's not a clinical fascination.

ELD: No, it's very personal. It's proprietary, possessive. After I found certain people in the book, I did do a little reading about them. Or I looked at photographs. To see something in a portrait; or to find a word, the sound of which I like very much; or to find a fact that, somehow, I know is for me—all of that is part of the work. But it's not systematic or exhaustive because I'm not a scholar and I'm not a journalist. It's all very haphazard.

CR: You mentioned the unconscious source of the book coming from a certain point within you, a point of despair. . . .

ELD: That's not philosophic despair, you understand. It's far more mundane—to try to get something on the page and see that it's not working or that it's only half there or that some people would think it's there but you know it isn't. When we fantasize in our daily lives, that's easy, because fantasy by definition is sufficient and compensating. But, the writer's fantasy is not complete until he can transmit it to somebody else.

CR: Do you have a sense of when your imagination is working and when it's clamping down?

ELD: Where it flows, where you find yourself going on and the writing generates more writing—there's your book. Mark Twain said at one point, "I don't write a book now unless it can write itself." That's what he was talking about.

CR: Do you rely on the routine of work to lead you to the book?

ELD: Without question. What else could be as reliable? And even after you have the book, even in the illusion that it's writing itself, you work to keep having it. There are very few pages in *Ragtime* that I didn't write a half-dozen times or more.

CR: How does the process end? Did you feel that there was a formal conclusion to the book?

ELD: The sense of the form of the book finally presents itself to you. I'm aware—perhaps this would modify my answer about the musical analogy—of a kind of speed-up in part four, as, for instance, the roll on a player piano will speed up as it gets to its end. There is a sort of intensification in much the same way musical show-offs will play a piece at a nice pace and then double the speed to show how fast they really can play. Despite Scott Joplin's warning. If there's a musical analogy, maybe it's really Charles Ives's music.

CR: Was *Ragtime* more difficult to write than your previous novels?

ELD: Well, each book has a different kind of life in you. Or your relationship to it is easier or more difficult. This book was hard work but the illusion I have of it now is that it was very easy to do; whereas I think I have worked harder on other things that I have done which, in fact, took just the same time or involved the same process.

CR: Each of your novels is in a different genre, yet you are political. How do you view the writer's social responsibility?

ELD: I think the writer, in a certain sense, picks up on what everybody is coming to know, and expresses on behalf of everybody else what needs to be expressed.

CR: Is art able to have an effect on history?

ELD: Auden said that art didn't change anything. He talked about all the anti-fascist poems that were written in the 1930s, none of which stopped Hitler. But maybe the poems weren't good enough. Or maybe the time to write them was before Hitler was born. I think it's very haphazard, but there are changes in consciousness that occur through literature. A book can give voice to a spirit, or substance to an attitude. I think Joe

Heller's *Catch-22*, for instance, was one of the books which created the possibility of the antiwar movement in the 1960s.

CR: As a writer, do you feel the need to protect part of yourself from media scrutiny? You speak of your imagination as something very organic, not to be articulated or defined.

ELD: That is a reaction not to the media, but to the kind of education I had, in which the practice of literary criticism was seen as the highest function that any human being could lend himself to. I grew up with the New Criticism and went to Kenyon College and studied with John Crowe Ransom and it was of course an invaluable experience, but it was something that I had to recover from. In order to write, I had to reconstitute myself. That faculty, that kind of analytical sophistication, is something that I had to turn away from in order to write. Faulkner made the point that nobody really wants to know how visceral writers really are, how intuitive, how they perceive at such a low degree of intellection in their everyday work. Critics certainly don't like to hear that their heroes have minds like compost heaps. [*Laughs.*]

CR: That's against interpretation.

ELD: If you will, yes. In my daily life, too, I tried to live plainly and without sufficient thought. All my decisions I make without sufficient thought.

PART II: *LOON LAKE*

CR: First I want to ask you, is Loon Lake an actual place in the Adirondacks?

ELD: There are over a dozen Loon Lakes up there, and several more in Minnesota, where the loon is the state bird.

CR: I know that often an actual location will start off your imagination.

ELD: We were visiting some friends and I hadn't been in the Adirondacks in many years, since I was a kid, and I found that I was responsive to everything up there. We were driving back to Massachusetts into the Berkshires. We were still in the Adirondacks and I'd passed a sign that said "Loon Lake." Suddenly an almost magnetic feeling for the place came to some point of shock when I sighted that sign, and I knew it was something for me. I didn't know why or how. We find things in the mind that we haven't been called on to use before. I knew about those camps, those retreats that very wealthy people built in the twenties and before. Morgan built a camp up there, and the Post Cereals guy, and Harriman had a place. They all did this, inventing the wilderness as luxury, as I say in the book. That's historically accurate. Then suddenly a situation occurred to me, which was of a private railroad train going up through these mountains and somehow carrying a party of gangsters. I don't know why that occurred to me or what it meant, but those were the images that the book began on, this train, with these people on it, and they were being taken to an Adirondacks camp of a mysterious man of wealth. That seems to be the way I operate. I find myself in a state of being terribly alert and feeling a response to something that I can't put into a predicament.

The first part of the book I wrote as a story to be read aloud and published in the *Kenyon Review* under the title "Loon Lake." That is now given to Warren Penfield the failed poet, as his poem. What was left out of the picture was the person watching the train as it went by, and that was Joe, the narrator. That came to me next, and I saw this kid hobo on the road in 1930 and somehow wandering to this little field beside the railroad track and seeing the train go by at night. The impact of this vision of an incandescent train going by with a beautiful naked girl looking at herself in the mirror, holding up her dress. Then I had the two main narrative intelligences of the book, Penfield and Joe.

CR: Joe came out of industrial Paterson. Did you choose Paterson because of William Carlos Williams's poetry or because of its history of industrial strife?

ELD: Paterson had some meaning for me, perhaps because I've read Williams and perhaps because I knew about the labor history of Paterson, which was a lot earlier than the thirties. I also like the idea of Joe's being accessible to New York, which has an entirely different kind of image connotation. It would have represented a step in his journey, which geographically is Paterson to New York, to upstate New York for the carnival, and then out to the Midwest and then back to Loon Lake. What I seemed to be doing was portraying a crucial nine months in the life of a very young man in the Depression, in which astonishing things happen and his fate is made. He composes himself in this period of time, from people he encounters and the experience he has. He's now reflecting on this period, forty or forty-five years later, as a man I guess in his sixties. He's a tremendous success and he can't help receiving, undiminished, the signal of this other guy, Penfield, whose life is a glorious failure. The question is why, what sort of ironic remorse is this? So it's the two lives played against each other. It's a novel about the sentimental education of Joe.

CR: The common thread is that Joe, primitive as he is, has an instinct about how power works.

ELD: He sees it in the carnival, the way that money is made from the poor, and even though he's having an affair with the wife of the carnival owner, his sensitivity is to the man, the owner, whose disregard of him is almost insulting. In one sense, Joe's life is a history of relationships with different women, and he moves throughout the book from one woman to another. The crucial identifications he makes are at the expense of women, and the final movement of his life was towards men, when the decision has to be made. I think that's a true picture of the corporate psyche.

CR: The opposing character is the failed poet Warren Penfield, trying to shape his life and his work, and yet they're always out of control.

ELD: I love that character. He's done all the wrong things, he's a miserable failure, but somehow there's glory attached to him. A sort of drunken, self-dramatizing, weak-willed romantic. This is never said in the book, but he even makes mistakes in terms of where he chooses to be in the course of history. The great expatriation was to Europe in the 1920s. Everyone went to Paris, and he, of course, ended up in Japan. Then, in the thirties, when everyone was going off to fight for the Loyalists in Spain, he was sitting in the Adirondacks drinking himself insensible. If you just think what the artists were doing, well, it's the history of a failed artist.

CR: The contempt with which he's treated at Loon Lake—do you see that as prototype of the artists' condition in America?

ELD: Well, I wouldn't want to be that schematic. But I'm satisfied that there's a picture of everyone in the book in terms of how they stand to infiltrate their place. There is some real truth and justice in this portrayal of the patronizing contempt with which Penfield is supported at Loon Lake.

CR: He has an affinity with and a dependence on the character I thought of as Amelia Earhart.

ELD: It should be clear by now that if I wanted to write about Amelia Earhart, I would have called her Amelia Earhart. This kind of woman seems to me a very resonant image of the thirties. Women were in aviation from the very beginning, very much earlier than the thirties—they were banging themselves up just the way the men were. But it wasn't until the late twenties, the early thirties, that the idea of the aviatrix heroine became a prominent cultural image. Amelia Earhart was one of them, and she was the most famous. But the idea of fatality attached to it is what attracted me. It just moved me to think of a woman doing that, the gallantry of it, before there was any general endorsement. It's the idea of this kind of achievement that interests me, rather than the specific history of one individual.

CR: *Loon Lake* is the wilderness as luxury, and yet the America you portray in that period as Joe crisscrosses the country is a landscape of despair, with the people exploited and downtrodden in the industrial upheaval that's the Depression.

ELD: Well, the Depression was a time of enormous suffering. Despite the New Deal, in 1937 there was another big dip and things began to fall apart. It wasn't until we started to make war materiel in the Second World War that we got out of it. It was an enormous crisis, and a lot of people just didn't survive it. I've been criticized as being preoccupied with this kind of disaster, and the attempt of people to get justice in their lives. But I think that it's insane to think that that's not part of us and our history, or that I make up that kind of thing, the Depression, the great industrial wars. I think it's amazing that people would be satisfied to write novels that take place in that kind of miniature landscape of the neurotic head. We all respond to different things, and I'm not interested as a writer in doing novels about someone's particular sex life or domestic difficulties. It just doesn't interest me. This is not to say that the preoccupation I do have is any more valid for the purpose of the novel.

CR: In this novel did you see a failure of the labor movement during the Depression?

ELD: There was a good deal of industrial espionage; that is historically accurate. As for what the labor movement is in the thirties, it continues to be argued by labor historians and scholars who know a lot more about it than I do. My sense of the thing is that the trade union movement kind of turned bad when all these settlements and contracts were made in the thirties.

CR: You see it as inevitable, in the capitalist system, to deal with those in power?

ELD: I think that in terms of the dynamics of the story I've written I've rendered something that's true: people do behave this way and it's true to them. I'm not a scholar. I'm not a historian. I'm not an intellectual. I'm a novelist. I think I have a different mode of thought that predates objective scientific thinking; that's why I deal in images and metaphors and things like the rhythm of prose. I invoke, as I write, feelings in myself, which, if I do my job well, will be re-created in others as they read. I wish I had some real conviction about who was right and who was wrong, and had a wonderfully simple schematic vision of what should be done, but I don't.

CR: Perhaps because of the last decade, the sense of social betrayal was present in my mind as I read.

ELD: I think we're all sensitive to that. But if we look back and try to find a time when there was no betrayal, it's pretty hard to find. There's always the assumption of some wonderful, shining, virtuous past. There have been virtuous men and virtuous moments when we've exemplified the best that we are. But it's also true that they've been shot down one way or another. At least in this country we have the burden of our constitutional ideals.

CR: In *Ragtime* the musical element of the composition was in the title and dominates one's approach to the book. I wanted to ask you about the construction of *Loon Lake.* You are using three narrative modes: poetry, a first-person narrative, and a mechanical computer-language printout of biographical data. The first two are intensely personal and of the era, but the computer is coldly contemporary.

ELD: Incidentally, I don't make any claims for what you call poetry. I would call it verse, and it is indicated as the output of a failed poet. [*Laughs.*] You don't start with any aesthetic manifesto, you just do what works. I went through many drafts of this book before I found what I wanted. In terms of the mock–computer language, I was using it and it felt right, and yet I didn't know what it was doing for the longest time. Then, of course, I found out in terms of Joe's life. He would be familiar with dossiers and computer files. You see the title of *Ragtime* as forcing a perception on the reader. Well, there's something equivalent here. I didn't figure it out, my wife did. She's a writer, and a wonderful reader. She said the book itself is the lake. I accepted that immediately. Of course that's what I am doing. People are always telling me what I am doing. I didn't know I tended to be interested in the past in my fiction until someone asked, when *Ragtime* came out, "Why are you always writing about the past?" Right, I do. I hadn't formulated that in my mind. Similarly here, I accepted my wife's idea. The book itself is the lake, so that all the different kinds of narrative in it, the shifts in voice and temperature, the jumping around in time, the discontinuity—one could say that the book is composed analogically to simulate the varieties of light and shade and illumination that you get in or on a lake.

CR: You meant the reader to come away with the sensation of looking into the lake. Your imagination is visual, isn't it, since you spoke of the pictures that began the writing?

ELD: That's definitely true.

CR: People often refer to your cinematic style, almost forgetting that your imaginative expression is verbal.

ELD: I do take exception to a too easy label of "visual." I think all good writing is visual, but it's also olfactory; it involves all the senses. Good writing is supposed to evoke sensation in the reader—not the fact that it's raining, but the feel of being rained upon.

CR: People are conditioned to see cinematic elements as they read, since it's the most powerful form of mass communication.

ELD: We've all learned something from film and from television that I think we'd be stupid to ignore.

CR: Are you interested in television?

ELD: Yes, the discontinuity of it. Someone criticized the discontinuity of a play. I said, "Well, watch TV news for five minutes." Anybody who does that knows all about discontinuity. What I think film and television teach writers is how little opposition they need as they tell stories. At this point in time it's possible that straight chronological narrative has the least energy of any kind of narrative. It's only when you jump around, play with time, be quite reckless with voice that you find that you lose energy with straightforward chronology or consistent voice. I tried to write a book observing all the rules—I tried to write *The Book of Daniel* that way, and it didn't work. It is only when I get to bust things up that I find the true form. Just in terms of your personal working experience, you do discover that certain things work now and others don't. You want to make the book happen, you want it to burst into blossom.

CR: You sound as if you were working on another novel.

ELD: I think I'm going to start a new book very shortly. I find that I have an enormous amount of energy at this point. Usually, there's been a period of about a year where I don't have any books in mind at all once a book is done. But now I find that I'm just the opposite. I have three or four competing senses, and one of them is beginning to occur with more frequency, and that is a state of susceptibility to the book I'm in. I'm going to be teaching for one semester in September at Princeton. I thought I might begin work. I don't want to know too much about why I'm in the state I'm in. But this book did good things for me.

CR: I know how sensitive you are to atmosphere and place. I was wondering if Sag Harbor, which is redolent of New England and the fantastical history of whaling, has sunk into your psyche. [Laughs.]

ELD: Well, it may have, but anyone who would write a novel about whaling has to be out of his mind.

PART THREE

Toni Morrison

TONI MORRISON BEGAN WRITING fiction in her maturity, and from the first she expressed the themes that she would explore and develop in her subsequent work. She has written a body of work that is unified by continuity and development.

She was born Chloe Anthony Wofford in 1931 in Lorain, Ohio, which is the setting of her earliest novels. She attended Howard University and received a B.A. in English in 1953, and a master's degree from Cornell in 1955. She taught English at Howard University, and worked as a textbook editor prior to writing fiction. But these are jobs she has continued, even as an established novelist. She is an editor at Random House, and is in great demand as a lecturer and teacher.

Toni Morrison published her first novel, *The Bluest Eye*, in 1969, followed by *Sula* (1973). Her reputation was established with *Song of Solomon* (1977), which was awarded the National Book Critics' Circle Award and the National Book Award for best novel. In 1981 she published the controversial *Tar Baby*.

In *The Bluest Eye*, a small Midwestern community is depicted through the eyes of a little girl, Claudia, during a cycle of four seasons. Her best friend, Pecola, prays for blue eyes, a special mark, the way her mother finds refuge in the immaculate kitchen, where she can forget her cross—Pecola—and her "Crown of Thorns"— Cholly, her alcoholic husband. In a drunken moment Cholly

Breedlove assaults his daughter. Claudia's answered prayer has the effect of an implosion that destroys her family and by extension heralds the eventual disappearance of the community.

Sula tells of the passionate and lawless Sula, the last of a matriarchal family. Nell, the narrator, is her complementary opposite, brought up in a strict Baptist household where every stirring of her imagination is disciplined. Sula's energy propels her out into the world, but the world drives her back into the community. Sula destroys her family and Nell's marriage, and she becomes an outcast.

Song of Solomon presents Macon Dead the slumlord and his bootlegging sister, Pilate, who are pitted in a duel that is carried into the third generation by the affair between his son, Milkman, and her granddaughter, Hagar. Within the conflicts of the black community, Toni Morrison introduces a secret society dedicated to retaliating, murder for murder, every crime against the black community. Yet this society misinterprets Milkman's quest for his African origins as a betrayal of their secret mission.

With *Tar Baby* the conflict between the races explodes, revealing all the underlying interrelationships between white masters and black servants. The Tar Baby is the black couple's niece (and adopted daughter), educated by their employers to a privileged position that places her midway between the two worlds. At the start of the novel, Valerian Street and his wife, Margaret, have retired from their confection industry in Philadelphia and are preparing for Christmas in their Caribbean retreat, "L'Arbe de la Croix." Their old butler, Sydney, and the cook, Ondine, uprooted and as yet unsettled in the tropics, await their adopted daughter, Jadine, as well as the son of the house. Suddenly, an intruder in the house creates a panic that dislocates each character and reveals a pattern of dependence, exploitation, and complicity between master and servants, servants and children, husbands and wives.

Jadine runs off to New York with Son, the young black intruder, only to be confronted by their incompleteness as individuals and as a couple. She will not compromise with his backward black world, and he cannot live in her white world. He becomes the rabbit caught by and sinking with the Tar Baby. Here Toni Morrison dramatizes his choice of death by Eros, or death by Psy-

che. The novel has a circular construction based on the cycle of
nature and the spiritual relationships of the characters to the laws
of nature.

These conversations occurred in Toni Morrison's office at Random
House. She is an impressive, strong woman, with an open counte-
nance and a sonorous, melodious voice. Her eyes are amber-col-
ored, of changing golden hue, and her face is extremely expressive,
with sudden shifts in tone and mood. Her sense of humor is dominant, and she mimics in expression and voice the different people
and characters in her conversation. But when she is deep in
thought, her eyes almost close, her voice grows quieter and
quieter, lowering almost to a whisper, and the quality of her conversation approaches that incantatory flow which is akin to the
lyric moments of her written style. Her response to the questions
are direct and forthright; she is eloquent about her beliefs and
kindly in her analysis of people. She reserves her mocking humor
and caustic wit for comment about herself.

Toni Morrison used the interview to explore and clarify her
own thoughts in the light of the interviewer's reading of the text.
The conversation took place in February 1981, prior to the publication of *Tar Baby*. Eight months later, after the reaction to the
novel had abated somewhat, we picked up our conversation where
we had left off, only to discover once again that there were at the
close still other topics not touched upon, such as her reading of
certain classics and her abiding interest in new black authors, as
well as what is for her the central issue of the black writer's feeling
sometimes that his or her work exists in a framework and conveys
an experience so unfamiliar to most of the reading public as to
seem like a translated text.

PART I

CR: What made you begin writing *The Bluest Eye?*

TM: I don't know. I never wanted to grow up to be a writer, I just
        wanted to grow up to be an adult. I began to write that book as a

short story based on a conversation I had with a friend when I was a little girl. The conversation was about whether God existed; she said no and I said yes. She explained her reason for knowing that He did not: she had prayed every night for two years for blue eyes and didn't get them, and therefore He did not exist. What I later recollected was that I looked at her and imagined her having them and thought how awful that would be if she had gotten her prayer answered. I always thought she was beautiful. I began to write about a girl who wanted blue eyes and the horror of having that wish fulfilled; and also about the whole business of what is physical beauty and the pain of that yearning and wanting to be somebody else, and how devastating that was and yet part of all females who were peripheral in other people's lives.

CR: Since your first novel is such a mature statement, clearly you are steeped in literary tradition, but I assume also in the great black novelists of the past.

TM: I was preoccupied with books by black people that approached the subject, but I always missed some intimacy, some direction, some voice. Ralph Ellison and Richard Wright—all of whose books I admire enormously—I didn't feel were telling *me* something. I thought they were saying something about *it* or *us* that revealed something about *us* to *you*, to others, to white people, to men. Just in terms of the style, I missed something in the fiction that I felt in a real sense in the music and poetry of black artists. When I began writing I was writing as though there was nobody in the world but me and the characters, as though I was talking to them, or us, and it just had a different sound to it.

CR: When you say that you feel these writers are explaining something "to me," are you referring to the fact that their work is morally informed?

TM: There is a mask that sometimes exists when black people talk to white people. Somehow it seems to me that it spilled over into the fiction. I never thought that when I was reading black poetry, but when I began to write. When I wrote I wanted not to have to explain. Somehow, when black writers wrote for themselves I understood it better. What's that lovely line? When the locality is clear, fully realized, then it becomes universal. I knew there was something I wanted to clear away in writing, so I used the geography of my childhood, the imagined characters based on bits and pieces of people, and that was a statement. More important to me was making a statement on a kind of language, a way to get to what was felt and meant. I always hated with a passion when writers rewrote what black people said, in some kind of phonetic alphabet that was inapplicable to any other regional pronunciation. There is something different about that language, as there is about any cultural variation of English, but it's not saying "dis" and "dat." It is the way words are put together, the metaphors, the rhythm, the music—that's the part of the language that is distinctly black to me when I hear it. But the only way for me to do it when I was writing was to have this kind of audience made up of people in the book.

CR: When I began *Song of Solomon* I thought, the King James Bible is the spine of this style.

TM: The Bible wasn't part of my reading, it was part of my life. In coming to writing I wrote the way I was trained, which was [*laughs*] scholarly bombast, so that I had to rewrite a lot. Getting a style is about all there is to writing fiction, and I didn't realize that I had a style until I wrote *Song of Solomon*. Yes, there's a formality and repetition in it, and I like that risk. I like the danger in writing when you're right on the edge, when at any moment you can be maudlin, saccharine, grotesque, but somehow pull back from it [*laughs*], well, most of the time. I really want this emotional response, and I also want an intellectual response to the complex ideas there. My job is to do both at the same time, that's what a real story is.

CR: You never had thought of yourself as a writer, yet you're certain of your artistic aims. Is it based on your reading as well?

TM: When I said I wrote my first novel because I wanted to read it, I meant it literally. I had to finish it so that I could read it, and what that gave me, I realize now, was an incredible distance from it, and from that I have learned. If what I wrote was awful, I would try to make it like the book I wished to read. I trusted that ability to read in myself.

CR: But tell me about the subject of your novels. In *The Bluest Eye,* for example, although Claudia is the narrator you switch the narrative point of view from first to third person. Yet it's the unfolding drama of Pecola which is the center of the book.

TM: I had written the book without those two little girls at first. It was just the story of Pecola and her family. I told it in the third person in parts, in pieces like a broken mirror. When I read it, there was no connection between the life of Pecola, her mother and father, and the reader—myself. I needed a bridge—the book was soft in the middle, so I shored it up. I introduced the two little girls, and chose an "I" for one of them, so that there would be somebody to empathize with her at her age level. This also gave a playful quality to their lives, to relieve the grimness. I had to go back and restructure all of the novel, and I introduced a time sequence of the seasons, the child's flow of time. I culled— from what I thought life was like in the thirties and forties—the past, whatever the past is. Once I realized that, I knew that I could not *not* write the book any more. After I had written it and "stopped"—that's the way I thought then—I still didn't know if I was a writer, but I knew that I always wanted to have writing to do.

With *Sula* I was obsessed with the idea, and totally enchanted by it. I was fearful that with *Sula* I was being bookish. It got hermetic and tight, which as a writer I now say. It may have been correct to have written *Sula* that way, but I know that when I wrote *Song of Solomon* it was more open and looser. That is more dangerous than writing in which every sentence has to be exactly right or you'll shoot yourself. I always thought that *Sula* was the best idea I ever had, but the writing was on its own.

CR: Were there family influences that eventually made you turn to writing?

TM: Life is very short—they couldn't think of that. When I graduated from high school, it was a huge thing. My mother had
graduated from high school, but not my father. They assumed
that all my life I should work. And I guess they assumed that I
should get married. It never occurred to me that I could get
married and not work. What was needed was skill. I had an
uncle who had gone to college, and I was surrounded by people
who had done extraordinary things under duress in order to survive. I didn't know it, but I think I had a feeling that I probably
wrote well, because when I was very little and we were asked to
write stories in classes, I just remember that I knew the teacher
didn't believe I wrote those stories. I thought that other people
didn't write well because they weren't interested.

Speaking of being a writer, when I mentioned to my editor,
Bob Gottlieb, after I finished *Song of Solomon,* that I was thinking of working less, he said, "Well, you should really make up
your mind that this is what you are going to be when you grow
up." [*Laughs.*] I said, "A writer?" Because I was convinced I
could never be without a job: I'm the head of a household, I
teach, I'm an editor, I write. I never equated writing with
money, as a living. When he said that, I thought for the first time
maybe I could just go home and write, as a job.

CR: These different jobs are important to you for reasons other
than financial stability. I know you've devoted yourself as an
editor to bringing out some very fine young black writers. Does
being the head of a household become part of your identity as a
writer?

TM: In terms of being a writer it's very stabilizing, being the
head of a household. I don't find it a deprivation. It also means
that when I go to write, I go there with relish, because of the re-
quirement of working at several jobs at the same time.

CR: Do you withdraw to a room, your own, or do you write in
your head before sitting down to work?

TM: I type in one place, but I write all over the house. I never go
to the paper to create. The meat and juice and all that I work

out while I'm doing something else, and it makes completing the chores possible, so I'm not staring off into space. Well, I might, but I also do the chores.

CR: In *Song of Solomon* the symbolism is different from psychological portrayal of the passionate characters, and different from the dream sequences or the lyrical moments. These different types of writing make me ask about the different aspects of your creative consciousness.

TM: I look for the picture in some instances. In order to get at the thing at once, I have to see it, to smell it, to touch it. It's something to hold on to so that I can write it. What takes longest is the way you get into the heart of that which you have to describe. Once I know, then I can move. I know that if the action is violent, the language cannot be violent; it must be understated. I want my readers to see it, to feel it, and I want to give them things even I may not know about, even if I've never been there. Getting to that place is problematic, that's the process. I remember how long it took me to write about the town that Milkman goes to, when he finally gets there. It took me months, and I could not begin. I could see it, but I wanted to write without going through long, involved descriptions of that village. Then I remembered the women walking without anything in their hands, and that set the scene.

CR: Your characters have dreams and waking dreams, but, also, spirits will come to speak to the characters. You differentiate that from the religious, which is often narrow and hard.

TM: As a child I was brought up on ghost stories—part of the entertainment was storytelling. Also, I grew up with people who believed it. When they would tell you stories about visions, they didn't tell them as though they were visions. My father said, "Oh, there's a ring around the moon, that means war." Indeed there was a war in 1941. I remember his saying that; now, whether he was also reading the newspapers or not, I don't know.

My grandmother would ask me about my dreams and, depending on the content of them, she would go to the dream book, which would translate dreams into a three-digit number. That was the number you played in the numbers game. You dream about a rabbit, or death, or weddings, and then color made a difference—if you dreamed about dying in a white dress or a red dress—and weddings always meant death and death always meant weddings. I was very interested because she used to hit a lot on my dreams for about a year or two.

CR: You mean she actually won money based on your dreams?

TM: She won [*laughs*], yes, she won. Then I stopped hitting for her, so she stopped asking me. It was lovely to have magic that could turn into the pleasure of pleasing one's grandmother and was also profitable. My dream life is still so real to me that I can hardly distinguish it from the other, although I know what that is. It's just as interesting to me and an inexhaustible source of information. I was very conscious of trying to capture in writing about what black life meant to me, not just what black people do but the way in which we look at it.

CR: Then the cycle of seasons, of birth and death, and the nature spirits that you use to structure your novels form your sense of the cosmology and of the psyche?

TM: It's an animated world in which trees can be outraged and hurt, and in which the presence or absence of birds is meaningful. You have to be very still to understand these so-called signs, in addition to which they inform you about your own behavior. It always interested me, the way in which black people responded to evil. They would protect themselves from it, they would avoid it, they might even be terrified of it, but it wasn't as though it were abnormal. I used the line "as though God had four faces instead of three. . . ." Evil was a natural presence in the world. What that meant in terms of human behavior was that when they saw someone disgraceful, they would not expel them in the sense of tarring and killing. I think that's a distinct cultural difference, because the Western notion of evil is to annihilate it. That may be very cleansing, but it's also highly intolerant.

CR: To return to your novels, your concepts are always so clear. Each novel has a circular construction. Does the idea come to you whole?

TM: I always know the ending; that's where I start. I don't always have a beginning, so I don't always know how to start a book. Sometimes I have to rewrite different beginnings. *Sula* began with Shadrack, so I had to write the part that precedes it. I always know the ending of my novels because that's part of the idea, part of the theme. It doesn't shut, or stop there. That's why the endings are multiple endings. That's where the horror is. That's where the meaning rests; that's where the novel rests. I suppose there is a strong influence of Greek tragedy, particularly the chorus, commenting on the action.

For me, it's also the closest way I can get to what informs my art, which is the quality of response. Being in church, and knowing that the function of the preacher is to make you get up, you do say yes, and you do respond back and forth. The music is unplanned and obviously not structured, but something is supposed to happen, so the listener participates. The chorus participates both by meddling in the action and responding to it, like the musical experience of participation in church.

I try to bring the essentials to a scene, so the reader, for example, can bring his own sexuality to that scene, which makes it sexier. Your sexuality is sexier than mine because it's yours. All I have to do is give you the lead, you bring your own perception, and you are in it. I don't have to use clinical language. I can say, "Son parted the hair on her head and ran his tongue along the part."

CR: You begin Tar Baby with Valerian Street, a retired candy executive, rather than with Jadine, who is the Tar Baby.

TM: But he is the center. He's not the main character, but he certainly is the center of the world. I mean, white men run it. He is the center of the household—toppled, perhaps, but still the center of everybody's attention—and that's pretty much the way it is. He is a rather nice man, not a wicked man. He has his serious flaws, as all of the characters have serious limitations, as all people do: trying to come to terms with each other, give up a little something, behave properly, and live in the world decently, maybe even love something, just trying to pick something out that's worth holding on to and worth loving. Sometimes it's a person, sometimes it's a house, or a memory. They are what they are and rub up against one another in that way. I chose, literally, the skeleton as the story of the Tar Baby. I had heard it and it just seemed to me overwhelmingly history as well as prophecy, once I began thinking about it, because it bothered me madly.

CR: Joel Chandler Harris, who recorded it, said that it was an African story told him by "Uncle Remus."

TM: I never read the story, but it was one of the stories we were told, and one of the stories my mother was told, part of a whole canon of stories. It's supposed to be a funny little child's story. But something in it terrified me. What frightened me was the notion of the Tar Baby. It's a lump of tar shaped like a baby, with a dress on and a bonnet. It's a sunny day and the tar is melting, and the rabbit is getting stuck and more stuck. It's really quite monstrous. The rabbit approaches it and says good morning and expects it to say good morning back. He anticipated a certain civilized response—he was a little thief—and when it didn't happen he was outraged and therefore got stuck and went to his death. Of course, as in most peasant literature, that sort of weak but cunning animal gets out of it by his cleverness. So I just gave these characters parts, Tar Baby being a black woman and the rabbit a black man. I introduced a white man and remembered the tar. The fact that it was made out of tar and was a black woman, if it was made to trap a black man—the white man made her for that purpose. That was the beginning of the story. Suppose somebody simply has all the benefits of what the white Western world has to offer; what would the relationship be with the rabbit who really comes out of the briar patch? And what does the briar patch mean to that rabbit? Wherever there was tar it seemed to me was a holy place. "Tar Baby" is also a racial slur, like "nigger," and a weapon hostile to the black man. The tragedy of the situation was not that she *was* a Tar Baby, but that she wasn't. She could not know, she could not hold anything to herself. That's what I mean by the prophecy: the twentieth-century black woman is determined in trying to do both things, to be both a ship and a safe harbor.

CR: All of the characters function very comfortably in their self-involved dilemmas until Valerian humiliates Sydney and Ondine and they explode against him and Margaret.

TM: The interdependence of employee and employer is clear, but the human dependencies of such relationships are not because of the artifice of jobs and wages. When you take that structure away, what you have left is very close interrelationships, sometimes seething rages; but you don't until you remove it and see what the relationship really is.

CR: Ondine feels morally superior to Margaret, and there's a complicity between them stronger than hatred.

TM: It's my view that one of the things that black women were able to do in many situations was to make it possible for white women to remain infantile. Margaret has been thoroughly crippled by her husband, who kept her that way, and Ondine helped. In a sense, such women are not innocent victims, but they really are victims of a kind of giant romantic stupidity.

CR: The complicity between the women—that is, about child abuse—is a theme that runs through all your novels.

TM: Certainly since *Sula* I have thought that the children are in real danger. Nobody likes them, all children, but particularly black children. It seems stark to me, because it wasn't true when I was growing up. The relationships of the generations have always been paramount to me in all of my works, the older as well as the younger generation, and whether that is healthy and continuing. I feel that my generation has done the children a great disservice. I'm talking about the emotional support that is not available to them any more because adults are acting out their childhoods. They are interested in self-aggrandizement, being "right," and pleasures. Everywhere, everywhere, children are the scorned people of the earth. There may be a whole lot of scorned people, but particularly children. The teachers have jobs, not missions. Even in the best schools, the disrespect for children is unbelievable. You don't have to go to the exploitation, the ten-year-old model and child porn—that's the obvious. Even in the orderly parts of society it is staggering. Children are committing suicide, they are tearing up the schools, they are running away from home. They are beaten and molested; it's an epidemic. I've never seen so many movies in which children are the monsters, children are the ones to be killed.

CR: Now you see a more impersonal attitude of, No room, no time for children.

TM: They have no apprenticeship. Children don't work with adults as we used to, and there is this huge generation gap. When my grandfather got senile in his nineties, he would walk off, not know where he was, and get lost. My job as a little girl was to find Papa, and we would. Some adult told us to go and we would bring him back, settle him on the porch, bring him walnuts or what have you. I remember I had to read the Bible to my grandmother when she was dying, and somebody assigned me to do that. They were caring for her, and I was involved in the death and decay of my grandmother. Obviously my mother cared for me, and I would do that for her; that is the cycle. It's important that my children participate in that. They have to take my mother her orange juice, and I don't have to tell them, because that's their responsibility. She can get them to do all sorts of things I can't. That's part of knowing who they are and where they came from. It enhances them in a particular way, and when they have children of their own it won't be this little nuclear you and me, babe.

CR: Sadly enough, I agree with you. But in your own novel, after the moral failure of the older generation is revealed, Jadine, it turns out, doesn't love Sydney and Ondine, who are passionate about her, any more than she cares for Valerian and Margaret.

TM: She is an orphan in the true sense. She does not make connections unless they serve her in some way. Valerian she speaks of because he did a concrete thing for her—he put her through school—but she is not terribly interested in his welfare. Ondine and her uncle Sydney are people she uses a little bit.

She is cut off. She does not have, as Thérèse [a spiritualist] says, her ancient properties; she does not have what Ondine has. There's no reason for her to be like Ondine—I'm not recommending that—but she needs a little bit of Ondine to be a complete woman. She doesn't have that quality because she can avoid it, and it's not attractive anyway. The race may need it, human beings may need it, she may need it. That quality of nurturing is to me essential. It should not, certainly, limit her to be only Thérèse with the magic breasts. There should be lots of things: there should be a quality of adventure and a quality of nest.

CR: That's adaptation for survival. This problem is true throughout society.

TM: This civilization of black people, which was underneath the white civilization, was there with its own everything. Everything of that civilization was not worth hanging on to, but some of it was, and nothing has taken its place while it is being dismantled. There is a new, capitalistic, modern American black which is what everybody thought was the ultimate in integration. To produce Jadine, that's what it was for. I think there is some danger in the result of that production. It cannot replace certain essentials from the past. That's what I meant when I said she cannot nurture and be a career woman. You can't get rid of the pie lady and the churches unless you have something to replace them with. Otherwise people like Son are out there, strung out. There is nowhere for them to go. I could have changed it around and it could have been a man in Jadine's position and a woman in his. The sexes were interchangeable, but the problem is the same.

CR: You describe Jadine as feeling lean and male, and since she is a character of will and decision, is there a male/female conflict within her? Does she unconsciously identify will power with being male?

TM: It has to do with being contemporary. The contemporary woman is eager; her femininity becomes sexuality rather than femininity, because that is perceived as weak. The characteristics they encourage in themselves are more male characteristics, not because she has a fundamental identity crisis, but because she wants to be truly free. Part of that is perceived as having the desirable characteristic of maleness, which includes self-sufficiency and adventurousness. For instance, Ondine is a tough lady in an older sense of that word, like pioneers, but she is keenly aware of her nurturing characteristics, whereas someone in Jadine's generation would find that a burden, and not at all what her body was for. She does not intend to have children. In that sense it's not an identity crisis in terms of male/female sexuality and personality. The impetus of the culture is to be feminized, and what one substitutes for femininity is sexuality.

CR: Then, with all of her education and cultivation, femininity for Jadine is the outward image; she is a model. Her focus is on herself, she's essentially narcissistic.

TM: Yes, absolutely. She is really about herself. The thing that happens to her in Paris, the woman spitting at her—even in her semi-dream state, Jadine knows what happened: somebody assaulted her image of herself.

CR: When she is in love with Son and returns with him to what you call his "briar patch," Jadine is alienated from his people.

TM: She feels left out from that environment. She is not afraid of the male world, but she is afraid of the female world. It's interesting to see such women who have gone away put into that situation. I have seen them extremely uncomfortable in the company of church ladies, absolutely out of their element. They are beautiful and they are competent, but when they get with women whose values are different and who judge competence in different areas, they are extremely threatened. It's not just class; it's a different kind of woman.

CR: But Son, for all his qualities, has no place in the black world, and is not equipped to face the white world.

TM: He has that choice. Either he can join the twentieth century as a kind of half-person like Jadine, or he can abandon it. He doesn't want to change. It's a no-win situation. He really wanted to go down, down, and come back up again—that he could control. He can't do it his way. Perhaps the rites of passage are wrong for him. There used to be a way in which people could grow up. Now it's free-floating—you're just out there.

CR: But he is the person in this book who is able to love totally, without reservation or condition. In each of your novels there's a character capable of selfless love, whose identity comes from loving another.

TM: I'm trying to get at all kinds and definitions of love. We love people pretty much the way we are. I think there's a line, "Wicked people love wickedly, stupid people love stupidly," and in a way we are the way we love other people. In *Song of Solomon* the difference between Pilate's selfishness and Hagar's is that Hagar is not a person without Milkman, she's totally erased. Pilate had twelve years of intimate relationship with two men, her father and her brother, who loved her. It gave her a ferocity and some complete quality. Hagar had even less and was even more frail. It's that world of women without men. But in fact a woman is strongest when some of her sensibilities are formed by men at an early, certainly at an important, age. It's absolutely necessary that it be there, and the farther away you get from that, the possibility of distortion is greater. By the same token, Milkman is in a male, macho world and can't fly, isn't human, isn't complete until he realizes the impact that women have made on his life. It's really a balance between classical male and female forces that produces, perhaps, a kind of complete person.

CR: In your novels the women feel responsible for the failures of the men. Is Jadine also responsible for what Son can and cannot do?

TM: Well, it's a dual thing. On one level, obviously, she is. She is the thing that he wants and he can't live with or without, as he immediately knew as soon as he saw her. This was the love he could not afford to lose; therefore he should not have it in the first place. But there is some complicity in him, also. He is derailed by this romantic passion and his sensibilities are distorted; he can't make judgments any more. When he looked at the photos that she took of his people, he saw what she saw and it could not revive what he had, and that's testimony to his frailty. All those images he carried around in his head and in his

heart should have survived her, but they didn't. He can't even
get to the briar patch by himself, and he no longer knows where
he was born and bred. Because it's in her world view, it takes
Thérèse to give him a choice. She gives him this mystical choice
between roaming around looking for Jadine and putting himself
in danger that is not dignified, versus the possibility of joining
these rather incredible men in the rain forest. I want him to be
left with a wide-open choice at the end. I also wanted to suggest
which one he chose by his asking her a second time, "Are you
sure?" could be "Are the men there?" Or, it could mean, "Are
you sure this is the island?" She says, "Yes, this is the place," and
then she talks about the men, and he asks her again, "Are you
sure?" She doesn't answer and he doesn't hear. When he climbs
off the rocks and stands up—nature has always been very sweet
to him anyway, giving him fruit—the trees sort of step back to
make a way, and then to have him go lickety-split is to suggest
the rabbit returning to the briar patch.

CR: I thought he was being betrayed by Thérèse, who was leading him to his death or his death wish. In your first novel, the
matriarch, seeing her son, a veteran of the war, turning into a
writhing fetus of pain from drug addiction, decides to put him
out of his misery and sets him on fire out of compassion and love.
But what you have just said makes me understand that the lawless characters you portray—Sula, Solomon, and Son—belong in
that other order of nature spirits, expressing a code of behavior
that is aristocratic because it is accountable only to the spirit of
nature, which is of African origin. My remaining question is
whether Jadine is a character who will be forced to make that
connection with the briar patch, even though love doesn't take
her outside herself.

TM: She has a glimmering. On the plane she thinks that *she* is the
safety she has longed for, that there is no haven, and being the
safety you have longed for is not only taking care of yourself; you
are the safety of other people. She thinks maybe that's what Ondine meant—there is the aunt metaphor about the life of a
woman in that stark warrior sense—but she is going back to
Paris to start from zero. She will have to, I think the word is

"tangle," with the woman in yellow. She thinks she is leaving
Ondine and all of that crowd, and she has to, but the issues are
still there. She now knows enough—she hasn't opened the door,
but she knows where the door is.

PART II

CR: Where do you see yourself now? After *Tar Baby*, where
would you place yourself in terms of your work as a novelist?

TM: Still in process, and I think that, if I'm lucky at all, it will always be that way. I want to learn more and more about how to
write better. That means to get closer to that compulsion out of
which I write. I want to break away from certain assumptions
that are inherent in the conception of the novel form to make a
truly aural novel, in which there are so many places and spaces
for the reader to work and participate. Also, I want to make a
novel in which one of the principles of the discipline is to en-
lighten without pontificating. It accounts for the wide-open nature of the ending of my books, where I don't want to close it, to
stop the imagination of the reader, but to engage it in such a way
that he fulfills the book in a way that I don't. I try to provide
every opportunity for that kind of stimulation, so that the narrative is only one part of what happens, in the same way as what
happens when you're listening to music, what happens when
you look at a painting. I would like to do better at this one thing
and to try to put the reader into the position of being naked and
quite vulnerable, nevertheless trusting, to rid him of all of his literary experience and all of his social experiences in order to engage him in the novel. Let him make up his mind about what he
likes and what he thinks and what happened based on the very
intimate acquaintance with the people in the book, without any
prejudices, without any pre-fixed notions, but to have an
intimacy that's so complete, it humanizes him in the same way
that the characters are humanized from within by certain activity, and in the way in which I am humanized by the act of
writing.

CR: By contrast to real life, for you the work of art permits this sanctuary.

TM: Exactly. It's a haven, a place where it can happen, where you can react violently or sublimely, where it's all right to feel melancholy or frightened, or even to fail, or to be wrong, or to love somebody, or to wish something deeply, and not call it by some other name, not to be embarrassed by it. It's a place to feel profoundly. It's hard to get people to trust those feelings in such a way that they're not harmful to other people.

CR: The function of fiction for you is extending those boundaries. I also have a strong sense of the continuity of your work. Does the writing of one work lead to the next? Your four novels form a coherent body of work.

TM: When I thought about what seemed next in an evolutionary sense, the most obvious way was to move from a very young girl to adult women in the second book, and then a man in the third book, and then a man and a woman in the fourth book. It was a simple progression, and because of the time in which they were placed, each one seemed to demand a certain form. I could not write a contemporary love story, so to speak, in the same meandering told-story form that's in *Solomon*. *Solomon* seemed to be very much a male story about the rites of passage, and that required a feeling of lore. In *Tar Baby* the lore is there but in a more direct, bold way than it ever was in *Song of Solomon*. Extraordinary people have things happen that are not literally possible in *Song of Solomon*, such as the absence of a navel on a woman. In *Tar Baby* that was done without even trying to make any explanation, so that I ran the risk of having nature itself bear witness, be the cause of everything that's going on. There are so many secrets in *Tar Baby*—everybody, with the possible exception of Sydney, has a secret that they don't want anyone else to know. Those secrets are revealed to other characters sometimes, but always to the reader. It begins with the most fundamental secret of all, which is that while we watch the world, the world watches us. It is the sort of secret that we all knew anyway when we were children, that the trees look back on us. So I put all of that on the surface of the novel in a way that is open to animism or anthropomorphism, whatever the labels are. Although the lore has gotten stronger, the narrative structure is more conventional and more accessible.

CR: Do you understand why the mythological aspect of your works puzzled people? It existed in certain characters in *The Bluest Eye* and *Sula,* and in *Song of Solomon* it's secret mythic history, but in *Tar Baby* it has suddenly manifested itself in the landscape.

TM: Well, one of the reasons it was not bewildering in the earlier books is, they may have decided that those books were distant in time so it's as if they were reading *Beowulf.* All three of those books are closed, back worlds; even though *Solomon* does come up to 1963, it's sort of back there somewhere. Also, it's a quest for roots, and spirituality. But in 1980, to take a person who was, after all, the kind of person that we ought to be, a fully integrated, fearless young woman, and to put that person—us— right next to the women hanging in the trees, may have been difficult because it means what I meant it to mean—those forces are still there now. It's not something that old people talk about, it is not back then, it is now—a violation of the earth, and the earth's revenge.

CR: Critics who didn't understand it seemed to suggest that it was a way out. I became conscious of the fact that the mythic element became a paradox, whereby going into the mythic the characters embraced death, but perhaps it was regeneration.

TM: I meant both. The risk of getting in touch with that world is that some part of you does die. You relinquish something, and what you give up is the person that you have made. But something else is revitalized. It's scary to contemplate, like the contemplation of death and change in the unknown. You discover you don't know it, and that's why it's so frightening. It is not codified the way the mythological world probably is codified. When Jadine is sinking in quicksand, she's terrified, and all the while above her terrifying creatures are watching. But they are benevolent and they are thinking religiously. Whenever butter-

flies or trees or anything speaks or thinks, what they think is
really quite loving. But people either ignore that part of perception, or cosmology, or life, or when they confront it they won't
comment. I suppose if one had a visitation of some sort, it would
be too terrifying to think about. Some forms of it lie in madness,
and you're frightened of that because it looks like you might not
get back. Even though there may be some incredible knowledge
revealed, we want to hang on to what we know. That view of the
world may be so narrow and so pitiful and so shabby and so
lonely that we die of starvation because we are not feeding off it,
yet this other, very rich perception may terrify us. But, more to
the point of your question, I thought of the origin of the myth,
the story, as being both history and prophecy, meaning it would
identify danger but it would also hold the promise that if one
fully understood it one would be free or made whole in some
way.

CR: But *Song of Solomon* does end in death. When I read *Tar
Baby* I understood Son's going towards the spirit world as also
rushing to his death.

TM: Well, in *Song of Solomon* I really did not mean to suggest
that they kill each other, but out of a commitment and love and
selflessness they are willing to risk the one thing that we have,
life, and that's the positive nature of the action. I never really
believed that those two men would kill each other. I thought
they would, like antelopes, lock horns, but it is important that
Guitar put his gun down and does not blow Milkman out of the
air, as he could. It's important that he look at everything with his
new eyes and say, "My man, my main man." It's important that
the metaphor be in the killing of this brother, that the two men
who love each other nevertheless have no area in which they can
talk, so they exercise some dominion over and demolition of the
other. I wanted the language to be placid enough to suggest he
was suspended in the air in the leap towards this thing, both
loved and despised, and that he was willing to die for that idea,
but not necessarily to die. Son's situation in *Tar Baby* is different, in that he is given a choice, to join the twentieth century or
not. If he decides to join the twentieth century, he would be fol-

lowing Jadine. If he decides not to join the twentieth century and would join these men, he would lock himself up forever from the future. He may identify totally and exclusively with the past, which is a kind of death, because it means you have no future, but a suspended place.

CR: Nor is it a wisdom or a power gained that can be brought back to the world, since the characters merge with the mythic landscape of the novel.

TM: No, he can't bring that back to the real world. I felt very strongly then—maybe that's what the next book is—that the book alone is the place where you can take that information, but in Son's situation and in Jadine's, it is literally a cul-de-sac. The choice is irrevocable, and there is no longer any time to mistake the metaphor. It seemed to me the most contemporary situation in the world. We are in a critical place where we would either cut off the future entirely and stay right where we are—which means, in an imaginative sense, annihilate ourselves totally and extend ourselves out into the stars, or the earth, or sea, or nothing—or we pretend there was no past, and just go blindly on, craving the single thing that we think is happiness. I was miserable and unsettled when I wrote the book, because it's a depressing and unlovely thought. I don't think it is inevitable. The ideal situation is to take from the past and apply it to the future, which doesn't mean improving the past or tomorrow. It means selecting from it.

CR: In the novels, you're evolving the mythology of black culture. Is it a mythology that you're retrieving out of a sense of urgency because you feel that there's a crisis in the culture? Has it already disappeared, or is it on the brink of being lost?

TM: The mythology has existed in other forms in black culture—in the music, gospels, spirituals, jazz. It existed in what we said, and in our relationships with each other in a kind of village lore. The community had to take on that responsibility of passing from one generation to another the mythologies, the given qualities, stories, assumptions which an ethnic group that is culturally coherent and has not joined the larger mainstream keeps very much intact for survival. The consequences of the political thrust to share in the economy and power of the country were to disperse that. Also, the entertainment world and fashion have eaten away at all of those moorings, so that the music isn't ours any more. It used to be an underground, personal thing. It's right that it should be larger now. It's done a fantastic thing, it's on the globe, it's universal. We can do it, and that's important. But what that means is, something else has to take its place. And that something else I think I can do best in novels. The mythology in the books can provide what the other culture did. It provides a transition, a way to see what in fact the dangers are, what are the havens, and what is the shelter. That is true for everybody, but for people who have been culturally parochial for a long time, the novel is the transition. The novel has to provide the richness of the past as well as suggestions of what the use of it is. I try to create a world in which it is comfortable to do both, to listen to the ancestry and to mark out what might be going on sixty or one hundred years from now. Words like "lore" and "mythology" and "folk tale" have very little currency in most contemporary literature. People scorn it as discredited information held by discredited people. There's supposed to be some other kind of knowledge that is more viable, more objective, more scientific. I don't want to disregard that mythology because it does not meet the credentials of this particular decade or century. I want to take it head on and look at it. It was useful for two thousand years. We also say "primitive," meaning something terrible. Some primitive instincts are terrible and uninformed, some of them are not. The problem is to distinguish between those elements in ourselves as human beings, as individuals, and as a culture, that are ancient and pure or primitive— that are there because they're valuable and ought to be there— and those that are primitive because they're ignorant and unfocused.

CR: A matriarch is at the center of each of your novels. Within black culture, do you feel that women bear the burden of living in a society where the men are more severely discriminated against?

TM: There's some problem with defining what men go through in
the culture of black people, or any group of people who have
really to work. Men identify with their ability to work and take
care of the people they are responsible for. People are what they
do rather than who they are. Now the work has been drained off,
and that's the economy in which we live. Also, work is being
split into little pieces, so you don't do a whole job but you do
part of it. You feel lucky to have any part in it at all. That is
devastating for the maleness of a man. So the women have the
domestic burden of trying to keep things going, on the one hand,
and also protecting the male from that knowledge by giving him
little places in which he can perform his male rituals, his male
rites, whether it's drunkenness, arrogance, violence, or running
away. It is a certain kind of fraudulent freedom, and destructive
perhaps. The man is not free to choose his responsibilities. He is
only responsible for what somebody has handed him. It's the
women who keep it going, keep the children someplace safe.

It's very interesting, because black women slaves in this country were not, by and large, domestics in the house, with the
headrag. They worked out in the fields, and they had to get to
the end of a row at the same time as, if not faster than, the men,
because there was this terrible totalitarian oppression of black
men and women as laborers. There was no question of "You
can't haul this sack, you can't cut down this tree, you can't ride
this mule," because women were laborers first, and their labor is
what was important. They were never permitted—even by their
own men, because of the circumstances—to develop this household nurturing of the man. They had this history of competition
with men in a physical way, meaning work, which was always
there, always. And out of that comes a sense of comradeship
among that other generation. I remember my parents and my
grandparents—I always knew somehow they were comrades.
They had something to do together. That does not exist now, because the work distribution is different. The man can't find work
befitting what he believes to be his level, so it changes the relationship between the two. What is valuable about that past is
not the fact that women had to work themselves into the grave
so early, but this little idea of what it meant to have a comrade.

It's not the mode of work, but the relationship of the work. A woman had a role as important as the man's, and not in any way subservient to his, and he didn't feel threatened by it, he needed her.

CR: This perspective you have comes from your own background. I remember you once mentioned that your grandfather remembered the days of emancipation.

TM: There are so many little feathers of stories about that. I never looked at it very closely, because there was so much misery way back then, but I remember he was a little boy under five, and all he heard was that emancipation was coming, and there was a great deal of agitation about that. Because he could feel the excitement, the fear, the apprehension as well as the glee, he knew something important was happening. Emancipation is coming! Nobody explained it to him—and he thought it was some terrible monster. And on the day when he knew it was coming he just went and hid under the bed. [*Laughs.*] Oh, poor baby. And then there were these other people I heard them discuss—their charm and traditions—they were Indians who were married to some slave people in my family. Some of them never made the transition from slavery. They were given land that was then taken away from them by the rapacious part of the culture that they could neither stand up to nor live with. Then there were others who were survivors, who got away with it, and made out in a flexible way. These things were talked about—the family, the neighbors, the community. They talked a great deal about Jesus—they selected out of Christianity all the things they felt applicable to their situation—but they also kept this other body of knowledge that we call superstitions. They were way stations in their thinking about how to get on with it and a reason to get up the next morning.

CR: I was wondering how you view the historical period of slavery. There are two cultural traditions. One is the Old Testament, tenet of the trial that forges an identity. The other is that of the Greek tragedies, that your most heroic people will be destroyed or enslaved. Solomon in flight is an Icarus figure.

TM: The heroic is hidden in the lore. The archetypes have this sort of glory, such as the triumph of this flying African. There's also the pity of the consequences of that heroism, so there's a mixture of terror and delight. In those figures and in those stories, the movement is away from the Brer Rabbit stories, being a kind of wit rather than power, but prior to that there are stories of wonder workers. I remember the story of a woman who was a worker on a plantation. She was sassy, she spoke up, was always being beaten and resold. She was powerful: at one point she was chained to a tree and lashed, and she let it happen. Then something snapped, I guess, and she pulled the tree out of the ground and with it beat the man and his dog. [*Laughs.*] That moment shows a really superhuman effort when we just say, "The hell with it," and let it out. The consequences of that woman's life, of course, were sad. There are hundreds of those stories, and they linger on. They were nourishing stories.

CR: In spirit this folklore is similar to the parables of the church, the hymns where there's the testing and the suffering.

TM: Being able to endure it. The connection with time in a large sense was the most important thing, to get through this because afterwards you can join all those others before you, and it would not be like this. The daily or weekly sessions in church were not only to give each other strength. It was the one place where you could cry, among other people who were also crying and whom you trusted to help you. With everybody else there, you were not afraid or ashamed to do it. You knew that afterwards you still had to get up and face it, but now somehow you could.

CR: You describe the bonding of the community in the church as the theatre of life.

TM: The society was there, the art was there, the politics were there, the theology was there, everything was there. That was the place where all of it was acted out, within a framework that was acceptable to them. There is so much in Christianity that makes it a very interesting religion, because of its scriptures and its vagueness. It's a theatrical religion. It says something particularly interesting to black people, and I think it's part of why they

were so available to it. It was the love things that were psychi-
cally very important. Nobody could have endured that life in
constant rage. They would have all gone mad, and done what
other cultures have done when they could not deal with the
enemy. You just don't deal with it. You do something that destroys yourself, or else you give up. But with the love thing—
love your enemies, turn the other cheek—they could sublimate
the other things, they transcended them. I do remember, there
were all these things that those people felt they were too good to
be, that they were above doing. They didn't commit suicide,
they didn't stone people, they just didn't—they were better than
that. What made them better was this very pure, very aristocratic love that made them the most civilized people in the world.
That was their dignity, how they transcended. And that part ap-
pealed to them.

I suppose if they had been untampered with, they could have
made out with the vestiges of that African religion that they
brought, because it survived in some forms, in ways in which
they worked, sang, talked, and carried on. Even now, Africans
have a way of saying, at least to people like me, that they feel
that other people's religions are an enhancement, something
they could incorporate. Some aspects of Christianity are very
exclusive rather than inclusive: it tells you who can or can't be
in, and what you have to do in order to be in. But the openness
of being saved was one part of it—you were constantly being re-
deemed and reborn, and you couldn't fall too far, and couldn't
ever fall completely and be totally thrown out. It was always
open for you, and there was something you could do to testify or
change your way of life, and it would be fine. Everybody was
ready to accept you. And also that transcending love, that quality, which is why the New Testament is so pertinent to black literature—the lamb, the victim, the vulnerable one who does die
but nevertheless lives. And of course there was that wonderful,
very strange Job, not his original wealth, but his steady, sus-
tained "I will not do that, I will not do that," all the way
through, and then finally the recompense. That's your test of
inner faith.

CR: What you're describing is the core of the culture after emancipation, which is in your earlier novels. But it existed within its own boundaries in a hostile society. Can you foresee an end to this prejudice?

TM: I really don't know. I write about what it must have been like when we just got here. There couldn't have been another slave society in the world with a Fugitive Slave Law. It could not work with the Greeks and Romans, because they all looked pretty much alike. But with the black people, skin gives them away. You could keep up the remnants and the vestiges of slavery far longer than it ever would have lasted if they had enslaved . . . suppose they had decided to buy Irish people and just spread them all about, as they did of course. Then when they stopped doing it you could sort of tell by the name or tell by the religion, but you couldn't have laws—Jim Crow laws. With black people, because of the physical difference, they could be seen as slaves, and subsequently are now viewed as the visible poor. We are perceived as the lowest of the classes because we can be identified that way. It wouldn't make any difference what we wore, or what neighborhood we lived in, we're still visible as that. The visibility has made the prejudices last longer. It's not because one is black that the prejudice exists. The prejudice exists because one can identify the person who was once a slave or in the lower class, and the caste system can survive longer. In Nazi Germany they found a way to identify the Jews by putting a label on them to indicate who they were. You know what I'm saying: they needed a mark. But here you have people who are black people.

CR: Do you think that the prejudices will erode away, or do you think they are always going to renew themselves?

TM: No, I think all your people think that because they're taught to. I think that it will last as long as the economy remains this way.

Paul Theroux

Often described as an expatriate or American writer in exile, Paul Theroux is neither, since he divides his time by spending summers on Cape Cod, where he grew up, and the rest of the year in London. He is distinctive among American writers in that his work is cosmopolitan in subject.

Paul Theroux was born in Medford, Massachusetts, in 1941. He attended the University of Maine between 1959 and 1960, then continued his studies at the University of Massachusetts, where he obtained his B.A. He went on to do graduate work at Syracuse University. A Peace Corps volunteer in Africa, he remained abroad as a lecturer in English, working in Kampala, Malawi, Uganda, and Singapore.

His prodigious output began in 1966 with his first novel, *Waldo*. This was followed by *Fong and the Indians* (1968), *Girls at Play* (1969), *Jungle Lovers* (1971), *The Black House* (1974), *The Family Arsenal* (1976), *Picture Palace* (1978), and *The Mosquito Coast* (1982). His collections of short stories include *Sinning with Annie and Other Stories* (1972), *Saint Jack* (1973), *The Consul's File* (1977), and *World's End and Other Stories* (1980).

It was in 1975 that he attained international prominence with a travel book, *The Great Railway Bazaar: By Train Through Asia*. It was followed in 1979 by the equally popular *The Old Patagonian Express: By Train Through the Americas*. His most recent travel

book, *The Kingdom by the Sea: A Journey Around Great Britain,*
was published in 1983.

The interview took place in the conference room of his New York
publisher, a book-lined room dominated by the enormous table and
chairs. Paul Theroux is of medium height, fair, with light-brown
hair, and dressed informally in tweed jacket, dark shirt, and wool
tie. His sunglasses, tinted a light blue, add the distinctive touch of

someone who has been living abroad. His approach to the interview situation was one of lively good humor, ready for anything interesting. He speaks rapidly, his voice having shed its New England tone for a slight "English" rhythm—which may be simply his natural vivacity and fluency. He is direct in his answers, and his wit is constantly at play with the subject of the conversation. As we sat across from each other in that windowless room without any sense of passing time, the conversation took its own course and had the frankness of an exchange between passing travelers.

CR: You live in England and summer on Cape Cod. What made you decide to live your life that way?

PT: Life in England, while very pleasant, is not something that engages me except as a spectator. I've lived there for almost ten years now, but I don't vote, and when something happens I simply get angry the way that one gets angry with an Istanbul taxi driver. I say, "Well, I'm not going to let that happen to me again," but I never think of changing anything. So it makes one cynical and dismissive. Every time I come back to the States, I see what possibilities there are. I have noticed how much optimism there is here, even in adversity, as opposed to the sense of demoralization in Western Europe.

CR: I assumed you were in England because it's more congenial to your literary life, and the detachment gives you a certain sense of freedom.

PT: I don't feel detached from literary life in England because a lot of my friends in England are writers. I know a lot of writers in the States, but I'm not part of any literary set. I'm not a natural joiner; very few writers are.

CR: Do you consider yourself an expatriate American writer?

PT: I wouldn't regard myself as that, because in the age of the standby fare there's no possibility for anyone to be in exile, or an expatriate. We live abroad in the way that, in another age, people went to the Maine woods. It's not hard to get to England, and it's not even hard to leave. I think the really expatriated people are people who don't have a country. They're uprooted people, or they're people who come from societies that are closing up. As an example, a lawyer in Ethiopia or Uganda or Malawi, where I was, might have some misgivings about putting up a plaque saying his name, Attorney at Law, in Addis Ababa, a place where people are shot every morning, where there's no rule of law, and a man with a sense of justice might find it very hard to live. That man is doomed to expatriation, and he just has to become a wanderer, to find a place that's congenial to him, where he can exercise his mind about things. Americans are not in that position.

CR: What originally made you decide to settle in England?

PT: I think of myself as temporarily domiciled there, but my reason was simple enough. I left Singapore in 1971, and I was determined, after the Foreign Service, that I wouldn't get another job, that I never wanted another job. My wife didn't feel that way: she said that she wanted to get a job. It was interesting that I, as a man, had decided that a job was oppression and an intrusion on my work, and my wife at the same time decided that the job was liberation.

CR: Your wife is in broadcasting. Is she a writer also?

PT: No. She is very good at producing radio programs. She had done it in East Africa, and she taught at the Chinese University in Singapore. When we left, I said, "OK, honey, you have a job, I'll shlep along; if you're going to get a job in London, I'll go," in the same way that a woman says to her husband, "Well, dear, yes, I guess you're going to be a bank president in Tasmania; I'll go along and make cucumber sandwiches for your colleagues." We landed in the English countryside at first, then we moved to London, and, just in the way things go, we discovered that we had a car, a house, children to educate, and we began to take on a sort of cultural baggage. It gets harder and harder to move. But I knew that as soon as I made a little bit of money I would buy a

house in the States and regard that as my home, as I always have.
I had a successful book not long after that, and I bought a house
on Cape Cod.

CR: Are you referring to *The Great Railway Bazaar?*

PT: Yes, that was really the first money, although the first successful book was *Saint Jack.* It wasn't a celebrated book, but it
sold a lot of copies. Money is a grotesque topic. It's simply that I
wanted a place in the States to call home and I wanted it to be
where I grew up. I will have spent four months here this year,
which means that I look after the children a lot.

CR: You come from a New England family of writers.

PT: I have two brothers who are writers and a third who is interested in writing. It's not a literary family, but it's a bookish
family. Almost more important than that, it's a big talking family where you really can't get in a word edgewise. It's not a
family where people are holding back, or in the corner with
their nose in a book, recommending the *Imitation of Christ*
bound in red morocco, or saying, "Here's a rare first edition of
Trollope's *Travels Across Australia.*" It's a family where there
are lots of ideas.

CR: Often isolation is the factor in making children turn to writing.

PT: I think children turn to writing after they've read something
that moved them. They really become infected with that virus,
and they want to do it. In a large family it's quite a natural thing,
because there's not enough space for everyone, so one's private
life is very strong. I come from a family of seven children. Virtually the only way we could express ourselves, since everyone's
talking at once, is through the printed word. I think the impulse
comes from talk initially, then from reading.

CR: Even though your people are from New England, from your
name I gather there's a richer cultural strain in your background.

PT: French-Canadian. My grandfather was the youngest of a family of nine boys. In 1885, when he was two, his mother was burned alive when the farm in Quebec caught fire. She threw him out of the window of the burning farmhouse into a snowbank, and they snatched him from it. At the age of thirty he eventually found his way to New Hampshire, along that route the French-Canadians take. All French-Canadians are found on that strip that goes through Maine, New Hampshire, and then down to Providence—they didn't get very far. I think they were hard-working but not particularly adventurous. They tended to difficult but unimaginative occupations, and he did that. He came to New Hampshire, and then got a job near Boston and started his family there.

CR: Are you passionate about Francis Parkman, who devoted himself to writing so beautifully about the French in the New World?

PT: Yes, very much. But I wonder if he was writing about *my* ancestors, because I think of them as very quiet people who would have stayed on the farm if life had been easier. I know that my grandfather left Canada because, after that fire, his father remarried, and he really hated his stepmother.

My mother's side of the family is Italian and equally interesting. My grandfather was an illegitimate son in an arrangement resembling that of *The Princess Casamassima*. There Hyacinth Robinson is the child of a servingmaid and a nobleman, and my grandfather was the son of a servingmaid and an Italian senator who was later ambassador to Japan, and who disowned him. My grandfather subsequently discovered his father's identity and how shabbily he had treated his mother, and said that he was going to kill him when he came back from Japan. He got a frantic letter from his father, saying, "I'll make it all right." He was going to be taken care of. Eventually his father tried to have him arrested, so he fled to New York. My grandfather was an anarchist at that period. He slept in what was called the Hotel Garibaldi, which was a statue of Garibaldi in Central Park under which all the Italian political people used to sleep. Then he went to Boston and started his family. Yes, it's interesting, but it's the interesting mess that a lot of American families are.

CR: It's interesting to find, in your family background, deracinated persons, because they are also characters in your fiction. Two of your books deal with travel by railroad. I'm more interested in the traveler. I was wondering what made you take those long journeys.

PT: They were mainly an antidote to the kind of solitude that I felt when I was writing. I've actually lived around Central Africa for five years, then Singapore for three, and I don't think of living in England as travel in any important sense. Well, I had felt slightly cabin-crazy after writing *The Black House,* and I thought, I've spent a year writing this book, I've got to get out. As a lark, I just thought, I'll go to Japan on the train, and tried to figure out a way of doing it. It all looks so simple now. At that time Turkey was no problem, the Orient Express still ran. This was a mere seven or eight years ago. Going through Iran was a piece of cake, going through Afghanistan was nothing. Now the Khyber Pass, all these places are walled up and bristling with machine guns, and it's all difficult. Yes, Cambodia was a slight problem then, but not a serious problem. Laos was no problem. Vietnam was in a period of cease-fire, which was interesting, not difficult. I could actually sit down in 1972 and get a map and say, "I'm going to go through Turkey, Iran, and all these places," and it seemed like a perfect way of spending three or four months, as a reaction against having spent a year writing a book, so I did that. Then a few years later I did the same thing, out of the same impulse, the sense of seclusion after writing *Picture Palace,* and wrote *The Old Patagonian Express.*

CR: While traveling, are you renewing yourself by changing your thought habits? Do you find yourself being more gregarious?

PT: In traveling you have to be gregarious. I have two ideas about traveling. One is that if you're writing, you have to offer yourself and create an occasion, and it's a very exhausting thing. It means arriving in a place and discovering as much as possible about it. You try to meet people casually, you try to talk to peo-

ple, you think, What the hell goes on here? Is this place worth
staying in? Who's here? What am I going to write about? What
is there to write about? You have to know something, so you look
hard. Well, I lived in England for quite a long time before I
began to write about it, simply because I wasn't traveling, I was
living in a house. I wasn't "on the street," prowling around.
When you're living in hotels and prowling around and taking
taxis and doing things, drinking, and generally moving around,
subjects offer themselves. I think that that kind of travel, as opposed to vacationing or residence, is critical. I've had vacations.
I've gone to Mexico and looked at the ruins and lolled around
and gone swimming, and I think, Three weeks have passed and
this has all been very pleasant. Travel is a twenty-four-hour preoccupation with trying to understand and see and take note. I
find that kind of travel is a very exhausting thing to do.

CR: I was wondering about how you define yourself as an ob-
server when you travel with the intention of writing a book?

PT: Well, it's difficult to define. The sort of travel that I do is like
writing a novel, but it's the opposite insofar as I'm outside and
I'm doing it with my feet, but the kind of discoveries that I make
are the discoveries that a man makes who is interested in the curious. You keep traveling because you keep discovering things.
When you stop finding things out, you go home. You get bored,
you say, "I've torn the heart out of this place, there's nothing
more to discover." The same thing happens with a novel, except
it happens when you're alone in a room working on a book.
You're writing about a character and you begin discovering
things about that character. Any man who knows in advance
what he's going to write about would be so bored that he'll bore
his readers, or he won't finish it. So I never begin a book—or
even a story, for that matter—knowing how it's going to end, or
knowing what I'll encounter along the way. I set off, first in *The
Great Railway Bazaar* and then in *The Old Patagonian Express*,
believing that I was going to find something out. I didn't have
the slightest idea of what I was getting myself into, so the ob-
server is one who's receptive to ideas and, insofar as possible, is
game for anything, and is offering himself so that things will

happen. If somebody says, "Are you interested? Do you want to go to the football game? Would you like to meet my sister?" you say, "Yes, yes, yes, yes, count me in, I'm your man, I'm alone, you know," and you're as plausible as can be. "Yes. That's right. Yes."

CR: In your short story "Acknowledgments" the researcher abroad looks up literary people and, being recommended from one person to another, makes it big. There's a contempt for that sort of person in your depiction of the professors of Amherst in London for the summer hunting down literary figures.

PT: Yes. During the vacations, in June, all English professors turn into writers and become predatory. They come to London, assume that everyone else is on vacation, and you get, "Oh, can you come to dinner? Will you have a drink?" They want to meet people, anybody, people who are dead, people who are alive, people who are half gaga, and, you know, they want to be in that world from June to September. Then September comes, they pack up all their memories, mementos, and anecdotes, and take them back to the English department.

CR: And write it?

PT: No, I think they talk them out. Do they do any writing? Perhaps a little.

CR: Is the American poet of the story based on W. H. Auden?

PT: I had Robert Lowell in mind, but Robert Lowell is mentioned as not being that man. I knew Lowell when he was besieged by people. The poor man, his face used to get pinched around the end of May, and he'd think, Oh my God, they're going to be coming through the woodwork pretty soon. And they were, in June. He had a whole battery of people he used to fend off, people from the English departments, and I won't say they killed him in the end, but he did die of a heart attack. Poor Lowell.

CR: In New York perhaps, and certainly in Paris, there's a whole bohemian world where people do not need to justify what they are doing. They are the leavening dough to the cultural scene, and the people you satirized could fit in fairly well.

PT: You can sit in a café in Paris or a pub in London and pretend that you're E. E. Cummings or Hemingway. There are those people living out that fantasy, who don't have Cummings's imagination or Hemingway's money or Ezra Pound's craziness. Britain and France are much more bourgeois than most people think. The fantasy really *is* a fantasy, and not much good work comes out of that kind of posturing. I have much more respect for people who live out that fantasy in out-of-the-way places, like Sri Lanka, or Papua New Guinea. These people end up having to face the fact that there is no fantasy and they're going to have to come to terms with this letdown and perhaps live there and make a few compromises, and so they do. I think more is learned from the simpler society, and not from the bourgeois, dinner-party-giving, indoor society. The story "Algebra" is about English writers who simply don't get out very much, and if you invite them to dinner they'll come. There are people, not many, who know that. The man in the story does. It's like finding out that Charlton Heston is lonely, or that Nick Nolte doesn't have a girlfriend. This fellow discovered that any number of literary luminaries were rattling around in the evenings.

CR: The lonely who are suddenly invited out to dinner are delighted to be asked. But by contrast, in your story "Zombies," the isolated writer is a prisoner controlled by people who seek her out. I thought I recognized Jean Rhys.

PT: That's a pretty accurate picture of her physically, and of her past, and what she was up against in her last years—people telling her not to write this, and did she really think that, and this is going to hurt your reputation, all sorts of rubbish. They were trying to tell her what she knew long ago, in the twenties. Sixty years ago, when Ford Madox Ford published her, people were saying these things to her.

CR: Did you know her well in her last days?

PT: Fairly well, but she had gotten to a stage in her life where she didn't depend on friendships except those ones that had worked for a long time. She wasn't looking, she wasn't trying to meet new people, that was the furthest thing from her mind. In fact, she was very serious about writing. She was a funny woman, and very vain and coquettish about her appearance. I liked the fact that at the age of eighty-odd she still wanted to appear attractive to men. I really did like her.

CR: What about the silence; did you have any insight into her long silence?

PT: Well, she says that she *didn't* stop writing, that she was still writing, that she was not only still alive, but she was at it. In fact, when she was rediscovered she had a book ready.

CR: That was *The Wide Sargasso Sea.*

PT: Yes. And I think she was living in the country, drinking, and had thought that she was forgotten. There are quite a few people who at a certain stage in life think, well, they've written all they have to write, the public has done its part, and they don't have a new book. And they fall silent. It's not real silence, because she even said that she wrote all the time, meaning that she wrote in her head. I believe that she did, that she saw things in literary terms. She was a very truthful person. J. D. Salinger appears to have fallen silent, but it would be a long shot to say that he's not writing. He simply is not appearing in print, but I'd bet anything that that man every day wakes up thinking of writing; he has ideas, and perhaps is trying to think of a way of ordering them, may even be writing. He doesn't become a sort of lumberjack simply because he's not appearing in *The New Yorker.*

CR: In the case of Jean Rhys, you mentioned her editor urging her to begin her memoirs, and *Smile Please*, those unfinished memoirs, were just published.

PT: She had started writing them but she was by then so enfeebled that she found it very slow going. She hadn't been back to Paris; she knew a lot, but to write the way she did was very exhausting and she physically wasn't up to the task of doing it; she didn't have enough lucid hours in the day to be able to write very much, so there's a lot of dictation. She was dictating for a while, and she wrote on her own, but it was a big job. I don't think that it's the whole story. She had a far more interesting life than appears in those unfinished memoirs.

CR: I had expected a fairly complete portrait of the period.

PT: You see, in one sense she wasn't a writer, she was like a chorus girl. I don't mean that in any belittling way, but she was someone who had—what did Blanche DuBois say?—"I have always depended on the kindness of strangers," meaning men, and she had. She liked men, and she liked being around them, so her libido and her loneliness and the kind of society that she required were somewhat at odds, I think, with the solitude—rather, the dreariness—of writing, because writing is pretty crummy on the nerves. There's no glamour in it. There appears to be some, but after a period of time you realize there's actually none, and then what do you do? You either go on writing or you capitalize on what you've already written. If you still feel like writing, you realize that it's going to keep you out of society. I think that she was gregarious and attractive and that writing required her to be reclusive and anonymous and so that was the division in her.

CR: What made you decide to write a story in Jean Rhys's style, "The Imperial Icehouse"? In your story the Jean Rhys character had been asked by her editor to delete one story.

PT: Yes. Jean Rhys didn't tell me what story she had been asked to delete, but I tried to guess at what she might have known. The short story is often a piece of mimicry, or like ventriloquism, it's assuming another voice, another posture; that's the fun of it, actually. You can just project or extend your mind and say, "I'm this other person." So I tried to write the fable and then tried to give it a link, because in this collection, *World's End*, I drew connections not only thematically but from story to story, with factual things. Miss Bristow in that story is published by the narrator of "Algebra." There are little connections between them, but that doesn't make a novel.

CR: The book is extremely well structured, since the title story, "World's End," refers to the next to the last story, "The Greenest Island."

PT: Yes, I hadn't thought how closely they dovetailed. There's a place in London called World's End.

CR: Dickens wrote about that.

PT: Yes, he did, and I think other people have. It's an actual district at the end of the King's Road which, when London was a lot smaller, appeared to be like the end of the world. In fact, there's a pub there called The World's End. The metaphysical image that one conjures up is of someone in Tierra del Fuego, yet in fact he's at the end of King's Road. That is, I think, a story about things closing up. The other, "The Greenest Island," has a character who is discovering that he can't get out of a relationship or leave a place. He and his partner are discovered as being like castaways. I find that attractive as an idea, not in the story, but in life—a place circumscribed by water in which there is a drama and people going there in search of something else. All those castaway island stories—*The Blue Lagoon,* a nice book; those Robert Louis Stevenson stories, *The Ebb-Tide, Treasure Island, The Beach of Falesa;* H. G. Wells's *The Island of Doctor Moreau;* or Conrad's *Victory*—interest me. I'm not saying the island is the world, but it has a perimeter and you have to work out your destiny within that small space. I think my story is about rejecting one thing and choosing another—discovering that you're rejecting one kind of entanglement, and choosing to be a writer.

CR: In "World's End" a man discovers that all the elements of his happy life—without his knowing it, through irony of circumstance—are the stages of his losing his world. It's a moment of realizing exactly what his situation is. The bleakness of it comes from the fact that there is no way out for him.

PT: What people find horrible, and yet it happens all the time, is that there's a child being privy to the domestic secret of infidelity.

CR: It divides children. . . .

PT: Millions of little kiddies are running around America—and
Europe, too—with the knowledge that their parents are liars,
they're corrupt, or that they're leading a double life. The children are supposed to keep the secret of Mummy's friend, or
Daddy's friend, or the divorce. It's a bit like *What Maisie Knew*,
except much more horrible because we want children to under
stand, so we in fact treat them as if they were older than they
are. They are rather fragile creatures who can't live with many
contradictions, and certainly want to know who they belong to,
and so it's *What Maisie Knew* with knobs on it.

CR: The saddest aspect of this story is that this man's love for his
son becomes so hysterical that he eventually uses the child
against his wife.

PT: You *do* wonder about the nature of his attachment. The child
is treated as a love object, as a possession, as a kind of mainstay,
as the proof of his own right decision. He represents too much to
the man. We *do* tend to use and misuse the people we love, and
to think of them as much stronger than they are, and people become burdened by this responsibility to be strong, flexible, and
able to handle all these contradictions. So the man is making a
grave mistake. But his worst mistake is corrupting the child with
this lie.

CR: By asking the child to spy on his mother. The common assumption is that children can grasp things that are explained to
them, when in fact they can only understand at the level of their
maturity. This story is contrasted with "The Greenest Island,"
and the paradox of the young couple's decision to separate, a
decision to affirm the sense of their destiny.

PT: The fellow in that story has the hope of youth. In that lovely
story "Youth" by Conrad, he says, "Ah youth!" How wonderful
it is to live, to dream, and go on. That's really what I envy in the
young, the fact that they have possibilities. It's the thing that I
loathe in Britain, as a matter of fact. You talk to a sixteen-year-
old, and he's like a little old man; his life is ending before it can

possibly begin. You ask, "What are you going to be?" and he'll answer, "Maybe I'll go into civil service." He doesn't say, "I want to punch cows," and "I don't know, be president," or the ridiculous but sort of touching ambitions that you get in American children. This guy in the story, being an American, is hopeful about his destiny. Perhaps this collection would have a different slant if it began with a story which is about hope and ended with one about horrible disclosure, but I did not choose that because I wanted to end on the somewhat hopeful note of someone marching into the world.

CR: On the island, the young couple cling to each other because she is pregnant, and reality finally forces them to make the decision to abandon each other and the hope of having a child.

PT: This story is set, although not very long ago, in another age, when such things were life-or-death decisions. You couldn't choose idly whom to sleep with. There was a kind of all-or-nothing about marriage, children, even about being a writer. Nowadays this isn't the case, and I think the world is much better for it. We are better for not having to make these drastic, life-altering decisions, or even thinking of everything as permanent. Things are not permanent, and there may be fluidity in marriage or children or even the occupation of being a writer. For example, when I was growing up, I found it very hard to admit to myself, and impossible to admit to other people, that I wanted to be a writer. Whenever anyone asked, "What are you going to be?" I always said, "A doctor." When I went to college I was a premedical student because it was inconceivable to me that I could be a writer. How do you become a writer? I never knew. If you told someone that you were a writer, they would say, "Well, what have you written?" You can't want to be a writer, you have to *be* one, and it seemed so final. That kind of decision of twenty years ago is not as crucial today. Today no one laughs when someone says, "I want to make a movie." A kid in high school might want to become Steven Spielberg. In fact, he might be working on *Gone With the Wind* down in the film seminar. No one who's nineteen years old now can imagine what it was like for a nineteen-year-old twenty years ago. Some people will read this story and think, Holy mackerel, where did this take place? Were things really like that? Like you or me reading Theodore Dreiser. The story which preserves a period as something vital, I think is something to value.

CR: What was the structure you had in your mind when fitting these stories together?

PT: The thread is thematic; it's the simple one of people being abroad in a metaphorical way as well as in a real way. I wanted to call the book *Overseas*, or *Abroad.* I wanted that sense of otherness of place in it.

CR: The title *World's End* certainly conveys that.

PT: It was a fortuitous title. But there were some stories that I left out because they were domestic stories, interiors, and had no suggestion of other places. Even the simplest story here, "Clapham Junction," has people mentioning life in Southeast Asia and China and other places, how it might have been and what they did and how they came back. They came back with these cultural impedimenta.

CR: What about the regional novel—Willa Cather, Faulkner, and that tradition?

PT: I read them, but I can't write them. Trollope is not regional in the Palliser series. The novels are localized in London, but Trollope went very far afield. He wrote stories set around the world, in Ireland, Switzerland, Italy, Australia, and so forth.

CR: But how do you react to a work that concentrates on one world and one place?

PT: I get terribly depressed when the place is always the same, the narrator's always the same, and the stories are similar. One of the saddest books I've ever read was *Dubliners*, which is all about Dublin, about depressives who are trapped, who can't escape, who can't get away, and at the end of *Dubliners* you want to cry for those people. I always read it with interest, but with an inability ever to connect or to see myself doing the same thing. The best example of a novel which I would be incapable of writing is *The Sound and the Fury*. The Faulkner novels are rooted deep in the ground. He mentions, in his sort of ponderous way, how the blood of these people watered these trees, and there were Indians and slaves and other people who prevailed in what was a whole world on what he called his "postage stamp of ground." Or a book like *The Story of an African Farm*, by Olive Schreiner—a lovely book, but you have to have spent twenty years on a farm in South Africa to write that book, and who in hell wants to do that?

CR: But what about the American writers such as James, who have that sense of place?

PT: He was the opposite of a regional writer, though. With James, there is a strong sense of place in his writing without your ever believing that his next book is going to be about the same thing. He didn't think *Washington Square* was important enough to put in the New York Edition, and yet I think that's one of his funniest, more readable, best books. I don't know how the regional novel ever gets written. I don't know what impels, I don't know what moves or what moved. Case in point: Faulkner had a hankering for Paris. He began life as a lyric poet, didn't he, and he created a romance, even told lies about the Canadian Air Force and Hollywood and so forth. He couldn't have written about Oxford, Mississippi, if he had never left. I don't understand how someone can be born in a place and begin writing about the place with any feeling or understanding without having left. One could never get by, being born in Ellsworth, Maine, and never leaving. Wright Morris I find an interesting writer, and he's from Nebraska. I don't know anything about his life, but he must have left. How can you know that something is worth writing about if you haven't seen anything else?

I think that Willa Cather was cosmopolitan in her travels, and that Mark Twain, if he had stayed in Hannibal, Missouri, wouldn't have written *Huckleberry Finn*. He was a tremendous traveler and went to what were then the Sandwich Islands, Hawaii, the Gold Rush, and then wound up in Connecticut. He wrote *Huckleberry Finn* because he lived in Connecticut, not because he went on living on the Mississippi River.

CR: Even books which we think of as created from one particular
place, such as *Wuthering Heights* and *Jane Eyre*, were written
after the Brontë sisters had gone to school in Belgium and returned.

PT: Right.

CR: Detachment is essential for a writer to understand the scope
of his or her vision. By contrast, as a writer you live abroad, but
you're also saying that you want your subject matter cosmopolitan.

PT: Yes, if what you mean by "cosmopolitan" is to break with the
preconceived ideas of American fiction. I don't think that break
is so radical. The example of Mark Twain comes to mind, because the interest in the possibility of a world—and I don't mean
"outer space," but simply other lives, other societies—has always been strong in the writer's mind. Bret Harte, for example,
was a consul in Germany. When you imagine Bret Harte, you
think of him as a poker-playing, cigar-smoking fellow standing
around while people are telling stories about the West. But he
was welcome in the drawing room, and when Twain met Henry
James and James said, "Do you know Bret Harte?" he said,
"Yeah, I know the son of a bitch." There was Mark Twain, who
you think of as so down-home, and chewing on a cigar. Well,
he's there at Lamb House talking to Henry James.

There's a writer's intensity of ambition, wanting to travel, see
things, do things, wanting to be active. I don't understand people who write a book and then hole up, and either live on their
reputation or don't want to write any more, don't want to see
any more. If I didn't write, I would still travel. I think I would
get around more, I would have quit more jobs, got more jobs,
been more places. Writing does keep you sort of in one spot, but
I envy people who can quit a job just like ripping off their
clothes and start somewhere else, going to Alaska or California,
or saying, "Let's try Brazil." That's a very enviable thing. I've always liked and almost admired these sort of freeloading, back-
packing hippies that you meet in Kabul. You say, "What are you
doing?" "Ah, looking." They're looking. That's a very likable

quality, and I think they have all the characteristics of a writer except they don't have pen and ink, or the typewriter. The temperament is the writer's temperament—wonderment, curiosity, and, physically, the willingness to take risks, actually going out. In bad writing that's evident as the internalization of an unwillingness to move. This person thinks highly of himself and doesn't want to stir. The New Yorker who doesn't want to leave New York, the Nebraskan author who's there in his cabin—that sort of person is missing a hell of a lot. . . .

CR: Which leads me to the final question. In your own travels, are you aware of looking for certain constraints, having limits set by an unfamiliar environment, or, in other words, looking for a constant in the unknown?

PT: No, but I used to find it interesting to be in societies which I thought of as simple. I liked living in places which were changing, either had been something, or were in the process of becoming something else, or were in complete decline.

CR: You're speaking of Africa?

PT: Africa, Singapore, Southeast Asia, places that were becoming decolonized, or facing the prospect of war, or just had a war. It takes a lot of stamina to live in societies like that. The people are at the edge, they have to become something: they have to face the fact that their society is collapsing, or will collapse. For a writer, observing this, or being in it, is never less than interesting.

CR: In some way you must be drawn to that edge, for your own reasons.

PT: To the idea of just wildness or emptiness, or social decrepitude—all of that is interesting. What's very difficult is that humor or satire only arises out of a society which has a strong social structure. The city in America in which people are the funniest with the least effort is New York. New Yorkers have a language of their own, and that's a sign they know how complicated their society is, and comedy can only arise out of this. Woody Allen is impossible in Britain or in Europe. He's the complete New Yorker. I also think he's a funny writer. New York is a place with such complicated rules, like certain primitive societies where the language is really complicated, formal, colloquial, in which you have to know how to address people, and where the danger spots are. So because of that some very funny books have been written here. The society in decline, or the collapsing one—the one in which rules are arbitrary—is not a funny one: it's a sad, desperate, anarchic one.

CR: Since you see the humor in the place so clearly, you must feel at home here in New York.

PT: In the way that everyone feels at home here. I wrote about New York in my novel *Picture Palace*. New York is shaped like an ocean liner, it seems to be steaming to sea, and New Yorkers are like people who have their sea legs, they know where everything is, where you can go, and what you can do, and everyone else is like a passenger on this great liner. We're all leaning over the edge looking at the East River or the Hudson River, and walking around the very geometric deck.

CR: Do you find this country "on the edge"?

PT: Americans, I've noticed, are casually cynical about leadership. We pay lip service to a kind of disrespect and always have. Before Kennedy was shot, very few people liked him, and no one remembers that now. He was the president, he was the person that you kick. But at the same time, people are dependent on leadership and expectant that their leader be intelligent. Somehow the casualness has gone out of our cynicism. These people really are incompetent, they really are doing things wrong. The only hopes that people have are straws in the wind: The United States is like the Catholic Church, with a Borgia Pope. Even though you have a Borgia Pope, a poisoner, an adulterer, a murderer, people still have faith, they'll keep on going to Mass. People think of the United States as an indestructible thing, but Reagan is an illiterate, a person who hasn't read anything and who doesn't know anything. He doesn't know as much as the people whose roles he assumed. All his life he's been saying things that other people have written. I suppose it has its comic side, but there's a kind of horror to the possibility of a president who is looking behind the camera into the audience—"What do I do now, how shall I say this, do I say this as if I mean it?"— which is grotesque, but perhaps what we deserve. I would say that of all periods to live in, this can only be one of the most interesting, and that, going through this period, whatever comes out of it in the next ten years, America will change radically.

CR: Do you feel very detached from all this? Or are you also caught up?

PT: I think that it's a convulsiveness that is affecting the United States, but however much it changes things here, it will change other countries much more. The people with problems are the Guatemalans, the people in India, the Third World countries. These people are doomed, because if we fail, and are made uncomfortable over the next decade, they will be falling into a bottomless pit. Think how much worse things have gotten in Africa. The great thing that happened in the sixties in Africa was that they became decolonized. They became free countries, but they are much worse off than anyone thought conceivable. Worse in terms of whether people can have the rule of law, can have a square meal, and all that sort of thing we haven't faced yet. I think that we will inevitably know what Western Europe knew in the years up to and just after the Second World War— real shortages, where gas costs five dollars or six dollars and they can't afford to drive to work, and may lose their jobs, and could not get another job. It's a frightening prospect, because it spawns desperate people. You can hate oppression, as V. S. Naipaul said, but fear the oppressed.

Robert Stone

IN EACH OF HIS NOVELS, Robert Stone pursues his questioning of America. He confronts the reader with the large issues of who we are, what we do to one another, what we do to the world, and how it comes back on us. Each novel reflects the moral and spiritual climate of the society.

Robert Stone was born in Brooklyn in 1937. He attended parochial school in Manhattan, then Archbishop Malloy High School, which he left to join the navy at the age of seventeen. There he became a Third Class Journalist for the Armed Forces Press Service. On leaving the military, he began writing poetry and fiction while working in the Merchant Marines in New Orleans.

His first novel, *A Hall of Mirrors* (1967), won the Faulkner Award. Its rootless, alcoholic protagonist, Rheinhardt, works as a newscaster for an evangelical radio station and cynically observes the financial and political interests preparing for a takeover of the city of New Orleans. This novel was eventually made into the film *WUSA* in 1970.

Robert Stone's second novel, *Dog Soldiers* (1974), won the National Book Award. *Dog Soldiers* takes the Vietnam conflict back to the United States by following the journey of a shipment of heroin. The brutal pursuit and defense of the drug through the desert of the Southwest is a catalogue of the broken dreams of the sixties. This became the film *Who'll Stop the Rain?* in 1978.

His most recent novel, *A Flag for Sunrise* (1981), presents the American presence in Latin America in the fictional country of Tecan. This ambitious work portrays a variety of Americans pursuing their goals as the economic, political, and religious upheavals tear the country apart.

For the past ten years Robert Stone and his wife have lived in Northampton, Massachusetts, where he teaches creative writing. The interview was set at my loft in Soho during one of his periodic visits to the city. The conversation occurred over two days, so that each of us would have a chance to return to what had been discussed.

Robert Stone is of medium height and build, with the ruddy complexion of the country life. His thinning red-brown hair and free-growing beard give the impression of an academician, or of an outdoorsman in town for the day. This is reinforced by his reserve and shyness. He is soft-spoken and precise in his choice of words, and has a wonderful speaking voice.

During this extensive interviewing, Robert Stone was disarmingly straightforward in answering the questions, which he often used to explore his own ideas.

CR: Your novels are set in New Orleans, on the West Coast, in the Southwest, and in Latin America. But you are that rare exception, a native New Yorker.

RS: Yes, I was born in Brooklyn and then moved to Manhattan when I was quite young, and grew up mostly on the West Side. My mother's family had been in the tugboat business in New York; not so much in the business but working on the tugs. I still have a lot of relatives in Brooklyn, in Broad Channel.

CR: I know you had a Catholic schooling. Was your family religious?

RS: My mother was a nominal Catholic with a real dislike for the clergy and for the church. Her family was Irish and Scotch.

CR: Was that combination of Scotch and Irish also Protestant versus Catholic?

RS: My mother's father was a Presbyterian; he was an alcoholic Scotsman who worked on the tugboats. My grandmother was an Irish farm girl whose family had been in upstate New York for quite a long time.

CR: It was she who wanted you to go to a Catholic school.

RS: I went to a parochial grammar school and to a Catholic high school. I really didn't get on with the Marist Brothers, and they didn't get on with me—we didn't relate to the fifties. It was the kind of Catholicism which doesn't exist any more, I hope. I just couldn't get it together in school, so I left high school without finishing it. Then I joined the navy when I was seventeen. I was a so-called minor enlisted man; I got out when I was twenty-one.

CR: Was this during the Korean conflict?

RS: No, it was in 1955 that I enlisted, and 1958 when I got out, so it was just after.

CR: Were you a journalist in the navy?

RS: First I was a radioman, but there is an official rank of journalism in the navy. You can be a hospital corpsman, or a journalist. Because I passed the test, I was officially certified Third Class Journalist. I had the insignia on my arm to prove it. Essentially I was a correspondent for the Armed Forces Press Service; that was my last year and a half in the navy.

CR: Was it right after that you worked in the Merchant Marines in New Orleans?

RS: I did a couple of trips out of New Orleans. Most of the work I did in the Merchant Marines was in fact pierhead work, unloading, because I had low seniority in the union.

CR: When did you turn to writing? Or were you writing all this while?

RS: I had always, on some level, wanted to write, and I had always been writing a little bit. I didn't do much when I was in the navy; I wrote one short story the whole time I was in. But I had won a contest when I was in high school. Because my upbringing was in what you'd call a working-class context, I had the impression that being a writer was unsubstantial and not altogether respectable. But it was basically what I wanted to do, even though I didn't realize it when I was younger. I always wrote. I always had a kind of narrative impulse to try to make sense out of things by telling stories about them, and I guess I also always had a certain facility with language and was always kind of in love with language. One thing that the Catholic school system did for me was to really teach me how to read and write thoroughly and grammatically. All this time I was mainly writing poetry. So in New Orleans I did things like read poetry to jazz, which was the thing of the time. The jazz, I suspect, was better than the poetry. My wife and I ended up taking the 1960 census in New Orleans. It really saved our bacon, because we were terribly broke. We got hired at a buck eighty a household to go all over town and just talk to the population of New Orleans—which is some population! What you would find behind a particular door would be completely unpredictable. It was a very interesting job, sort of fun, even though all it consisted of was taking down names, ages, and so forth. It was fascinating to see the city on that level and be able to go into everybody's house and figure out their story; marvelous.

CR: New Orleans is the setting of your first novel, *Hall of Mirrors*. Had you started writing it at that point?

RS: I wasn't ready to write a novel at that point in my life. I started the novel when I must have been about twenty-six, and prior to that I had not enough sense of life lived in time, the shape of people's lives; there was no pattern that I saw in things until I got to be that age. When I was twenty-one, twenty-two, I was not Carson McCullers—I did not have any vision, I just didn't know enough.

CR: How did you start the actual writing of *Hall of Mirrors*? Was it when you were involved with Neal Cassady and his friends?

RS: Marginally, because Janis, my wife, was a waitress in the
Seven Arts Café on Ninth Avenue, and that was a hangout for
everybody. She had a day job in the RCA Building as a guide. So
she would get out of her uniform and put on her black stockings.
We both worked nights. I would get out of work about one a.m.,
and that's when I would run into the poets and musicians of the
late fifties. LeRoi Jones, as he was known then, and Gregory
Corso would read there, for example. Our living in the Quarter
in New Orleans is the genesis of *Hall of Mirrors*. When we
moved to California, which struck us as a marvelous sybaritic
place where you could live cheaply, that's when we met Ken
Kesey and his friends. I was in the process of writing *Hall of
Mirrors*, and that process was sort of interrupted by this encounter with all these people, and I spent a lot of time doing funny
things in my head and hanging out.

CR: Were you also dropping acid at the time?

RS: Yes, with the result that the book, which began as a traditional, realistic novel in the manner of Dos Passos or Steinbeck,
began to change as my perception of reality was altered. I don't
know how much importance to ascribe to that. It would be
wrong to say that I started it as a realistic novel, took a lot of
drugs, and then it went funny—that's not really true. It probably
would have taken a lot of the turns it took anyway. It changed in
my hands as I worked on it over a long period of time. I was
never sure that it would be a finished book. I expected it would
be one of those ongoing novels that you're always writing, writing for the rest of my life, and it would never be finished. I made
a contribution in that direction by not working on it for a long
time. I finally left California, where I had a fellowship at Stanford, because I was having a terrific time but I wasn't getting
any work done. I came back east, and the writing of the novel
was interrupted by periods when I would have to go to work. I
would work for twenty weeks, and I would go on unemployment. Sometimes I would take turns with my wife—she would
work and I would work on the book. That's the slow way to do a
book. Rather to my surprise, it did get finished in '66, and it
came out in August of '67.

CR: *Hall of Mirrors* deals with alcoholism. Is that something you felt was a literary subject? That was a popular romantic concept.

RS: In a way, it's something that I'm trying to get away from. I was in the drug culture—not so much the criminal end of it, although you always run into some pretty bad people sooner or later. The drugs that run through all my stories and in my novels are a reflection of people I knew who did take a lot of drugs, so that I am really reflecting what I've seen around me. People are constantly drinking, they're constantly doing stuff throughout the book, but that's what these particular people would do. In the case of my protagonist, Rheinhardt, there's a lot about him that represents the shadow part of my life, in the sense that it wasn't my life but, in a way, it could have been. I inflicted on Rheinhardt all the things that I was afraid would descend on me so that he was literally my scapegoat; he was a kind of alter ego. I didn't make the choices that he made. I did everything else that he did. I more or less stopped drinking a lot, which I used to do. I was a kid who went to school drunk in high school, and I quit doing that.

CR: The culture of the fifties had a romance with drinking.

RS: Drinking was it and, as you say, it was romantic. And it was my first novel. I don't think I was ever an alcoholic, but if I hadn't made the choice not to be, I would have drifted that way, as had a lot of other people that I knew, such as Kerouac and a lot of lesser-known people around the scene, whether in New Orleans or in New York.

CR: Someone was telling me about the drive you took in the desert. Tell me the story.

RS: Tom Wolfe describes a ride I took with a guy named Ken Babbs and his wife and children who were aboard. We drove from Manzanillo to Nogales, Arizona, all the way up Route 5. We were doing lots of speed, smoking lots of grass, and wildly hallucinating on the Mexican desert. We kept seeing these machines which looked like road monsters. Once we encountered this thing standing in the road—it became necessary, if we were to continue, to drive right into it, and we had this moment of sheer terror when we thought that we were either about to drive into another dimension or into this beast—we were going to do a Jonah and disappear into the belly of the creature. Somehow we got through the ride. Neal Cassady, in those days, was pretty shot—I never knew him at his best. He was gone on stuff like Methedrine, so he never shut up—he just went on and on, out of his head.

CR: Could you still distinguish the charisma that made so many writers captivated by him?

RS: Well, I have used Cassady-like people in my books, but I was not captured by the romance of Cassady. He looked and seemed to me like a guy who'd done a lot of time. I read *On the Road*, and I see how Neal was like the hero, but he was somewhat older than me and I always had the feeling of a guy who's on his way to being—I hate to say this—but on his way to being an old-time street guy, short of breath, who was really hustling to keep up with these younger people. I've seen some of the movies that Ken took and it really showed in that footage—how old and pained Neal looked in those days, and how everybody around him was so much younger and just full of this infinite energy. He was taking all that speed, in my opinion, basically to stay up—to get in there with these crazy kids. I remember an encounter between the people in the bus and Jack Kerouac, somewhere on Madison Avenue. Cassady was driving the bus, and Kerouac, Ginsberg, the Orlovskys, and a couple of other people, including a guy who claimed to be Terry Southern and wasn't, were in this party. Kerouac had reached the stage of being very alcoholic and embittered—boy, he hated us. He was jealous that Ken Kesey had grabbed Neal as a bus driver. These people were just a bunch of California hippies. He did not see us as angels, seraphs, and all the terrific things that he saw his own generation as. It's true, in a way we were the opposite—we were a lot healthier and California-like; we were just not a New York number. There was a lot of the hayseed, cowboy element in Kesey that clashed with the Eighth Street commando—an East/West

Coast cultural clash of ages. Kerouac was eloquent on what jerk-abouts we were.

CR: But Neal Cassady affected all of the Beats, and, as a young writer, could you identify with their experience of encountering someone much more raw with all his poetic vitality?

RS: Their encounter took place in the forties. *On the Road* is set in 1949, to a large extent. They were young people at Columbia who were encountering, in Cassady, the American West, the outlaw and the life of the road. I can see how the young Cassady could appeal to them. He just knocked them out by being such an American original. I don't think their attitude towards him was patronizing, but I think there was something of the discovery of the genuine, unschooled American. Their perception of him was aesthetic—they were seeing all those traditions reenacted in one individual. In a way, he was always performing for intellectuals. He had this role of American original thrust on him, and enjoyed it, and always, on some level, had to work at it. Which doesn't mean that their friendships were false or that their feelings for each other weren't valid; there was a lot of mutual respect.

CR: Were you writing prior to *Hall of Mirrors?*

RS: I started writing *Hall of Mirrors* in New York in '62. On the basis of the beginning of it I got a fellowship at Stanford. When I went to California, it was like everything turned Technicolor. California, in 1962, was a different world, of course. Somebody described being in San Francisco as like being stuck on an escalator in Lincoln Center. There were people there who had gone there to get away from crime—it sounds absurd now. But it was a much more easygoing place than New York. The sixties hadn't really happened yet. The worst and the strangest thing around was us. We were, when you come right down to it, pretty harmless.

CR: Did that affect your writing?

RS: Yes, it did. It's hard to say, but I think it did affect my writing, because it changed my life and circumstances and it gave me a view of what is practically a different kind of culture. It changed my perspective, it enlarged my experience. It made me think, as acid did, made me consider questions of reality—the difference, as somebody said, between words and silence. It also brought back what I think were a lot of latent religious feelings in me that I had really turned my back on. What got me into trouble at school was my rather naïve, militant atheism. But, in fact, I was basically religious. Even though drug mysticism is a vulgarism of the real thing, I think it did make me come to terms with my own religious impulses. There is some element of the religious in almost everything that I've written.

CR: In *Hall of Mirrors* your style is all there, and it won the Faulkner Prize for a first novel. I was wondering if you had a sense of coming into your own when you were writing?

RS: Well, I was creating myself as a writer in that book. I put everything that I knew—or claimed to know—into that novel, as one will with a first novel. That book was like a process—rather than being something that I sat down over a period of time and wrote, it existed in my life and parallel with my life for a number of important years. I was learning to be a novelist in the course of writing it, I was developing a style, and I was also pursuing a vision of things. I wasn't sure what I was after when I began it, but as the characters came into existence and I began to play them off against each other, I realized that I had attitudes about the relationships between people. I had something to say about how people are with each other—how they seem to promise things to each other and, most of the time, don't come through, or come through and don't quite manage it, or come through in the face of expectation and sense. The attitude towards the world and towards fear and towards violence were things that I had something to say about. By the time I was halfway through it, I really had myself and my novel. It sounds funny to say, but it has to be true about any novel: it's something that you make up as you go along. With *Hall of Mirrors*, I knew pretty much how it would end, but a lot of what was in the middle I didn't know. If you'd asked me then what I was writing about, I would have said, in a kind of Kerouac-like romantic vein, America. If you'd asked me if I had a writer I was emulating, I would have said Gogol. It would have been presumptuous to say all those things, but I was trying to make a statement about America.

CR: With Rheinhardt, you first introduce the potentially psychotic character that he reveals himself to be, which is something that fascinates you. Where does that aspect of your fiction come from?

RS: The affectless person is a person that fascinates me. That's the result, in a way, of when I was young. I spent three years in an orphanage, basically because my mother was schizoid—she wasn't a sociopath or a psychopath in any sense of those terms, but she was schizoid. I grew up, in those years, with people who were going that way—these affectless, institutionalized sociopaths were the people right around me. When I was in the navy at seventeen, there again I ran into military people like that. Those things frightened and fascinated me. There are people like that always with us. There's an American way of being like that, which I presume differs from the French or German or English way of being like that. Is it too much to say that there's a little bit of that person in everybody? I think it is too much to say that, but maybe there's a little in me.

CR: Do you see it out there in the culture?

RS: Exactly. Because of the lack of tradition and the general rootlessness and transience of American life, that character plays a larger role, is more in evidence, and is, to some degree, celebrated. That character is a contributor to the American experience. Not only have we the Frontiersman and the Puritan and the Outlaw, but we have the Sociopath as a major cultural type, and there is a certain reverence for him in American society. I think what I was trying to do was to recognize the importance of the rootless, affectless, emotionally crippled individual in American life.

CR: Rheinhardt is both a brilliant musician and a confidence man in his ability to infiltrate any society, and yet he chooses the derelict's life of a drifter.

RS: He's able to live in it, like a fish lives in water, because he's chosen it. Rheinhardt is a man of tremendous spite who has rejected his own talent because, as he says, he feels he lacks the energy and manhood. By that I mean that he just doesn't have the moral substance to be what he should be—a great musician. In an act of spite, he leaves his family, leaves art, and, ultimately, leaves good. He chooses the bad. Spite is what drives him to destroy himself, to move towards all the forces of darkness because he's turned his back on everything positive—all the things of light. I was once going to call that book *Children of Light,* and I wish I had.

CR: I focused on the fact that his intelligence is always used provisionally. He knows, without thinking about it, that he can do a newscast, and still he prefers the oblivion that drink promises.

RS: His dynamic is perception, and that's the one thing he can't turn off. He's doomed to witness and to be intensely aware of what is going on around him. His condemnation, this doom that he's going towards, is all the more painful because of his self-awareness. Every time he deliberately makes an immoral choice, he is aware of the difference. There's a constant process of his choosing the darkness. He has to experience doing that.

CR: From the narrator's point of view, neither Morgan the social worker nor Geraldine is innocent. Is that also part of your vision?

RS: They have their price. They're both hungry, they're both victims of spiritual hunger, and they both come into contact with Rheinhardt, who is on his way as far down as he can possibly go. Geraldine has the bad sense to fall in love with him, which is, of course, going to sweep her away. Her price, in a way, is him.

CR: Your characters are helpless but the society explodes. Was that a political statement?

RS: No, it's a surrealistic ending. At the time I wrote about the riot, before '64, as best I recall, there hadn't been any. I was carrying things to their logical, absurd conclusion. Unfortunately, the logical, absurd conclusion turned out to be what happened.

CR: Was that ending also a resolution for you as a writer?

RS: I take satisfaction at having done it. I haven't read it now in a couple of years. But I remember it very clearly, because it was harrowing to write. When Geraldine died it was like a death had really occurred. It really upset me, and I stopped writing for over a month while at that scene. There is humor in the book that I can't help bringing to bear, because it's one of the ways that all of us get through life. Emotionally, it really knocked me out—the years of writing it—it was like a rock. By the time I'd finished it, I was in a different place, and in a different head. I was living in the real world and I was living in a fictional world. Reflections of my real experiences, my feelings, my politics, my attitudes towards people and towards life and towards America were all going in there.

CR: Was that when you went to England?

RS: After that I went to England. I was trying to begin another novel and I didn't know what the novel was. I had a wonderful time in England; I was drinking too much, partying too much. Then, of course, Vietnam was in progress. It began to occur to me that if my subject was America, and if I was going to be faithful to the subject that I had chosen, I had better get over there. I knew I was going to have to write about people who had been there. I got accreditation from a now defunct English imitation of the *Village Voice* called *Ink* to go to Vietnam as a correspondent.

Nineteen seventy-one was an odd period in the Vietnam War. It was not a time of intense combat, although there was some near Saigon and up north. I think my going out to the line, which I did on the back of somebody's motorcycle, was really a gesture. I just thought, I can't really stay in Saigon. If this was going to have any validity, I really should get out there and see the line. So I did. Somebody like Michael Hare saw twenty times as much combat as I ever did. Michael really paid his dues over there in a way that I didn't, but I thought I had to pay some dues, so I went out.

CR: In Saigon, while reporting, did you consciously look for the subject of a novel?

RS: Well, I really didn't know quite what I was after. I was writing for *Ink* and I had a good, close, scary look at the drug scene and the black market in Saigon, partly because, more or less by chance, I ran into some people who were connected with the shady side of Saigon, and the shady side of Saigon was quite as frightening to me as the stuff that was going on on the line in 1971. It was the time of Vietnamization, and American troops were being taken out of Vietnam. The ARVNs were still fighting and dying, to speak of the allied side, and certainly the other side was. But the love of combat was not intense for most people. Then I began to see what this book was going to be and who these people were going to be.

CR: Were the people there trafficking more desperately?

RS: A surprising number of respectable people, or apparently respectable people, were involved, to some degree or another, in both drugs and gold. A lot of people carried things back and forth to Laos, for example, or carried gold from Laos—and that includes diplomats and civil servants, members of the press corps, and the military, too. There was a lot of profiteering, more than one might think. There was a large press corps, and some of it marginal. I am by no means speaking of everybody, but there were plenty of people in the press corps who were into drugs—who were using them and, to some extent, dealing. By 1971, there was a heavy drug scene.

CR: While you were there, did you have the images of war that we did here, watching it on TV every evening?

RS: We were all part of the antiwar movement, but I was getting my perceptions of the war through the medium of the English press and television. That is why I think, when I came to America, I saw the impact of the war on the whole country more clearly, because I had been away, and I hadn't been experiencing it as a gradually increasing thing. It was still going on when I came back in '71, the same year that I had been over there, and came back to what was the beginning of post-Vietnam America. To me it seems that, with the war and the drug explosion and everything that happened in the sixties, the world seems so different than it was before the Vietnam War, before the drugs, the music, before all that wild thing went through. It's almost like living in the aftermath of a revolution—as one might talk about "before the revolution" and "after the revolution." This is a different country. It's easy to confuse one's personal circumstances with circumstances in general, but that's the way it seems to me.

CR: Since so much of your information came from outside this country, did you find double motives as you focused in on the book?

RS: It was this corrupting force that even those honestly involved in it—who, from traditional motives, participated in the war—were involuntarily contributing to the corrupting of American society all the way through. What was worst in America was acted out. What is best about America doesn't export. Yet I have to say that a funny thing happened to my antiwar position as a result of being over there. It wasn't that I stopped being against the war, but I began to feel about it in a different way. Suddenly it was not something abstract; I knew what it looked like and I knew what it smelled like and I knew more about Vietnam than I had known, and it occurred to me that the other side, who had always been my good guys, were, in fact, not such good guys after all. I began to encounter and to hear about some of the atrocities that they perpetrated. One feels one is taking leave of one's senses to talk about whose atrocities were worse. But the image of the North Vietnamese or the Vietcong soldier as representative of humanism and progress, which a lot of us allowed ourselves to entertain, was not a correct one. I began to feel an ambivalence that was reflected in the book. Suddenly there was no more a question of right or wrong, there was just this awful event. In V. S. Naipaul's *A Bend in the River,* two characters are talking and one of them says, in effect, "Sometimes it seems as though there is no right or wrong here." The other character says, "It isn't that there isn't any right and wrong, it's that there isn't any right." That's the way I felt. It is extremely difficult to discover where right is. It keeps disappearing—you think you see it and you've got it in your hands, and then you don't—that old ambivalence comes down and you're compromised. It's just that the ambiguities of life are infinite. Everybody's talking morality, but there aren't a whole lot of people trying to practice it.

CR: Were you also disillusioned by a lot of the leaders of the antiwar movement?

RS: Yes, I was. I think that one of the lessons of the sixties, the war and that period, was that so many of the leaders of the alternative societies or the alternative methods—those systems and ideas which were offered—were quite as ready to lie and as corrupt in their way as the leaders of the so-called establishment. All the leaders, all the gurus that I'm aware of, turned out to be questionable. So where was the true way? It wasn't there. There was damn little that one could do, and life was, finally, as it always is, a lonely and dangerous business in the last analysis.

CR: The character of Hicks becomes the protagonist even though Converse is convinced that he's a psychotic. This paradox you created in *Dog Soldiers* is a recurring theme in your work.

RS: Hicks is absolutely determined to be true to himself and to what he perceives to be his code. His code may be assembled—it's homemade—and some of his sources may be vulgar, but he's going to act morally in his own terms. That makes him look crazy to somebody as relativistic as Converse. Sometimes he does violent and impulsive things, which he then regrets, but he's trying to follow his own code.

CR: By the time you introduce Hicks and he encounters the criminals of the heroin traffic, he becomes a warrior, and the war is brought back to America in the book.

RS: There's more than a grain of truth in it. The social fabric—to coin a phrase—was struck a blow, either as a result of the war or as an indirect result of the war, that it hasn't recovered from. There was an undermining of the society, and it was partly economic and it was partly spiritual. I think everybody must be aware that this society is a whole lot shakier now than it was before that war. I was trying to examine the process of that blow's falling on America in *Dog Soldiers*. *Dog Soldiers* is about a whole lot of dreams that went bad. It's about people pursuing sensation and experience for their own sake; people doing things that they did both in Vietnam and in America, as they still do—doing things that they never thought to see themselves do in the name of experience.

CR: What is heroin?

RS: It's not only a manifestation of moral sleaze. If you want to take and abstract all human desires and make a paradigm out of them, that would be the pattern. It activates the pleasure centers of the brain. It is pure abstract desire. It takes the place of money, sex, and company. It's a magic and powerful substance; traditionally, a gift of the gods, and also a curse. It is a substance that is charged with its own mystique. If you've ever read junkie poetry, people have this love for heroin and they fear it. People speak of it as though they were speaking about God. It is the Big H—a mixture of love and adoration, and it's really awful.

CR: In Hicks's total distrust, did you see the war as catching up with and destroying the counterculture that grew out of the protests?

RS: Yes, it finally did. Another thing that *Dog Soldiers* is about is that nothing is free. There was America having this party at the same time as the war was on. We were going to do three things at once—we were going to fight a successful war in Asia, we were going to reform society, and we were going to have a terrific party at the same time. That just wasn't so.

CR: Were the authorities, the hijackers, and the narcotics dealers reflecting your feelings about the government?

RS: The characters are not themselves officers of the law, but they are the kind of people who are always around them—stoolies and gofers. They are the place where the cop meets the criminal subculture. They represent that side of the law. I was using a situation that was true about certain law-enforcement officers, agencies, and individuals, as a reflection of the general corruption and uselessness that I was seeing in the government. I am not a radical, and I think the American Constitution is one of the great documents of the eighteenth century. In theory this system is terrific, and in practice it has a lot of good things about it, but I am not an admirer of the American government.

CR: From the Vietnam era we have a distrust and a fear of power.

RS: I have been observing power in its application through all my novels. I am suspicious and fearful of organized or institutionalized power, whether it is "alternative" or "establishment." I have learned, and I hope that others have learned, the truth of the old dictum—"Trust is good; not to trust is better." It's a brilliant proverb.

CR: You portrayed the corruption of society in all your novels, so that your view is of the underside of events.

RS: I have an attitude towards institutions and power, and I really suspect that, down deep, nobody knows what the hell they're doing. A lot of correspondents in Vietnam, when they were writing about the war, would say, "We're writing this up and it gets put in neat columns of print, and we are attempting to make sense, or we are making sense, of something that cannot be made sense of." In a way, all life is like that, in that most people are more like chimpanzees than they're like Socrates, including myself. Our collective perception of what we're like is considerably at variance with what we're really like. We are cleaning up our own act in our collective perception of ourselves. That has its amusing aspects and its terrifying aspects, but I believe that is the case. It is very hard for us to put one foot in front of the other, so to speak. It is very hard for us to behave rationally, let alone well.

CR: In the way you portrayed how Hicks died in the desert, did you see him as a martyr of his own code?

RS: Yes, in that he insists on coming through. In remaining true to himself, he does terrible things that he would never have thought that he would do. The violence of his nature emerges in the pursuit of his own code, and it becomes an end in itself. It becomes something beyond morality, something more important than life. He's just determined to live up to this construction of himself, and that is in a way noble but also pathological.

CR: There's an element of rage against America in characters such as Hicks. Does it represent an essential trait of the culture?

RS: They are, in their way, particularly American characters, and they represent a number of forces in the society, in the myth and the reality of America. There is a lot of rage against America, and it is there for the obvious reasons. I love America, so it enrages me—if I didn't, I wouldn't be so angry, nor would I make America my subject.

CR: Who are the writers you read and learn from?

RS: The first person who gave me what I would call a literary experience, who taught me something about how language works and what writing is about, oddly enough, was Carlyle. I must have been in the eighth grade when I read Carlyle's *French Revolution.* My first reaction to it was "I can't understand a word of this, it doesn't make sense to me, what a strange way of writing this is." But as I read it, I began to really enjoy it and I began to understand it more. It really struck me as most unfamiliar, provocative, and strange. That was the first time that I was really struck with language. I learned about the variety of textures that prose could have, about the liberties that could be taken with language, that one could depart from the conventional rhetoric of English and in so doing produce a strong effect.

And, of course, Dickens. The characters in his books are in a kind of alternative world that you can get into, and when you're into it you're really seeing it. Someone described Dickens as a visionary; his imagination is so visual and so verbally skilled that you cannot refuse his reality, and you know, by reading him, that his experience of his fictive world was very rich and immediate and present. He was obviously immersed in his books. That's his greatness. He was afraid of so many things as a Victorian, but writers as different as Dostoevsky and Kafka saw themselves as attempting to emulate Dickens. He really has a sense of evil—he just never forgot that blacking factory. It must have terrified him—the prospect of tumbling into the proletariat in the Victorian age of primitive accumulation. You can imagine that it must have been scary for him, but it did him a lot of good as a writer.

When I was a teen-ager I read Dos Passos's *U.S.A.* trilogy, and I still have a habit of beginning to write about many different characters. When I was in my early twenties I found the reading of Kafka's *The Trial* a revelation. Finally, I think the writer who influenced me the most, even though I don't share anything of his vision, was Conrad—as a storyteller. I learned the art of the novel from Conrad and Scott Fitzgerald: the novel as being full of strategic as opposed to tactical considerations. There's nobody writing, under a certain age, who wasn't influenced by Hemingway. My favorites are, I think, every writer's favorites— that is, Beckett and Borges. They are the greatest writers in the world to me.

CR: What are your work habits?

RS: My work habits are fairly rigorous. I start early in the morning. I'm usually out in the woods with the dog as soon as it gets light; then I drink a whole lot of tea and start as early as I can, and I go as long as I can. Right after I wake up, I feel I'm at my best; I feel like all the systems are going. I exercise regularly, I don't drink a lot. That's perhaps one of the reasons why my characters are always drinking and taking drugs, because I am not.

CR: Is Mrs. Stone also a writer?

RS: No, she's a social worker.

CR: And do you read your material to her?

RS: Yes, she's always the first person to read it. I use her if I'm uncertain, if I have trouble with something I'm writing. Writing is a constant process of decisions, and as a writer I feel I have to make the decisions. Once in a while, something will be too close

to call and I will take it to her. Among civilians, it's only my wife
who will read it.

CR: Nabokov once said that he wrote for a small group of people,
most of whom were friends. Who are your books written for?

RS: Somebody who is like me but obviously cannot be me. I have
to trust the hypothetical reader. I am trying—in a good cause—
to crowd people out of their own minds and occupy their space.
This is an incantatory process. I want them to stop being themselves for the moment, I want them to stop thinking, and I want
to occupy their heads. I want to use language and I want the
language to reverberate and I want to use the white spaces between the lines. I want it to be the total experience that language can be. That's my ambition. I may not always do it, but
that's what I'm trying for. If I didn't write for people, my proper
business would be meditation. But my business is writing for
people. To me, it's an act of affirmation.

CR: Critics have commented on the originality of your style. Can
you define your particular style?

RS: One doesn't consider style, because style is. I can see myself
not being able to write because I'd be thinking about Style. Style
is form. My style of writing is part of my way of being, and it's a
reflection of what my mind is like and what my relationship to
language is.

CR: Faulkner once said that he owed his style to a fifth of bour-
bon.

RS: I cannot write intoxicated in any way. Somebody once asked
Ken Kesey, "Well, you're a young man and you've written two
major novels in a short period of time. How have you been able
to do that?" He said, "Speed."

CR: Do you work things out by rewriting?

RS: I'll write a very rough first draft of every chapter, then I will
rewrite every chapter. I try to get it down in the first rewrite,
but some chapters I can't get quite right the third time. There
are some I go over and over and over again. For example, the

Naftali chapter in my last novel—I must have done it five times. There was always too much of something. It was too long, or it was too short. It was either too sentimental or too lacking in sentiment. I couldn't get it right.

CR: What mistakes do you rewrite out?

RS: If you've been writing for a while, you begin to indulge yourself; you begin to think that minor things of concern to you are going to be of concern to everybody.

CR: When you work, does your imagination begin with language or with images?

RS: In imaginings, when I'm walking down the street, I begin to make language of it at a fairly early stage. I make it verbal. Language is a code system, and for writers it's their medium, so I begin to impose language on phenomenology very quickly, because it is how I make sense of things. I like to write dialogue, so I'm always listening to people talking. But there are some people that you should listen to and there are some people that you should watch, because you're going to learn more about them that way than from what they say.

CR: Does the material of the novel create its own form, or do you begin with a sense of structure?

RS: I think I have a sense of structure at the beginning. I am not certain what will happen in terms of specific incidents, but I have a sense of the rhythm of it. When you begin, it's a little open—what the ultimate beat is going to be. As soon as I know who the people are and as soon as I begin to write, I can sort of catch the beat. One is improvising when one writes, and you pick up in the same way a musician starts to improvise and detect the inner structure of what he's playing—that's the way I think it works in the writing of a novel. You pick up the beat.

CR: Are the strange and frightening things you write about the things that you fear?

RS: It's a commonplace idea, isn't it, to be drawn to the things you fear. The reader and I will consider how strange and frightening things are and we will laugh about it, having no other alternative, and thus transcend it and assert the positive part of our humanity and perhaps make it less fearsome. If you read Beckett or see one of his plays, it seems as though he is pushing despair, but the strength of his insight leaves you feeling kind of elated and comforted by the fact that there is a sensibility that is aware and can go down to that depth and bring up pure art. I want to share that sense of the terrifying nature of things with my hypothetical reader and, as a result of our sharing it, produce a positive experience that gives rise to hope and transcendence. That's what I'm trying to do.

CR: That's art as sublimation?

RS: Well, sure it is; it's what Malraux described, as in all art. It's a response to the silence; it's a response to loneliness; and it's also reassembling our lost God. It's part of the process.

CR: How did you go about creating a whole country for *A Flag for Sunrise?*

RS: It's not so hard to create a country. All you've got to do is think of a name for it. [*Laughs.*] I don't want to be facetious in my answer. I wanted a combination of countries to go with what I had seen and what I wanted to do. Tecan is representative of all those places in the world, particularly in Latin America, that are beset with the American presence and that are ill-governed. People die and they are unhappy with the world. So it is what it is—an unfortunate Latin American country—and also it is the world and things as they are.

CR: I was wondering which specific countries you had in mind for Tecan?

RS: It's not a portrait from life of prerevolutionary Nicaragua, nor is it Honduras, nor is it Guatemala, but in certain ways it resembles all those places.

CR: Was this a subject you had in mind for a long time?

RS: Well, I once gave a reading at a university and ended up with a thousand dollars in my pocket. I thought, I've got to go somewhere, where shall I go? I found out there was this flight down to San Pedro Sula, Honduras, so I thought what a gas it would be if I got on a plane to San Pedro Sula. I expected a town out of *The Wages of Fear,* and that's exactly what I got. There it was! I started traveling from there by bus, met some people, and ended up, after some weeks, in Costa Rica. In the course of that trip, just listening to people, keeping my eyes and ears open, I became aware that there was a lot going on down there that was extraordinarily interesting. So I went back.

CR: What were you sensing there?

RS: The situation began to remind me of Vietnam. I was sensing the American presence in the undeveloped world, and I was again seeing this vaguely irrational sense of mission which Americans are consumed with when they are about their business in the undeveloped world: anthropologists, missionaries, contractors, deserters, crazies, druggies—various people.

CR: Was it all out in the open, and were they all visible?

RS: They were all visible to me in the course of my several trips. In 1976, when I set out, the Nicaraguan revolution had not begun, nor was it expected. No missionaries had been murdered; these things occur in revolutions. So I've been overtaken by events in the worst way again. It was not due to any great prescience on my part, because anybody who was down there at that time could feel those things in the making.

CR: It's not surprising that you mentioned Conrad before. *Nostromo* deals with a revolution in a Latin American country. Were you thinking of that novel?

RS: No, I wasn't. I haven't read *Nostromo* in a long time, and I tried to put *Nostromo* out of my mind. It was not in any way a model or even an influence, nor is it one of my favorite Conrad novels. I admire *The Secret Agent* and *Victory* and *Lord Jim* and the beginning of *Under Western Eyes,* which I think is marvelous.

CR: Is Graham Greene a favorite of yours?

RS: He is not a favorite of mine. When I went to a Catholic school, I was always abjured to read him, together with Evelyn Waugh and various other Catholic writers, for the salvation of my soul. While it's true that we both have guys in white cassocks staggering around under palm trees, the similarities really do end there.

CR: I was thinking of the preoccupation with the moral concerns of your cast of characters in *A Flag for Sunrise*. The book opens with Father Egan, in his despair, encountering such extreme violence, and that's the drama that unfolds.

RS: One of the things that I want to establish, for my purposes, is the *homine lupus*. I want to deal with extremes of brutality, yes, that the innocent suffer at the hands of people or forces driven by ignorance and greed. It's against that background of innocent suffering that the action takes place. It's representative of life in Tecan with a vengeance. It is the place that Father Egan has to start from, where he stops being a declining, cowardly, aging alcoholic and begins to reach out towards God for the first time in years. It practically costs him his sanity. The constant memory of this not only shakes his soul and fills him with terror, but it also moves him out of despair towards the numinous. This element of the numinous is always there for all of the characters in their various ways, just on the edge of their vision. They're always getting little glints of what may or may not be God. All of them are pursuing something beyond themselves. Holliwell thinks, Well, in the end, is there justice? Pablo, in his primitive way, is after it, and Sister Justin is after it in politics, and she finds it's not in politics but in martyrdom. And all these people are striving for and occasionally glimpsing a transcendent realm which they desire passionately. Everybody's after a new morning: What do we have to run up and salute tomorrow?

CR: That's the meaning of your title.

RS: Right.

CR: Holliwell discovers that all these people have been through Vietnam and are doing the same things in Latin America.

RS: Such a brotherhood exists, and he is part of it and so are those others. It's like a recurring dream, not quite being able to remember the past and being condemned to repeat it. It's a condemnation, on the wheel of existence, to relive, in a much more frightening and a more dramatic way, Vietnam. It's as though he's paying dues that he didn't necessarily pay the last time.

CR: When you have him make those statements about American culture—is that parallel to your ideas that the worst is exportable but the best is not?

RS: It's a lament for an America that may be lost, a lament for the integrity, for the grandeur of the inner spirit of America— it's a lament for that which takes the form of a diatribe.

CR: When Sister Justin sleeps with Holliwell, is it a gesture of despair more than of love?

RS: Love is such a strange thing—it has so many crazy forms that some loves are reflections of despair. Holliwell says they are both looking for a warm, soft place, in every sense. They're looking for shelter. They don't know if there is such a thing as love—how much of a word it is, and how much of a real thing. But she doesn't consider herself to be a nun any more, and he is going to probably assume that she can act out a rejection of her vows.

CR: In the same way as Father Egan despairs of God.

RS: She despairs of God and turns to man and finds God. One of the things she has to do is go the whole distance in rejection.

CR: Catholic priests and nuns know that despair is a sin, and their training arms them against entering that state as your characters are driven to do.

RS: The underlying loss for everybody is Gnostic rather than Catholic. In Gnostic theory we are all lost, all separated from our true selves—we are components of a divine entity. The myth of Gnosticism predicates this great battle between good and evil, where some divine being was destroyed in a cosmic destruction which created the world and created us. We are the ruins of a vanished God and our necessity is to reassemble that God.

CR: The escaped killer, Pablo, journeys down to Tecan. Is that just another aspect of the American presence?

RS: In some ways, I'm thinking of what Porfirio Díaz said about Mexico: "Poor Mexico, so far from God, so close to the United States." But every time this colossus of the North turns on the edge of its bed, poor little Tecan is practically overthrown. This American presence—its turns cause all this upheaval—it's almost unaware of itself, unaware of its effects. It doesn't specifically mean to cause harm. It's serving its own interests as it sees them, but it is inflicting great hardship and great harm on Tecan. It's a due bill coming up for payment. We've been getting our bananas, we've been getting our potassium to stave off our sense of existential dread, we've been sending in Marines, pushing people around in Central America, and we're going to eventually have to pay the price of it. It's already happening.

CR: The whole structure of the American presence in Vietnam is moved to Latin America.

RS: Right. They're doing their job in the same way that the Soviet police state proceeds. It acts. It spies on its people, it tells them lies, and it does that while, at the same time, rationalizing and justifying its doing so. All its officers, all its functionaries do what they always do. The sum total of that is by way of being a misfortune of the country. There's no exact parallel there, but it is rather the same with the Americans who deal with Tecan; they're doing things that they've always done.

CR: Both Lieutenant Campos, who preys on young women, and his American counterpart, the child murderer, confront Father Egan. You have these blind, deadly forces turning to a spiritually bankrupt priest for help.

RS: They're both part of Egan's parish now, because of what he witnessed and collaborated in—this is his ministry. He is now a party to the most fearful side of humanity, and that is where his mission lies as a priest now. Father Egan has found his way to this kind of Gnostic mysticism which presumes that all material existence is flawed and basically evil. These men are both, in their separate ways, human pathology, and at the same time rather innocent, like forces of nature. They're wounded humanity who do evil without particularly wanting to. Again, it's that disconnection between impulses, between motivation and its result. So he's confronting another failure of humanity, the flaw in things as they are.

CR: In the scheme of nature within the novel, the landscape is reflected by the offshore reef where each character who dives down experiences terror.

RS: But this is nature, and there is a predator down there. It's more than a shark, it's more than a killer whale, it's an elemental force. Perhaps the opening to hell. The implication on a realistic level is that there's a shark or killer whale there. But this is where Father Egan dropped the body of the girl. What's down there is evil itself. I was thinking of the speech in *Richard III* where Clarence, just before they drown him in the butt of malmsey, says, "I have passed a miserable night, / So full of ugly sights, of ghastly dreams, / That, as I am a Christian faithful man, / I would not spend another such a night, / Though 'twere to buy a world of happy days." And he describes his dream, which is of a thousand men that fishes gnawed upon, and skulls with jewels, and so forth.

CR: You suggest the coral reef inside man—is that something you've perceived?

RS: Yes. It's in imagination, because brain coral looks like brain tissue when you see it. It's enormous and round. This idea that the mind is an undersea thing, going deeper and deeper, is something that came to me one day when I'd been up for about thirty-six hours.

CR: The sea is the image of the subconscious.

RS: This is the undersea reflection of the world. How do the fish live in the sea? As men do on land. So the bottom of the sea, to me, means primary process of nature, nature being most itself. Although it is innocent, it is full of dangers and also frightening. It's a paranoid nightmare of looking over your shoulder. No matter how beautiful it is, you're always on the watch for some dreadful monster.

CR: Contrasted to these blind and innocent forces of nature, there's human history, which your characters try to grasp. What is your concept of history?

RS: It's a bitter and ironic reflection that Holliwell has from his experiences. He understands it now, if he didn't before. Anyone who has been witness to history and its aspects should be proof against surprises, will not be affrighted by anything that happens. He's talking about Vietnam, and he's talking about what happened in Tecan, and he's talking about history in general. Everybody's giving their interpretation. Sister Justin, who is coming into a kind of Marxist frame of mind, is after the same thing. Whether one is religious or whether one is a Marxist, one is committed to the idea of history as positive. It's Christian dogma that the world is not evil, that the world is good, it's God's creation. The combination of Darwinism and the Christian world view is the essence of Marxism. So these characters are fighting to maintain their view of history as a positive force and I am carrying through my skepticism, not only about religion and humanism but about history as a positive force.

CR: The irony is that in the end Holliwell and Pablo, adrift in a boat, become the absolute mirror images of each other. Is this duality about the underlying anarchy of human nature?

RS: What one would have thought as the most likely thing is what happened. Holliwell, who certainly doesn't want to kill anybody and certainly doesn't see himself as a violent person or murderer, kills Pablo. Pablo thinks that his spiritual education is still in progress and he's going to be saved. For reasons which Holliwell can justify, but which obviously are unknown to Pablo, Pablo thus becomes this innocent victim. There is a kind of mirror. As unlikely as it seems, they have much in common—the murderer is murdered. All the killings that take place are a reflection of the violence of that part of the world. There, realities are stripped, and, without any veneer over things, it is a primary process. In places like that there is much seeking after God and yet the feeling of His tremendous distance.

CR: I was wondering, what are the implications for you?

RS: It reflects, I guess, my own attitude towards the state of God and man—the possibility of, the absence of, the unknowableness of, or presence of God. Whether He is there or not there, He certainly is physically extant and physically absent.

CR: How far away are you from any kind of faith, really?

RS: I'm not much crazier than anybody else, but I'm not much saner. So, I thought, I'm really feeling crazy today, I think I'll go see a shrink. I called my GP and asked, "Who's a good shrink?" He gave me this guy's name. He was everything that a psychiatrist should be: a Jewish psychiatrist who was very together, very humane. I went to him, and I talked to him, and he said, "What you need is religion. What you should do is to go to Uttar Pradish in India, because in Uttar Pradish the ground is holy and if you walk on it—the ground is so holy that the vibes coming up from the ground will clear up your head."

Scott Spencer

SCOTT SPENCER'S NOVELS HAVE the theme of an isolated young man's attempt to shape a life for himself, in terms of love, power, or success. In each work a dramatic conflict is established between unconscious motivation and the character's actions on the larger stage of societal values.

Scott Spencer was born on September 1, 1945, in Washington, D.C., and grew up in Chicago. He attended the University of Illinois, and he obtained his B.A. degree in 1969 from the University of Wisconsin at Madison. His earliest publications were articles for the Chicago *Tribune, Harper's,* and *Redbook,* and short stories written under a pseudonym.

His first novel, *Last Night at the Brain Thieves' Ball* (1973), is a black comedy about a psychologist's ambitious research project to know, and therefore to control, his subject, which is all of American society. Paul Galambos abandons an academic career to join the secret organization NESTER, a think tank dedicated to research for the purpose of manipulating the nature of American desires.

In *Preservation Hall* (1976), his second novel, Virgil Morgan contrasts his happy marriage and successful career as a management consultant to that of his father, a failed composer. His dread and complete repudiation of his father's way of life is symbolized by Preservation Hall, his country retreat in the wilderness of

Maine. Ironically, it is in this haven that he destroys his perfect way of life.

Scott Spencer's third novel, *Endless Love* (1979), is David Axelrod's story of falling in love at sixteen with Jade Butterfield. His total surrender to adolescent passion leads him to espouse the Butterfields as a surrogate family. When they banish him in order to limit his affair with their daughter, David devises a puerile trick. He sets a fire he believes he can contain, with the intention of appearing heroic to them when he comes to the rescue. Their home is destroyed and their family life irretrievably altered. This love shapes the course of David's life and determines the person he becomes. The novel was made into a film by Franco Zeffirelli in 1981.

Scott Spencer and his family live in a postwar brick apartment building in the West Village, where the irregular streets crisscross to form small islands of green, irregular-shaped parks and playgrounds. Their apartment is spacious and light, comfortably furnished in country golden-oak. On the walls are sketches and paintings by Coco Dupuy, his wife, who was leaving to work in her studio just as I came in. The view from the window is a pattern of dominoes made up of the tarred roofs and chimneys and green treetops. We scheduled the interview for the afternoon when Scott Spencer would have finished his work for the day, and we met on two consecutive days so that we could pick up what had been discussed previously. Scott Spencer gives a boyish first impression— slender, strong, with open features, blue eyes, and thick head of light curly hair. He has a ready grin and is quick to react to the absurdities and humor of any situation. The conversation was taped in his workroom, where all evidence of typewriter and papers was enclosed in his rolltop desk. Scott Spencer was disarmingly responsive during the interview but always incisive and witty. He speaks rapidly in a pleasant, gravelly voice, bringing his thoughts to a frank conclusion.

<hr>

CR: When did you begin writing *Endless Love?*

SS: I started on *Endless Love* around the time *Preservation Hall* came out in 1976. My wife, Coco, and I moved to Vermont and I went on unemployment compensation, which I felt was my version of the National Endowment for the Arts grant. I began writing the book and worked on it for two years out there, and after we ran completely out of money we came back to New York. I got a job here and then finished the novel.

CR: Was it a book that came to you whole, or did it go through stages?

SS: I have a thousand pages of that book; it's my curse. I'm trying desperately to avoid it in the book I'm working on now. If I could think, maybe I wouldn't write. It's very hard for me to think about these things realistically and to make intelligent mental plans for my work. I'm always stuck with the process of writing something through, seeing what I like and what I don't like, and starting it again. The one thing I always had was the title, *Endless Love*, from the Delmore Schwartz poem, and that was the feeling I wanted to convey in the book. That kind of miasma, that sense of what I wanted to happen emotionally to me and to the reader, is essentially unchanged. But how to go about it was something I attacked from a dozen different angles. I started it as a third-person narrative. It began with the young people meeting for the first time. But I didn't get very far; I never wrote the book all the way through. I would always write about a hundred fifty pages and then get that nauseous feeling that I was going in the wrong direction. You can tell because when you begin your day's work it doesn't seem ready, you have to shake it loose, and when I get the narrative right everything's alert and waiting for me the next day. It is in its place.

CR: So do you have a set working routine?

SS: I work every day, from ten in the morning till I'm done with my pages. I try not to write beyond a certain point. It's my experience that if I write too much in one day it kills a couple of days' work for me after that. I like to keep myself to three or four pages a day.

CR: Was the first draft a total loss?

SS: Yes. It went around describing so many things, and was getting to be a cluttered domestic book. I was led into having to describe things that were merely necessary. I felt that the book

contained so many narrative obligations that it was tiring me out
and making me bored with it. Finally I said, "I want to write a
book that only has good parts. I don't want one paragraph in this
book to be something that I'm not completely excited about
writing."

CR: You didn't want to give background information?

SS: Background information, descriptions of time passing, setting
up room after room after room and getting people in and out of
those rooms—this was probably the most tiresome thing in writing. It's the one thing that movies do better than writing. You
can't do it in the third-person naturalistic flow. You get so deep
in ordinary reality.

CR: Was there also a second draft?

SS: To use an irony that I certainly didn't have at the time, I said,
"I love all these characters so much. I think they all should narrate it." And I went quite a ways into doing a *Rashomon* construction, with each person narrating. David's parents had large
sections. Actually it turned out to be good for the book. For
instance, I had sixty or seventy pages about David's parents'
meeting and their experiences in the Communist Party during
the thirties, and how Arthur helped Rose get her divorce from
her playboy husband, and all that. But after about three hundred pages I realized nothing had really happened yet, except
that an enormous amount of detail had been given and there was
a lot of feeling through it. There were rhapsodic passages that
I completely loved. Some of them I managed to smuggle into
the final draft. But it was impossible to follow what was going
on.

CR: What was your focus in separate voices? Which character
were you drawn to?

SS: I was always drawn to David, but he was the most ignored of
all my characters. I was waiting for him to emerge from all these
voices. The major problem I had was that this boy, who was basically the catalyst for the action of the novel, was opaque and
totally withdrawn. As verging on the operatic as he is in the final

draft, he was until then virtually as silent as John Wayne. I don't know what caused that. I suppose he was my own imagination waiting, watching, and trying to make some sense out of the events.

CR: How much time did you spend on each of these versions?

SS: Roughly speaking, a year, a year, and then a year.

CR: So in the third year you realized you needed a first-person narrator?

SS: I just tried it out of sheer desperation. I had returned to New York thinking that I'd come back with a book. And I had come back with a bunch of pages that weren't remotely a book. I had never even gotten to the point in the book where the house caught on fire. At one point I had some fairly bad ideas, that the fire should only be alluded to as some terrible thing that had happened, and then towards the end you would walk by the house and see this thing, charred planks hanging on nails and still smoking, and think, Aha! Well, this was probably the corniest idea I've had. One night I thought, Let's immediately put this behind us and start off with a fire and see how that works, and let the boy narrate it. But not from the necessary lack of perspective that you have when you're seventeen, and let's look back and feel it with an older heart. Then his voice was immediately there. And I don't think I ever looked back after that. It wasn't easy to write, but that draft went all the way through. That was the first time that I could end the book.

CR: When you say "never look back," did you have a sense of where the narrator was at the beginning?

SS: I actually think I did have a sense, but it was a secret I kept from myself.

CR: You knew that he was purged, but you didn't know.

SS: Yes. I could tell by his voice that he was purged, and he had a sense of some strength and regret. I knew that I wasn't going to write this book from the perspective of somebody who is in the bus station waiting for the next Greyhound because he had a new clue where Jade might be. I never knew definitely how the book was going to end until I actually wrote the end.

CR: When you start working, do you have an intuition or feeling of the germ or mode of the story?

SS: I think the primary thing is an intuition, though not really a picture, but some surge of emotions. In *Endless Love* I did have the image of a boy having breakfast with a family, and sleeping with the daughter of the family. It reminded me of something I wanted to read, but no one had written it yet.

CR: The feeling of the Delmore Schwartz poem was the catalyst, or the starting point, when you began.

SS: It's a voice for me. It's my habit to deal with my feelings, my intuitions, by sitting down and noodling away at the typewriter. How do I make a bridge between my conscious mind and my unconscious mind? The only way I've learned how to do it so far is by finding a tone of voice, by writing.

CR: What is that sense you have of writing the book you want to read?

SS: What I meant facetiously is that it really comes from the idea of when I want to read a certain kind of book. I think that's why I feel divorced from *Last Night at the Brain Thieves' Ball*, because with *Preservation Hall* and *Endless Love* and the book that I'm writing now I really want to read the book. In a way, it would be almost as though I would be very jealous and shocked if someone else wrote them. But I feel a need to have a certain experience, to see certain feelings displayed, to see certain ideas pursued, and at one point or another I make the audacious choice of appointing myself as the person who can conceivably do that. Now it's become quite natural for me to say, "Well, OK, this is the book you want to read and that's what you ought to write."

CR: Is that still very close to your sense of yourself? For example, in that picture of the family around the breakfast table, was that you in the picture?

SS: In that particular picture it was me.

CR: And then the narrative voice that you finally established is also tied to you?

SS: I think it really is quite tied to me. I think it's one of the reasons why, aside from fault in design, I couldn't do that *Rashomon* structure. It really is very difficult for me to pretend to other voices. I mean, the voice that I write in is in fact my voice. That's how I think and talk to myself as it comes out on the page.

CR: That's the raw material. Is it a mimetic process in the final work? Do you find this character, or does the character work itself out in the process?

SS: I think that it really is like "method acting" in a certain way. I read the work out loud to myself and try to believe it. The rhythm and the style are totally important to me. I'm not interested in public readings and don't like them. But I can't bear the idea of writing something that wouldn't read well, that wouldn't have certain musical qualities to it.

CR: From your description, initially I think the impetus to your work is very dramatic. I can see why Franco Zeffirelli saw a film in it, since that's his medium. What happened when the novel *Endless Love* was made into a film? Did that take you back into the work, into yet another version of the work?

SS: I think that *Endless Love*'s becoming a film cut me off from the work.

CR: Because someone else wrote the script?

SS: As soon as I realized that it was out of my hands, I think I emotionally cut off from it. I didn't want to be upset, and so I kept the book at arm's length.

CR: But you were consulted during the making of the film, weren't you?

SS: Not really. I was in that fake way, such as their asking me, "What do you think of Elizabeth Taylor?" I was actually quite pleased when I learned that they had hired Judy Rasco to write the script, because I happen to be a fan of hers. I read her book of short stories called *Yours, and Mine.* But I never forgot that it was basically an enterprise, that anything was likely to happen. When they hired Brooke Shields it was immediately going to be a different kind of film. So, as much as my curiosity would allow me, I kept away from it.

CR: What was your reaction to the filming?

SS: My reaction to the actual filming was a kind of old-time socialist's reaction. I said, "Well, here it is, a time of recession, and look at all the jobs I've created. These lines of trucks and all these cameras." It was just an astonishing feeling. I said, "Gee, there I was in some drafty Vermont farmhouse living on ninety dollars a week, writing away on a wobbly table. Now machines are running, big electronic cables are crawling like cobras in the middle of the street, and traffic is being stopped." It was all just astonishing.

CR: The power of what you had created?

SS: Yes, the ripple effect. But I never forgot how much of it was a fluke, and how much of it was because the title was great.

CR: I have asked you about the mimetic in your imagination. How was it to see young actors portray your characters?

SS: When I actually saw the movie I had sedated myself mentally and distanced myself as much as I could, but it was an astonishing thing to see something that I had created being acted out and seeing strangers pretending to interpret things that I had made up. I suppose, in some primitive way, you have some little Punch and Judy show going on in the frontal lobes as you're writing, you have these little characters talking back and forth to each other. Then all of a sudden you turn around and you can go into a darkened room, a beam of light comes streaming out of a hole in the back wall, and there it is on the screen. Again, I was dazzled by the strangeness of it all, of seeing this young actor pretending to be David Axelrod and walking around setting fire to the house. It's embarrassing in a way.

CR: How could it be embarrassing?

SS: Well, I've never been one of those people who can go into the bookstore and ask, "How's my book doing?" or "Where's my book?" or "Do you have my book?"

CR: Or "Why isn't it in the window?" Why?

SS: I feel quite shy about it, that books are private, it's an intimate relationship. The fact is that one reads a book alone, one writes a book alone. It's like a secret sign language between the author and the reader, and it seems a little distorting and shocking to have the lights put on it, and to have it blown up and suddenly be a terribly casual and public thing. For instance, I recently got a Betamax and I was looking through the catalogue of films available and saw that *Endless Love* was now available for home cassettes. They had a little thumbnail sketch of each film, and it said of *Endless Love,* "Permissive parents let their children do anything they want and things get out of control." Frankly, the feeling I got from this whole experience was not of enormous power but one of insignificance, that I had been working very hard to create something and someone swooped down upon it, like a crow that sees something shiny, and took it away. I didn't feel that I had, with that film, reached deeper into the collective mind of America. I felt that they had used it to their own purposes. It made me think that if I had been more powerful they wouldn't have dared to do that.

CR: Are you saying that it made you feel that the writer is expendable from the work?

SS: It did. I needed to be reunited to it. I was very glad that I wasn't in New York when the film was coming out. The first I saw of it was before they'd taken the scissors to it, and they had to do some last-minute emergency cutting because of the censors, the ratings board. Then, when I was at the public screening that Franco Zeffirelli had the night before it opened, it was really tough to see it.

CR: Did you at some point connect the fact that the film is a public interpretation of your book with the fact that in some way it's indeed a testimony to the way someone, or the industry, reads the book? It's not your sort of reader, but it is a "reading" in that other sense.

SS: I really don't think that it is. Now that I've had the experience of adapting someone else's work for film, I can tell you that at a certain point you don't give a damn what's in the book. You're trying to make a movie. You're not trying to do justice to the book or even reflect it. Doing a script certainly gave me a perspective. But I guess my perspective while it was happening was just to try not to be too caught up in it. I read about James M. Cain that when an interviewer asked him, "What do you think about what Hollywood did to your novels?" he said, "Hollywood didn't do anything to my novels. They're right over there on my shelf." That's the truth of it. Hemingway's idea of the way you sell your book to Hollywood is that you drive to the California state line, stop, have them throw the money over the state line, and then you throw the manuscript, grab the money, hop in your car, and drive away. I tried to keep that larcenous, cynical view as much as I could, because I thought that's what it would take to get me through, and it worked. It would be ridiculous to put myself into this crybaby position of pointing to the screen and then pointing to my heart—"What have they done?"—because it was basically a financial decision. So I figured we could just let it go.

CR: After the novel, you became caught up in scriptwriting. Did that experience also affect your next novel?

SS: Well, everything affected the next book I was going to start on. The success of *Endless Love* affected the next book I was going to start on because I knew I didn't have the kind of privacy I had before, or that I imagined I did. Maybe I do. Before that no one really knew that I was writing another novel, and it wasn't a matter of any particular importance to anyone else, and I felt the total anonymity chafed against me, as it does all writers. The public reaction to *Endless Love* immediately put me into competition with myself—"I sure hope the next one meets with that kind of success." And with that bald-faced utterance, I ripped the pen from my fingers, broke it in half, and basically didn't work for about a year.

CR: Was there something else—another reaction, or a private reaction apart from the public—that was affirmed?

SS: I think there was a feeling of my life's having taken an unwarranted spurt forward when I wasn't really totally ready for it. A good description of the pace of my life was Priestley's idea that one ought to take little Japanese steps, and that was really how to proceed. I liked that idea; I still rather like it. And I felt that my stride had been completely broken.

CR: So how were you able to get yourself back into the imaginative state of writing fiction?

SS: I just needed a little time to stop worrying about it, enjoy what I had done, and then just look around and feel that it was my turn again—that no one had heard anything that I had to say.

CR: No, you assimilated the experience and felt you wanted to get on with it.

SS: I assimilated it, I stopped caring about it in any particular way. I felt that I didn't need to compare what I was writing to it any longer. The public's response to the novel is impossible to evaluate. It's dependent on so many things. You know that I'll write better novels that will get less attention and that will make less money and get less praise. I think that's just the way things are, that every once in a while the public focuses on a piece of work and it's hard to say why it happens.

CR: What is the direction of your next work?

SS: I really need to believe that the work I'm doing now represents some kind of advance from the work that I've already done. I feel that the second book is better than my first. And my third book is truer than my second. And I certainly feel that the book I'm working on now represents growth for me.

All of my writing life I've been trying to write in the third person. I feel it's an idea of the dignity of the novel that makes me think it ought to be in the third person. I have such respect for the kind of novel that gives us a complete picture of the society in which it takes place. The vision of life can be hinted at, you can get intimations of it from a first-person narrative, but it can't be given as fully as in the third person.

CR: The novel I admire most would be Proust's, which is basically in the first person, although the whole world is there, too. You define it as a question of scope.

SS: It's a question of scope and history and to find out what I understand about the moment and how we are connected to each other. It's not something completely lacking in my books, but it's hard for me to do it justice.

CR: Behind the dichotomy are there two separate concepts of the writer, or of who you are, or ought to be, as a writer?

SS: I suppose there really are. I suppose that's part of the crisis that I went through in this book—the idea that one wrote more responsible and useful books in the third person. I was imposing an idea of myself onto something which was much more genuine, which was what I really wanted to do.

CR: Speaking of this hypothetical third-person narrative, is there something of the scope of this country or this society that you absolutely want to do and artistically want to make your own?

SS: Is there a territory I want to cut out for myself here? Well, I suppose there is some idea left over from childhood—I don't mean to call it that as a way of denigrating it—that writers operate as part of the conscience of the society that they live in, and it's a job that's better done, is more obviously done, by writing novels of a scope that shows how we are all connected, that demonstrates this interdependence between people, and illuminates how the dispossessed are crucified and how the wicked and undeserving go on being wicked and all the more undeserving. There are things that I feel are genuine responsibilities of writers, and certainly of writers who feel the way I do. Now, when there's very little public discourse about equality and justice and fairness and decency, if a writer does feel that way in his personal life he has a responsibility to demonstrate these concerns in his work. And I take myself to task for not really having done that. It's a question of conscience versus impulse. Because, frankly, my impulse is to write whatever I want to write. I don't enjoy writing so much that I can write a whole book because I think I ought to.

CR: You are not speaking about the fact that art is morally informed. Yours is a political consciousness of the novel's function. Is that part of your formation as a writer?

SS: I really found politics through literature. I think that's why I keep coming back to this idea of the responsibilities of people who create. Even in reading someone like Allen Ginsberg when I was fifteen years old, the sense of his conflict with the society and all his references to the history of conflict made me feel that I was somebody, a part of tradition. When I asked my parents about this, it was at that point that they began revealing how much of their life was political.

CR: What were their political commitments?

SS: My father was a CIO organizer, and he also organized mine workers in Pennsylvania. My mother was a radical in the thirties and forties and is still involved in the important issues.

CR: What was the impact of their beliefs on your development?

SS: Well, it certainly has colored my whole life and way of thinking, but I think that they wanted me to be whatever I was going to be.

CR: Did you always want to be a writer? Did you start writing as a child?

SS: I think I wrote my first novel when I was eight. I remember it quite well. I wrote a novel about a horse that was captured by the Nazis in Tunisia, and he was picked up and rescued and rehabilitated by an American film crew filming a Buster Crabbe desert epic. Then I wrote a novel about separated twins. *The*

Prince and the Pauper had a tremendous influence on my imagination. The difficulty of being an only child is imagining yourself as another person. I think that with siblings you can do it more readily, because you almost see yourself as another person, but you don't see that when you're an only child. You are left with imagining yourself as another person almost as a necessity.

CR: Did you have imaginary companions as you were growing up?

SS: I don't remember talking to myself except once. It's a terrific example of how children can be their own psychiatrists. When I was eight, nine, ten years old, I would get out of the shower, slick my hair back, and sort of wipe off the medicine chest so I could see myself, and then begin talking to myself in the mirror. I didn't think I was talking to myself. I thought I was looking in the mirror because the show had begun. I was a son coming to avenge his father's death and going into this place and saying, "I am his son, now you must be punished, you cannot do this to a man like this and not be punished." But I realized I was staring into my own eyes and I was completely in this final Oedipal fantasy of killing my father and punishing myself for it at the same time. Always in the rather comforting form of an Edward G. Robinson film.

CR: Were your parents involved in the arts?

SS: My parents are both first-generation Americans and both looked up to art; and we always had books around.

CR: So they had that love of culture?

SS: My father [Charles Spencer] wanted to be a writer, and then went on and did other things and now is a writer. He wrote a book about his twenty-five years as a steelworker, *Blue Collar*, which was published in 1977.

CR: So that he was able to return to some aspirations that he never lost touch with.

SS: There is no question that a part of me wanted to be a writer because they wanted me to. I don't see how I can escape it. I remember once, as a young boy, I asked my father what the word "uncanny" meant, and he said, "Well, you know, Jackie across the street has an uncanny ability to fix things. Carl has an uncanny ability to be an athlete, and you have an uncanny ability to write stories." I was very relieved to be named in the litany of the boys with uncanny abilities.

CR: Your talent was an accepted fact at home. Were you writing in college?

SS: Yes, I was. I used to write for quite a while. And when I was fifteen I stopped writing and I read. When I started to write again, I didn't know where to locate myself culturally at all. I'd been very political for the part of my life between the ages of fifteen and twenty. At eighteen years old I was the executive secretary of the Illinois Socialist Party. I was expelled from the Socialist Party for writing a document that was insulting to International Social Democracy.

CR: Were you politically active at least through your college years?

SS: I severed my ties from all my political friends because I felt that I was on a treadmill. I had no idea why I was doing what I was doing and what my beliefs were.

CR: Were those also the years of the drug culture?

SS: I think there's certainly nothing like taking a drug that will focus you fairly intensely on all the danger and majesty of what one calls the "self."

CR: Did that start you writing?

SS: College was really my first time away from home. I think that's really what it was, being completely on my own. That's when I started writing again, but I had really no voice. It was so filled with fanatical flourishes and complete insecurities. I felt certain that if I were to endure the scrutiny of others at a time like that, it would have had a demoralizing effect on me. It was very hard for me to tell people that I even *was* a writer. In college I never worked on the literary magazines or took a writing course, and I would hang around with people who wanted to be writers and they all talked about who is a genius and what it felt like to be a genius, and I don't think that six of them knew that I ever put pen to paper, and I wrote all the time. But it just was something that I felt—perhaps with my background, my character—shy about. And I really didn't need the validation of somebody else saying, "Yes, you're a writer."

CR: Who were the writers you were reading when you got started?

SS: I revere Nabokov and feel that I've learned a large portion of what I know about writing from reading him. I read to learn how everything is done, and I've learned from strange sorts of things. I remember after reading Gide's *The Counterfeiters*, which is not a book that I liked, I said, "I think I know how to write a novel now." There was something about the way in which the book fell short that I found completely illuminating. I certainly learned a lot from reading Hemingway, such as how to withhold information and that wonderful lesson of how to seduce the reader into accepting your frame of reference, those methods of tilting the world so it gets curious looks and falls into place, and then, once you have that, you have so much freedom. You can take the piece in so many odd directions and not feel that you're all by yourself. Hemingway makes people who never cared about blood sports and all that accept it as an important experience and valid metaphor for human interaction and a way of discovering our place in the world.

CR: I wanted to ask about who you read because your first novel reminded me of *The Crying of Lot 49*.

SS: I liked *The Crying of Lot 49* very much. It is this neat, eccentric little invention that somebody has made, a Rube Goldberg machine, completely entertaining. What interests me in *The Brain Thieves' Ball* is the false confession. The one book that most influenced my writing of *The Brain Thieves' Ball* is a book that doesn't resemble it much, Nabokov's *Despair*, in which the narrator, in unburdening himself to the reader, reveals more about the truth of the situation than he himself knows. It enter-

tained me so thoroughly with suppressed laughter that I wanted
to do something like it.

CR: *Brain Thieves* has another element, a black humor. People
tend to forget the comic or ironic aspect of your work.

SS: *Brain Thieves* is my only comic novel so far. When I brought
it to my publisher, had I not been so naïve and so grateful to be
published, I would have fled when I realized that everybody
there took it as a serious cautionary tale. I thought to myself,
Well, they're misreading it here, but when it comes out, whatever reviews it gets will correct this ridiculous misunderstanding. The first review they got was from the *Library Journal*,
which said it was the most frightening book since Orwell's *1984*.
I said, "God, I'm sunk! No one's getting it."

CR: Was it based on the behavior-modification experiments of
psychology that we subsequently learned are applied in advertising or propaganda?

SS: I think that the impetus in writing the novel came from a
friend who, after living a completely bohemian, ragtag Lower
East Side experience, suddenly felt that it was time for him to
take some realistic steps, so he got a job at IBM. He showed me
around one day, and I saw these crazy-looking geniuses sitting in
their cubicles, staring off into space with these printouts around
them. You can be eccentric, ingrown, what we thought of in
high school as a hopeless mass of tangled nerves and with
flipped-out theories, but there's actually a real place for you.
More than you yourself, more than your friends or anyone who
loves you, there's someone who knows how to use your strangeness. Someone else has a larger, sinister picture, and will fit you
into that almost frightening human ecology in which individu-
alism is just a trick done with mirrors. When we think we're
being most ourselves—that's what consumerism is.

CR: The narrator has split from his wife and family, and abandoned his teaching career, and he's painfully aware that his
imaginative ambitions put him outside of reality. Is he like that
hopeless bundle of nerves you saw at IBM?

SS: Paul, the narrator, is slightly less gifted than he imagines himself to be. What separates him from humanity is his unpleasant ambitions for himself. I think it's his desire to feel unique that makes him so dangerous.

CR: There's his wild ambition of "discovering America brain by brain," and the irony is that he's exploiting sex and all the natural human appetites in order to control them. Is that the brain thief in the novel?

SS: It's a continuing puzzle for me, what is this thing called "free will," and how much of it is just instinct and how much of it is rhetorical, part of our ideological fight with the other half of the world. I don't know how much of what we choose is really chosen, and I suspect it's rather less than we imagine.

CR: In his drive for power, were you satirizing the function of the imagination?

SS: I've always found it easy to satirize social scientists. I had a job once sloshing through those printouts when I was in high school, and I did door-to-door interviews. The whole idea of human data is both frightening and contemptible to me, and not all that difficult to satirize. I don't see novelists as demented or power-hungry. I should think that there would be no greater cure for megalomania than writing a novel.

CR: In the end he comes to a sense of himself because he is studying sexuality, and that makes him want to break out of this prison which is NESTER and the organization he slavishly devotes himself to.

SS: I've always had that old-fashioned belief that one's sexual instincts are humanizing. I think it also probably does make him horny. "What am I doing here, when my subjects are having so much better a time than I am?" He says, "I want a life of my own." So he passes from the voyeur's phase into his own life.

CR: The somber note is struck when the price of his own freedom is mutilation. At the time of writing it, what made you feel that the narrator had to pay a price for his freedom?

SS: There seemed to be no way for us to have any fond backward glance at him, knowing what he was capable of, knowing what he allowed himself to do, unless we said, "OK, he's paid for it. Let's see what he makes of the rest of his life." We would know to look at him that he was a thief. His hand is cut off, because that's the punishment for being a thief.

CR: "An eye for an eye" is a ruthless sense of justice. It's without the spiritual dimension of forgiveness, salvation, redemption.

SS: The need for justice and the thirst for it seem so fundamental in human psychology that to interrupt it and to avoid it is really to do something strange and destructive to a character.

CR: Do you also believe that psychologically mutilating oneself, taking down one's power, and hiding is a method of survival and a way of being left alone?

SS: Certainly within the family people survive by hiding, and since we all come from families, we clearly take this habit into the world with us. I think fundamentally it's not a way to survive, and that people who fall into that habit are people who end up being hurt.

CR: Did the writing of *Last Night at the Brain Thieves' Ball* change what you were trying to do in your novels?

SS: I write one book at a time, and what I learned from writing *Last Night at the Brain Thieves' Ball* is how to get from the beginning to the end of a novel. I was learning how to write, and I think in an accountant sense I didn't want to disturb my store of personal vision for a novel written with the skills I possessed at that time. I have always been shy about being a writer. I wasn't ready to commit the double audaciousness of trying to publish a novel and also having a subject that I cared deeply about. I needed the ironic remove of writing what I considered essentially a dark entertainment.

CR: *Preservation Hall* begins with the relationship of Virgil, the narrator, and his father, Earl. Why does this novel of lost love begin within the family?

SS: I think the essential preoccupation in *Preservation Hall,* which I can link to *Last Night at the Brain Thieves' Ball,* is the man who fundamentally does not know if he's good or bad. This mystery within himself, this heightened awareness of exactly how mixed his motives are, begins with the relationship between him and his father. It's the inevitable place where the book should begin. Learning to live with the good and the bad in yourself means knowing how you are connected to others, either as an open and loving person or as a reserved and unkind person.

CR: Amorality is not a viable state for your characters.

SS: In my rather oversimplified view of things, amorality is that sheet we throw over things we don't want to fully look at and evaluate. I don't know what exists outside of the moral sphere. I don't see how things could. Some people call amorality things that aren't explained by traditional views of what's right and what's wrong and what's moral, but that's not amorality.

CR: For me, it's when a person doesn't evaluate what he does and feels no necessity to evaluate. Virgil has a sense that his destiny is outside the run of common humanity. Luck is on his side, and he feels that life is going to spare him the failures of his father, and he has an aversion to the people who are helpless in the face of events.

SS: What Virgil calls luck is ruthlessness. He feels that somehow chance has separated him and allowed him to prosper. But it's what he fought for and desired above everything else. He didn't win the lottery. He organized his life in a certain way, and then he's left with the prospect of having to disorganize his life.

CR: In his ruthlessness, is the central theme the ruthless in love?

SS: The ruthless in love? I was much more interested in the ruthlessness than in the love. He is someone full of such suspicion about what life had to offer, and what his place in that world was going to be, that he needed to order his own existence as rigorously as possible, and he also needed to have a quite physical dependence on his wife's presence.

CR: What leads to their buying Preservation Hall in the wilds of Maine?

SS: It's the metaphor for his whole ordered life. He would look at a place like Preservation Hall as a way of getting away from the effort of his life. He makes a retreat for himself that is an unconscious duplication of the effort and bad faith that placed him in a position of moral discomfort in the first place.

CR: You investigate the disowning of the father, or parent, by the child. The artistic parent is something you're going to explore in other works.

SS: I'm more interested in the unrealized parent than the artistic parents. Most people's hopes are just to make a living and do well and to have a family and to have love. But artists have a temptation to want things that are really quite outside of the normal human contract—to have recognition, to have that sense of importance. That sense of how frustration and injured pride pass from generation to generation is completely interesting to me.

CR: Is there an equivalent, then, between the father's unrealized aspirations and the son who realizes false aspirations?

SS: Earl is no fool. He knows that he cuts a ridiculous figure and, rather than go through the pain of thinking it himself, he passes this knowledge to his son and lets him think it.

CR: When Earl finally marries Lillian and the two stepbrothers meet at Preservation Hall, was Virgil killing a part of himself in the accident that cost his stepbrother's life? You say he has to start life all over again, and that's when he tries to return to his wife. Is that the quest for love?

SS: It's a quest for love. It's a quest for a kind of emotional spontaneity and openness to approach someone without trying to hide the fundamental fact that he can't live without her. He no longer has the illusion of being autonomous.

CR: With Tommy the stepbrother you introduce the element of incarceration or imprisonment that runs through your work. I was wondering what the significance of that is for you?

SS: To an extent, it's just the reality principle. It's the embodiment of how short is the leash that we're on, and how temporary and unstable daily life is. I once had the traumatic experience of being arrested in Spain for no reason whatsoever. The Spanish law is that you cannot keep somebody in jail for more than two weeks without bringing charges against them. I was in there for twenty days and it was mind-boggling. Compared with an American prison there wasn't much problem at all, no violence. At first, it was in a little town and they didn't even have a jail there, so I was locked in somebody's barn for three days until they brought a big bus and took me to the city, where I was in jail for the duration. It really wasn't so bad. I played chess out in the courtyard all the time. It was more like a dorm room with bars, and we were there in our room from six in the evening to six in the morning and outside the rest of the time. There's no more painful and vivid demonstration of where the self ends and the world begins, and how much of the world is in you and how much of you is in the world. It all seemed so perfectly and yet so grotesquely characterized by the experience of institutionalization.

CR: It's not a case of Cain versus Cain, is it?

SS: Virgil's life was a temple of reassurance where he could go and feel safe. I think he has despair of ever really becoming real in his own eyes. I think that it's a need to be authentic. In Virgil's case, he was raised by unrealized people, and these people used him as a mirror. He was never given any validation as his own separate person, and he came up with a hollowness, acting as a kind of bell jar in which sheer desires could rage. So his need is to crack this and to try and build a self.

CR: In *Endless Love* the narrative voice has inherent within it a life or a destiny that's been completed, and my question is whether that's the element where your ideas of fiction come together within the voice—that is, this individual life gives shape to the novel.

SS: The way it gets worked out for me, writing in the first person, is basically spending a lot of time thinking about the character, writing about the character, and, in that sense we were talking about, the mimetic sense of pretending to be the character, until an entire life unconsciously takes shape within me that I can express in the character's voice and in the few actions that the book will permit him to commit. In that way I try to suggest an entire life that lives inside of the society that he comes out of. That's as close to the idea of a third-person narrative as I can get in the first person. It's the storing of detail in that Hemingway sense of knowing about six times as much as you finally write. The full curve of destiny is something that I like to leave as sketchy as possible for myself. I try to know as much as I can about a book before the beginning, but I never know exactly where it's going to end.

CR: But then you do have a sense of the destiny of the characters.

SS: I certainly have a sense of their past. I certainly have a sense of what they are and what they need up to the point of the novel's beginning. I don't have the ability to map out how they're going to change and what they're going to make of themselves by the time the book is over. That I actually work out as I'm writing. I don't know why I do this exactly, but I feel a need to maintain a kind of artificial blindness.

CR: Isn't that to prevent the novel from becoming predictable?

SS: I still suspect myself of a certain schematic frame of mind which I like to negate by denying myself certain information about what's going to happen. I feel my character is extremely logical and orderly, and these traits, if they become too prominent, can take the life out of a novel.

CR: Isn't that combination of qualities what enables you to go deeply into their rationale and still retain the sense of order?

SS: Yes, because I have it inside of me to do this. I always know what time it is. Even when I took LSD I knew what time it was. I know how to live with my own complete unreasonableness. I was raised in a certain way that enables me to do that. One of the reasons that I didn't have much difficulty in learning how to write screenplays is that I have a good sense of structure. I can burrow into something and know in the back of my head when things should stop because it's gone on for too long and "don't forget you have to go to point b and point c and point d, too, and when you want to be there."

CR: Does *Endless Love* reflect your own idea of the home?

SS: Either rigid or anarchic? I think that the families in both of those homes were headed by people whose lives were to a large extent unrealized. And the domestic relations were distorted by that fact. In the Axelrod home, their emotional peak had come and gone and they were sort of living in the ever-more-faint reverberation of their best moment. Whereas in the Butterfields', they felt that they had just missed a chance to be who they were supposed to be, so were frantic to catch up. I don't know if either of those is necessarily all that a family can be. I feel a little optimistic and defensive since I now have my own family.

CR: The narrator's home is that of an only child who is almost an equal to his parents, and the narrator finds that unbearable; I was wondering if that reflected what you were trying to say?

SS: I always thought that David's problem with his parents was not that they treated him too much as an equal but that they never told him the truth about anything. I thought that the key to his feeling about his home was that his parents were like captains of a sinking ship and he was the passenger, and every time they turned around they put on this false smile and said, "How's dinner?"

CR: But what is it that they're trying to shield him from?

SS: They have completely lost their sense of direction in life. They don't know what they are doing from one day to the next except out of force of habit. They have become very uncomfortable with each other and feel somehow embarrassed about their life.

CR: What about the father's social ideals?

SS: I don't think this ever found its way into the book, actually— that the father felt the Communist Party had ruined his marriage; that his wife spent the best part of her heart in that, and when that ended she withdrew from passion because she'd been cheated, betrayed, and exhausted by it. He felt the ardor that he was capable of had never been tapped by this marriage. That's what made him rather susceptible to the rather strange example set by his son.

CR: Is that the opposition between devotion to a cause and loving the individual?

SS: It's very difficult, I think, to be involved in politics and not use it as a way of slightly dehumanizing yourself. Finally, politics has only a passing interest in what we *really* are like.

CR: In *Endless Love* you begin the narrative at an earlier age. David is younger, and talking about the discovery of life. He falls completely in love with Jade, and you are dealing with a particular stage of love. It's a sexuality that is a discovery of the world they share. But at the same time, because of their age, you're also dealing with the explosive element of narcissism. I was wondering why you pitched the experience at that age?

SS: David was lucky enough to realize that if he was ever going to be anything like what he felt he could be, he would have to find another family. On a certain level, he would have been just as happy to be Jade's brother as her lover. The important thing was to find an emotional situation that would crack the mold and allow him to see what was fundamental inside himself. When that opportunity is suddenly taken away, the need isn't satisfied yet. So the need could become atrophied—he could say, "OK, I don't need it after all. I'll do something else, I'll do what's expected of me"—or, if he were a different sort of person, he would maintain his loyalty towards himself and to what he believed was right. You can't negotiate that.

CR: Being neither, he'd rather destroy them than to recapture them.

SS: I don't feel that he wants to destroy them. Certainly he didn't
want to kill them when he set that fire. He needed desperately to
demonstrate how serious this was. Because it happened to David
and Jade when their socialization wasn't complete, when they
hadn't gone through the necessary discouragements and chas-
tisements that teach how to live within certain boundaries, there
is really no limit to how far they can go.

CR: In terms of the self-absorption of adolescence, is the sexual
drama at the level of narcissism, where Jade and David are aspects of each other because, as you said, they're not socialized
really?

SS: I think that when we do completely join ourselves to another
person, we see ourselves just as Blake saw the world in a grain of
sand. I think that's a fundamental truth. I think of narcissism as
negating another person in favor of yourself. I don't think that is
what happens between David and Jade.

CR: What you capture is that whole initial experience of love
where one just uses oneself and the other person.

SS: I don't really think selfishness is that close to narcissism. He
was a boy with a fairly complicated, boring personality who
knew that he wasn't the person he could be, and was very happy
to take instructions in being a completely different kind of person. But David, once he enters the Butterfield family, acts as a
reflection of all its missing, unfulfilled needs for different members of the family—and in that sense shows up all the cracks in
that structure. He's found another den of unrealized lives.
There's no way to live in this world without having foisted upon
you some level of inauthenticity. Life is just too trying and too
disappointing for us not to become defensive and artificial.

CR: When he's institutionalized, is that again your concern for a
price?

SS: He is a spendthrift and price is no object. He's willing to pay
and pay and pay. It doesn't really matter to him. He knows that
what he wanted was a good thing and could have been right for

Jade. It is the central concern of his life, and everything else is diminished because of that certainty. It is the only authentic thing in himself and it's the only thing that's completely his. If he were to let go of that, he would have nothing.

CR: Once he gets out of the hospital and looks up the family, he's accused of luring Hugh to his death. Is that an act of murder?

SS: I never thought of it as an act of murder. I felt more that when you are living outside of the agreed-upon human contract, nearly everything you do is scrutinized and seen in a special light, and if anything goes wrong you are immediately to blame for it. But what makes it an intolerable act for the rest of the family is that they realize that Jade has to begin facing to what degree she has been using David all along as her avenging angel.

It is her revulsion against the moral lassitude of her parents and the fact that she has somehow conspired to bring this person into their lives to expose the family and, taking it a step further, to really destroy them. Thus it was Jade herself who set fire to the house. It was Jade who set her father a-trot as he was walking down the street with his ridiculous new girlfriend.

CR: When David and Jade are reunited in that hotel room and they're making love all day, covered with menstrual blood, is that love or is that war? That's where sexual passion crosses over the boundaries into annihilating the other person, as well as oneself, in sex.

SS: The reason that sex is so important is that we are not quite ourselves when we're making love. We're not ourselves in the sense that we don't speak correctly, we don't recognize the same rules of spatial distance; we become elemental, and that's rather desperate. This desire to strip away makes this reunion as thorough and fundamental as could be. It turns the body inside out. I don't believe that David was trying to destroy her in any way.

CR: I wasn't asking if it was angry sex.

SS: The menstrual blood on his hands and on her has a double meaning because of the fact of Hugh's death. It's the way in which the circumstances of our lives color the impulses of our lives. Blood had been shed, and it was not a shared fact between them that David, however tangentially, had something to do with it.

CR: When David and Jade go off to live together, there's the question of whether she's rehabilitating him or merely domesticating him. So that the idea of love and slave comes out of that phase. He's literally in the dog house when he is reduced to that bestial, elemental thing. The problem is, was he always the dog?

SS: You mean the difference between love and masochism, because he wasn't. After Hugh's death, David couldn't be honest with Jade any longer. It injected a destructive fantasy into their relationship. Also, she really was no longer prepared to have the kind of relationship he wanted. So, at that point, he really was by himself. Without one other person to join him in that cutting loose in the intensity of love, it did turn into something slavish, unbalanced, and condemned.

CR: When I read that scene I thought of Djuna Barnes's *Nightwood*, where Robin goes from a vegetable state to an animal state without ever touching the possibility of becoming a human being. I wondered about David's total regression and his decision to be more and less than he was, so that he ends up again incarcerated at the end.

SS: I never saw the final conclusion as being altogether pessimistic. I felt that David wasn't mad at the end, and he had managed, to some degree, in his own mind, to behave heroically on his terms. He can bring a real wisdom and a real tenderness to whatever is next for him.

CR: Was this novel a celebration of first love or the tragedy of first love?

SS: The original vision that I had of the young man having breakfast with the family really was a very pleasant vision, and I think that at a certain point, it involved a sense of wanting to write a book that didn't have any sort of dramatic thrust, and it was just a kind of poignant vision of love in families and out of families and overlapping relationships. I think somewhere there is a possibility for happiness and peace and understanding that I haven't been able to express. It's just an intuition. One has momentary glimpses of some profound and joyful unity. It would be wonderful to hold it and to express it.

Charles Ruas was born in Tientsin, China, in 1938, and educated at Princeton University and the Sorbonne in Paris. From 1968 to 1975 he taught French language and literature at Columbia University, and from 1974 to 1977 he was director of arts programing at radio station WBAI in New York. He has translated works from the French—among them, Michel Foucault's study of the life and work of the surrealist writer Raymond Roussel.

A NOTE ON THE TYPE

This book was set in Caledonia, a type face designed by William Addison Dwiggins (1880–1956) for the Mergenthaler Linotype Company in 1939. Dwiggins chose to call his new type face Caledonia, the Roman name for Scotland, because it was inspired by the Scottish types cast in 1833 by Alexander Wilson & Son, Glasgow type founders. However, there is a calligraphic quality about Caledonia that is totally lacking in the Wilson types. Dwiggins referred to an even earlier type face—one cut in 1790 by William Martin for the printer William Bulmer—for this "liveliness of action." Caledonia has more weight than the Martin letters, and the bottom finishing strokes (serifs) of the letters are cut straight across, without brackets, to make sharp angles with the upright stems, thus giving a modern-face appearance.

W. A. Dwiggins began an association with the Mergenthaler Linotype Company in 1929, and over the next twenty-seven years designed a number of book types, the most interesting of which are Metro, Electra, Caledonia, Eldorado, and Falcon.

Composed by American–Stratford Graphic Services, Inc.,
Brattleboro, Vermont.

Printed and bound by Maple Press, York, Pennsylvania.

Designed by Tasha Hall.